THE CIRCUS KINGS

University Press of Florida

Florida A&M University, Tallahassee
Florida Atlantic University, Boca Raton
Florida Gulf Coast University, Ft. Myers
Florida International University, Miami
Florida State University, Tallahassee
New College of Florida, Sarasota
University of Central Florida, Orlando
University of Florida, Gainesville
University of North Florida, Jacksonville
University of South Florida, Tampa
University of West Florida, Pensacola

THE
CIRCUS KINGS

Our Ringling Family Story

Henry Ringling North and Alden Hatch

Afterword by Fred Dahlinger Jr.

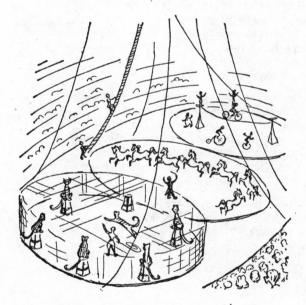

Drawings by Allene Gat Hatch

University Press of Florida
Gainesville/Tallahassee/Tampa/Boca Raton
Pensacola/Orlando/Miami/Jacksonville/Ft. Myers/Sarasota

13 12 11 10 09 08   6 5 4 3 2 1

Library of Congress Cataloging-in-Publication Data
North, Henry Ringling, 1909–
The circus kings: our Ringling family story/Henry Ringling North
and Alden Hatch; foreword by Fred Dahlinger Jr.
p. cm.
Originally published: Garden City, N.Y.: Doubleday, 1960.
ISBN 978-0-8130-3311-2 (alk. paper)
1. Ringling Brothers Barnum and Bailey Combined Shows.
2. Ringling Brothers. I. Hatch, Alden, 1898– II. Title.
GV1821.R5N6 2008
791.3—dc22   2008018562

The University Press of Florida is the scholarly publishing agency
for the State University System of Florida, comprising Florida
A&M University, Florida Atlantic University, Florida Gulf
Coast University, Florida International University, Florida State
University, New College of Florida, University of Central Florida,
University of Florida, University of North Florida, University
of South Florida, and University of West Florida.

University Press of Florida
15 Northwest 15th Street
Gainesville, FL 32611-2079
http://www.upf.com

To John, who filled a father's place and
smoothed my way with gaiety and affection.

ACKNOWLEDGMENTS

There could hardly be a more interesting and delightful occupation than collaborating with so many of the North family in writing the story of the circus. We include all of them in this tribute. Brother John Ringling North supplied many of the most amusing and valuable stories. Mary Salomé Wadsworth and her husband, Randolph L. Wadsworth, added great sections to the manuscript at "Mother's crumbling mansion" on Bird Key, as we ransacked huge piles of memorabilia to authenticate this work. And Charles Ringling's daughter, Mrs. Hester Ringling Sanford, was likewise gracious.

Many other people contributed to the story from their crowded memories. Among them: Arthur M. Concello, once the world's greatest living aerialist and now executive director of the circus; Pat Valdo, personnel director, who has served the circus for almost sixty years; Mrs. Alice Ringling Coerper.

Because of these efforts, we believe that this is the most authentic account possible of the rise, the glory, the tribulations, and the renaissance of the beloved American institution which is known, not without justification, as The Greatest Show on Earth.

February 1960

CONTENTS

Part I
SON OF THE CIRCUS

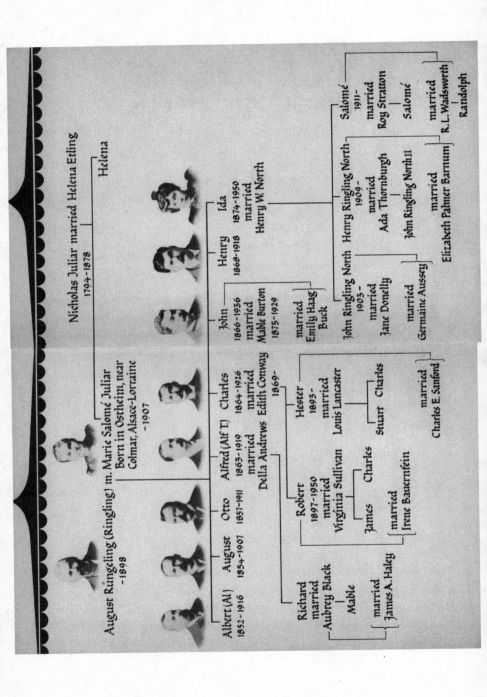

Nicholas Juliar married Helena Etling
1794-1878

Helena

August Ringeling (Ringling) m. Marie Salomé Juliar
Born in Ostheim, near
Colmar, Alsace-Lorraine
-1907
-1898

Albert (Al)   August   Otto   Alfred (Alf T.)   Charles   John   Henry   Ida
1852-1916   1854-1907   1857-1911   1863-1919   1864-1926   1866-1936   1868-1918   1874-1950
                                                  married   married   married   married
                                                  Della Andrews   Edith Conway   Mable Burton   Henry W. North
                                                                    1869-   1875-1929

Richard   Robert   Hester   married
married   1897-1950   1893-   Emily Haag
Aubrey Black married   married   Buck
│   Virginia Sullivan Louis Lancaster
Mable   │
married   James Charles   Stuart Charles   John Ringling North   Henry Ringling North   Salomé
James A. Haley │   │   1903-   1909-   1911-
            married   married   married   married
            Irene Bauernfein married   Jane Donelly   Ada Thornburgh   Roy Stratton
                              Charles E. Sanford   married   John Ringling North II   Salomé
                                                        Germaine Aussey   married   married
                                                                                Elizabeth Palmer Barnum   R. L. Wadsworth
                                                                                                                Randolph

CHAPTER I

CIRCUS-BORN

The circus is a jealous wench. Indeed, that is an understatement. She is a ravening hag who sucks your vitality as a vampire drinks blood—who kills the brightest stars in her crown and who will allow no private life to those who serve her; wrecking their homes, ruining their bodies, and destroy-

ing the happiness of their loved ones by her insatiable demands. She is all of these things, and yet, I love her as I love
nothing else on earth.

The circus can be generous, too, especially to children.
Sometimes I think that my brother John, my sister Salomé,
and I had the most wonderful childhood ever. Imagine growing up adored and spoiled by six uncles who owned not one
circus but a whole flock of circuses, including the two outstanding ones of history: Ringling Brothers and Barnum &
Bailey's "The Greatest Show on Earth." That slogan, which
we adopted in 1919 when we combined the two circuses, was
a stroke of sheer genius on the part of the master showman,
Phineas T. Barnum. It was also true; for I firmly believe that
Ringling Brothers–Barnum & Bailey is still The Greatest Show
on Earth.

My love affair with the circus began at the age of three,
when my mother, who was the Ringling brothers' only sister,
took me to see the show in the Coliseum in Chicago. For so
small a boy it was mainly a gloriously exciting, spectacularly
bespangled scene of utter confusion. But out of that riotous
afternoon my memory holds one picture as clear as though
it were immortalized in Technicolor.

It was, I imagine, the climax of the show, the grand finale.
While elephants, horses, giraffes, zebras, camels, and clowns
circled the auditorium and aerialists flew gracefully through
the air overhead, a magnificently caparisoned white horse was
led onto a platform in the center ring. The fifty-piece band
burst into frenzied circus music as the platform with the horse
and his brilliantly uniformed attendant began to rise slowly
upward. Higher and higher it went, past the rigging for the
aerial acts, past the highest wire, on up to the shadowy dome.
Glittering in the glare of a white spotlight, the horse was
dwarfed to pony size by the immense height. He remained
suspended at the zenith for a breathless moment. Then the

spot went out and the platform erupted in fountains of golden fire and jets of bursting stars from a tremendous display of fireworks.

Looking back, I strongly suspect that my uncle Al Ringling, who was equestrian director of the Ringling show that year, had dreamed up this fantasy and also engineered it. Even then I thought it was a strange thing to do to a horse.

From the moment of my indoctrination I lived and breathed circus. At that time, in 1912, we lived in Baraboo, Wisconsin, where my mother and uncles had grown up and where the original Ringling Brothers Circus started on its long road in nine wagons, on one of which was a cage containing a moth-eaten hyena, the precursor of all those thousands of "Savage, Man-Devouring Denizens of the Jungle" which have traveled with our show. By the time I was born we had gone a long way from that unhappy hyena. The Ringling show now traveled in an eighty- or ninety-car train commanded by one of the uncles, while Barnum & Bailey toured the country in an even longer one, also directed by a Ringling uncle, since they had bought that circus from James A. Bailey's widow in 1907.

My uncles, the seven Ringling brothers, had also gone a long way from poverty-stricken country boys who had dreamed of owning a great circus and made their dream come true doubled in spades. Uncle Gus died in 1907, two years before I was born, so I never knew him, but the others were living in considerable splendor, each according to his taste. Besides their fine houses in Baraboo, some of them owned large estates in what they considered more civilized parts of the country. In addition, Uncle Charlie and Uncle John had pleasant winter houses in Sarasota, Florida, where I spent part of my childhood.

The only one who did not live part of the time in Baraboo was Uncle John, who became the most famous of them all.

Having achieved one ambition by masterminding Ringling Brothers' purchase of Barnum & Bailey, he was just starting to build the great financial empire which made him, for a time, one of the richest men in the world. But even he always returned to Baraboo for Christmas, and for the brotherly conclaves in which the affairs of the circus and of everything else pertaining to the family were decided in roaring, shouting, acrimonious arguments, which, once settled, were never reopened, as all the brothers confronted the rest of the world with complete unanimity.

These big, lusty, gusty uncles of mine dominated the life of the little midwestern city they had literally put on the map, and they also dominated the lives of their wives and children; and my mother and my father—Henry Whitestone North—and John, Salomé, and me. But they were very kind to us.

After my uncle Al died in 1916, when I was seven years old, the conclave of uncles decreed that we Norths should live in his great, turreted, Renaissance-style mansion, half castle and half château, built of Lake Superior sandstone. I have fond recollections of that house. The interior was as magnificent as its imposing, if doubt-inspiring, façade. The parlor and music room had silk damask walls. The dining-room ceiling was covered with real gold leaf. The library was paneled in dark lustrous wood. There was a big ballroom in the basement and, of course, an amply stocked wine cellar. Behind the house were extensive stables, where Uncle Al, who was a fine horseman, kept the beautiful riding and carriage horses he loved so much.

When I was growing up, Baraboo was a true circus city. The Barnum show wintered at Bridgeport, where it always had, but Ringling Brothers still had its winter quarters in Baraboo. They were an elaborate establishment that ran along both sides of the street beside the Baraboo River. There were many long brick animal barns and stables, a wardrobe building, electrical department, machine shop, wagon shop, and blacksmith's shop, where the broad iron tires for the wagon wheels were forged and the horses shod. At this time our press agents claimed that the show had 1002 horses. I cannot be sure, for I did not count them.

In addition, there were always about twenty-five or thirty wild animals in the menagerie—seven or eight lions, half a dozen tigers, a white leopard, two or three giraffes, a rhino, a couple of hippos, llamas, zebras, monkeys, and baboons— and a great many camels, which were used very effectively in the spectacles and parades. Now there is hardly a camel in any circus in America because of the Department of Agriculture's restrictions on importing them from disease- ridden countries. There were also thirty to fifty elephants.

As a small boy I had the run of Winter Quarters, and most of the personnel of the circus from Jim Pepper, who drove the lowly gilly wagon, to whatever lovely aerialist or equestrienne was queen of the back yard were my friends. I was especially fond of Cliko, a tiny African Bushman less than four feet tall. His real name was Franz Tyboch, and he had been captured by the British during the Boer War. He joined our circus in 1913 and remained with it until he died at an estimated age of over a hundred. Malvina Hoffman made a bust of him in her ethnological series for the Field Museum, as representing a Kalahari Bushman. Cliko was completely illiterate but a wonderful mimic who could imitate everyone in the circus. In civilian life he liked to wear a raccoon coat and a derby hat, with a cigar almost as big as he was sticking out of his mouth. For the circus side show he wore a leopard skin over one shoulder, a pair of socks rolled down to the ankles, and ordinary walking shoes. In this extraordinary costume, he'd come roaring out of his tent as the people were leaving the Big Top, uttering fearful yells and native war

SON OF THE CIRCUS

whoops in the loudest voice I ever heard and performing his conception of an African war dance.

This frightening creature was, in fact, a sweet and gentle man who loved all small things. The midgets were his close pals and when I was a small boy he was very fond of me. He'd let me pull his kinky hair, which would stretch out a foot or more and, when I let go, snap back like a rubber band. He called my brother "Johnny" and me "Bonny" to save the bother of adding an entire new word to his limited vocabulary.

Frank Cook, the circus lawyer, legal adjuster, or "fixer," adopted him, and by what political machinations I'll never know—since Cliko could not read—got him made an American citizen. I'll never forget Cliko's joy when he heard the news. He came bounding up to me on the lot and shouted, "Bonny, me American citizen now, no more nigger son of a bitch."

The animals were my friends as well, and I often went to call on them in the big brick barns where they were housed through the rigorous Wisconsin winter. Katy the giraffe I loved dearly; in fact, I have always been particularly fond of giraffes. Then I would run through the cat house, where all the jungle animals were kept, greeting my friends in their cages, but circus-wise enough never to get within paw reach, for you never trust the cats. Indeed, any old circus hand knows that even the friendliest animal will have a bad day and take it out on unwary humans, so you never stand where a giraffe can kick you, or an ape clutch you, or an elephant trample. Every now and then someone forgets these cardinal rules and loses an arm or gets booted twenty feet through the air into a hospital bed. Seeing it happen, as I often did, was a strong object lesson. I loved my animal friends, but treated them with great respect.

Most of all I loved the elephant barn filled with the huge friendly creatures. I even loved its overpowering musky-aromatic smell. When I was a little boy, there was tremendous excitement at the birth of a baby elephant. All the elephants we had were born wild in the jungle, since it is almost impossible to rear one in captivity. They will breed all right; but the mother elephant will kill her baby—as sentimentalists think, to spare it a life of captivity.

On this occasion Uncle Charlie and our family physician, Dr. Kelly, were determined to save the elephant child. They were close by at the time of delivery, and as soon as the little thing was on its feet they tried to get it away from its mother. Unfortunately for my uncle's plans, the five-ton principal of this maternity case became violently agitated, trumpeting loudly and thrashing about. Uncle Charlie told me that at this point he saw her leg chain begin to part. He dove through a small hatch in the door of her stall with Dr. Kelly close behind him. They landed on their faces in a great pile of elephant manure. The mother elephant bashed her baby to death.

Undoubtedly the greatest thrill a boy could have was to ride the circus train. When Mother was a girl she often traveled with her brothers in their private car. In those days they did not have a car all to themselves; part of an ordinary Pullman was used for living quarters and the rest of it was a dining car for the management and star performers. But by the time I came along, the uncles were more luxurious. Uncle Charles had a splendid car called the Caledonia, furnished in magnificent red plush and gold, with real lace curtains. It was a perfect example of "Early Pullman." In 1917 Uncle John outdid him. The Jomar, built especially for him by the Pullman Company, was the longest private car in the world. It, too, was a lush example of railroad interior decoration: fine mahogany woodwork fretted into intricate designs, brass chandeliers with Tiffany glass shades, a double brass bed in Uncle John's stateroom and a smaller one in Aunt Mable's.

The food aboard was magnificent. As I shall tell, Uncle John ate only two meals a day, but they were gargantuan.

Both uncles usually invited us children to ride for a week or two on their trains. That was my time of sheer delight. Days and nights were equally exciting. Going to bed at midnight after the show in the railroad yards, decorated by the ruby and emerald signal lights and full of puffing monsters and clanging bells and the fine wet smell of steam. Waking in the night to feel the rumbling wheels, or perhaps alongside the section with the menagerie aboard, lions roaring, seals barking, and camels gurgling angrily. Then morning, getting up as soon as possible and skipping across the tracks to where the wagons were unloading from the flats, and hooking a ride to the show grounds perched on the box of a lion's cage. By the time I got there the Big Top, which traveled in the second section, was going up in a scene of splendidly co-ordinated confusion. An even thousand men were working like demented ants around the huge rolls of canvas, some lacing the sections together while others guyed out the center poles, which weighed several tons each, and then erected the thirty-six blue and fifty-four red quarter poles and one hundred twenty-four yellow side poles needed to support the six-pole top. Working elephants pushed and pulled with intelligent strength—before the days of tractors we could not have gotten the Big Top up at all without them. The canvas alone weighed seventy-two tons—or so our publicity department always claimed, but it was really only sixty-three tons, wet, about thirty tons, dry.

After superintending the work of the boss canvasman, I would dash around to call on my side-show friends, or into the huge cookhouse for a fine big lunch. By that time the elephants would have hauled the bail rings up to the peak of the poles, the side walls would be raised, and the Big Top ready for the aerialists' rigging and the folding-seat benches, or "bibles." The parade was about to start.

When I was about eleven, John, who was seventeen, was already working with the circus during his summer vacation, and I had the tremendous thrill of seeing my splendid big brother ride by in the parade dressed up as a Napoleonic hussar.

I attended every matinee and evening show and never got tired of it; for I had already identified myself with the circus. I was part of it then and always. But I was deprived of one inalienable right of every American boy. Never could I work my way into the circus by distributing handbills or carrying water for the elephants. Nor could I enjoy the delicious risk of sneaking in under the walls of the Big Top. Naturally this was impossible with our own show; but sometimes when an opposition circus played a town near Baraboo, I would ride my pony ten or fifteen miles to try my luck. It did not work. Even in the tents of mine enemies I was invariably apprehended and escorted to a front-row seat in a box opposite the center ring.

At midnight, very tired after the evening performance, I went back to find the Caledonia on her siding in the yards and crawl into my bunk. Mother was a tremendously good sport about the real risks an active boy might run on such a disjointed journey. She had been indoctrinated so successfully herself that she wanted her sons to have a part in the great national institution which the Ringlings were proud to have given America. The only thing she worried about was the tricky business of running around the railroad yards at night. "Be very careful of those tracks, Buddy," she said to me the first time I went off with Uncle Charlie. And almost the last time I saw her, as I was taking the train out in 1950, she said, "Buddy, please be careful in the railroad yards. Watch those trains, they're dangerous!"

The uncles gave us ponies almost before we could walk. The first one I remember was a tiny Shetland called Minnie. John induced that pony to climb up to our attic playroom on the third floor of the house. It is quite easy to get a horse to walk upstairs but another thing to get him down. My father almost had to carry the poor thing. Our next pony was Maud, and Uncle Charles Ringling gave us a beautiful little cutter, exactly like a real one but pony size. What fun we had driving over the snowy Wisconsin roads with our silver sleigh bells jingling! Most fun of all was the tiny clown police patrol wagon that the midgets drove in the circus. I'd go over to Winter Quarters to borrow it, hitch my pony to it, and drive all over town with the gong clanging furiously.

My favorite pony was Dandy, whom I got when I was five years old. Dandy was a beautiful black-and-white pony, who lived to a great age for a horse. When I was twenty-one and a senior at Yale, I made a special trip to Baraboo to call on him just before he died.

Salomé was afraid of the ponies, though she had to have one anyway, but I always loved to ride. I used to go for wonderful rides with my cousin Henry, who had a pony named Robin L. One of the great tragedies of our childhood was the day we went to the pasture to get Robin L. and found him lying stiff-legged under a tree. He had been struck by lightning. But Henry got another pony and we continued our excursions.

It seems strange for a child, but one of my favorite rides was to the cemetery in Baraboo. It was, and still is, a beautiful place, situated on a hill with a fine view of woods, the lake, and rolling farm land. Even as a little boy I had many friends there—old Civil War veterans with whom I'd marched in the parades. My grandparents were buried there and later my uncles. So I would go and call on my friends, riding Dandy up the hill to that burying ground which had no terror for me, but only a sense of beauty and companionship with people I had loved.

At an early age I naturally wanted to be a performer in the circus—an equestrian, of course. I can remember riding bareback when I was so small that I had to stand on a pail or a pile of rocks to scramble aboard my Shetland pony. Of course, I had some fabulously expert coaching from the famous equestrians in the show, and I got tolerably good. I could lean out of the saddle and pick up a handkerchief from the ground. I could ride standing up—and fall off standing up, too, but it was a fine trick when it worked.

Brother John, the businessman, used to put on a children's circus every spring with half the kids in Baraboo as performers. It was a real professional job. In those days the circus owned its own concessions. Sid Rubeen, who was in charge of them, was a soft touch for us, and he would supply us with whips, and birds on sticks to whirl around, paper toys from Japan, funny hats, canes, and balloons to sell outside our circus. Incidentally, having an ample supply of circus whips around the house was a mixed blessing. Mother used to spank us with them when we were naughty. We borrowed our costumes from the wardrobe department—one year we were all Roman gladiators. Of course, we charged a stiff admission, and looking back on it I believe it was worth the money, for surely no other children in the country had so much experience and assistance.

Playing as we did in the circus back yard, we naturally picked up some rather startling language. John was especially proficient in the profane—and still is. When he was about eight years old Mother became worried about his language and asked the Episcopal minister, the Reverend Clark A. Wilson, to speak to him. The good rector approached John on the street one day and said, "John, I feel I must talk to you about something I've heard that isn't very nice."

Very respectfully John said, "Yes, Mr. Wilson?"

"I hear you've been using very naughty language."

"Who told you that?" John demanded.

Full of tact, Mr. Wilson said, "A little birdie told me."

Whereupon John indignantly observed, "I'll bet it's one of those God-damned little sparrows!"

In fact, the sparrows were a curse in Baraboo. With so many animals around they throve and multiplied exceedingly, and here again John showed his financial acumen. The livery-stableman, Mr. Holsapple, injudiciously offered the boys with BB guns a penny apiece for every dead sparrow. As a result they were thinned out considerably. When the hunting got poor, John took his gun over to Winter Quarters, where due to the enormous manure piles there was probably the greatest concentration of sparrows in the United States. He knocked off a hundred or so, put them in a basket, and carried them back to the livery stable, where he surreptitiously spread them around and then ostentatiously picked them up. It was very good business while it lasted.

A little later John had a change of heart. He became for a time very devout. His musical talent made him a great addition to the choir of the Episcopal church, and he was made crucifer. I can still see him leading the choir into church in his red robes, with dark curly hair, and shining eyes fixed on the tall golden cross he carried.

John could not wait to begin working for the circus. He started at the age of twelve, hawking those same whirly birds, pennants, and whips which we had sold at the children's circus. But it was the real thing now, and he rode the train.

While we were growing up in Baraboo the circus made another great leap forward. In 1919 the uncles decided to merge Ringling Brothers and Barnum & Bailey into one tremendous combined circus which would in truth justify the name of The Greatest Show on Earth.

It was the great show of the twenties in which both Brother John and I got our baptism of fire. A freshman from Yale, John joined the train in Baltimore. His advent was less than impressive. To test his mettle Uncle Charlie had put him on the advertising car as a billposter, a job which required him to get up at 5 A.M. Looking back with amused irony at the brash young man, John describes himself as reporting aboard wearing a camel's-hair jacket and a flashy vest. He carried a Malacca cane and a saxophone. As he walked down the fusty, paper-littered car between berths occupied by weary, unshaven men catching cat naps in dirty undershirts, one of them said, "Here comes a guy who thinks Manual Labor is a Spaniard."

The first morning, John crawled out of bed in the murky dawn of the railroad yards. Empty and disconsolate, he teamed up with a Dutchman and pasted bills on barns, boards, and telephone poles all morning. By noon his mettle had been tested—to the breaking point. He said to himself, "This is ridiculous," and took a taxi to the Belvedere Hotel, where he sent a telegram to his college friend, Theodore Buhl of Detroit:

"If you still want me to visit you wire me one hundred dollars here."

To pass the time of waiting he went to see Charlie Chaplin in *Dynamite*. By the time the picture was finished, the hundred-dollar reply was at the Belvedere.

Thus John disappeared from the circus train and from the family ken. When he did not show up in a day or so, all the Ringling resources were marshaled to find him. Mother was reasonably calm, but Uncle Charlie was in a swivet and Uncle John in a lather. Meanwhile Johnny was cruising Long Island Sound with Theodore Buhl and his mother in her yacht.

Now, this anecdote is not intended to imply any lack of enthusiasm or perseverance on the part of my brother. No one was—or is—more dedicated to the circus than he and no one is willing to work harder. But Uncle John would have understood, as Uncle Charlie did not, that giving a person of Johnny's temperament a dull job, and making him get up at five in the morning to boot, was pushing him too far.

John rejoined the train with what he considered a proper job—selling tickets—and worked hard at it. Indeed, he rode the train every summer for six or seven years and learned more about the techniques of handling a modern railroad circus—the day-by-day, hour-by-hour minutiae of ten thousand things that must be done at every stop—than ever Uncle John knew. Even when John was married and made $28,000 in a single winter selling real estate in the Florida boom, he still went back to his fifty-dollar-a-week job on the circus train each summer.

It was only natural that some of the managerial employees should regard the advent of young Johnny North in the role of heir apparent with eyes turned a bilious yellow by jealousy and fear for cherished perquisites. But it was typical of the underlying violence of circus life that they expressed their disfavor by trying to frame him. That year Johnny was in charge of checking the receipts at the front door and the registers of the concession department, which naturally put a considerable crimp in any funny business that might be going on. This, too, may have supplied a motive.

It happened after I, too, had joined the show, and it was my first apprehension of perils other than physical ones in my chosen career. The plot was hatched, while Uncle John was in Europe, between one of the staff managers and the man who was one of the detectives. It was particularly cruel, since if it had succeeded it would have left an ineradicable stain on my brother's reputation.

The detective, whom for the purpose of this narrative we shall call Turnip Bunson, announced one day that six hundred dollars in one-hundred-dollar bills was missing from a wallet he had left in the staff car. Then he just happened to remember seeing young Johnny North coming out of the staff car, which he did not live in. Of course, Johnny might have been looking for his kid brother, said Turnip. . . .

Rumors ran through the company like poisonous snakes. Most people did not believe them, but there was an element of doubt evident in sidelong looks of embarrassed eyes.

Meanwhile the manager worked subtly to spread the poison. He dropped into Lillian Leitzel's private dressing top, where she reigned as queen of the back yard and received callers in the afternoon between shows. Bringing the subject around to Bunson's loss, he smoothly suggested that while he himself was giving Johnny the benefit of the doubt, there was a doubt. . . .

Dear little Leitzel, with whom we had been friends since childhood, leaped at him shrieking curses that made razorbacks stare in envy, and Alfredo Cadona, who was lazily lying on a sofa, sprang like a white panther. The manager saw murder in his eye and took off. Cadona chased him right through the Big Top.

Not all our people knew us so well. Distrust hung like a tangible cloud between us and our friends and fellow workers.

Johnny was angry and hurt, but too experienced a circus hand by now to go off his rocker. I was outraged. I was working during my summer vacation from Manlius, a military school where the code of honor was as strict as at West Point. It was almost incredible to my unscarred mind that anyone could be so base as deliberately to try to blacken another's character. Even more incredible was the idea that people could believe so mean a thing of John. All my love and loyalty to him set my brain boiling like lava in Vesuvius before she blows her top. Which I came close to doing.

Johnny tried to calm me by saying, "Now don't get excited. Six hundred dollars is a pretty important loss to Bunson. Perhaps he really believes I took it. Perhaps a lot of people do."

"They can't, really," I said incredulously.

Johnny grinned. "Maybe not really yet," he said, "but they will soon."

"What can we do?"

John never lacked decision. "I'm going to have W. J. Burns send an operative down here to find out the truth."

In the circus you cannot even think of doing something without everyone knowing it by a marvelous sort of mental telepathy. The moment Johnny thought of hiring that detective a small miracle happened. Those six one-hundred-dollar bills reappeared in Bunson's wallet just like a magic bunny. He explained that they must have been shoved under a loose lining in it!

This was only the first of the many crises and betrayals which John faced and overcame in his climb to the pinnacle of the circus world. Others far more dangerous and bitter confronted him. It was partly due to his hard schooling in the bare-fisted, knife-wielding, groin-kicking back yard of the circus world that he triumphed over them. But schooling would have meant nothing without his qualities of imagination, courage, bullheaded persistence, outrageous optimism, and dedication to our great family enterprise. It was these coupled with that hard, youthful experience which enabled him to win our circus back from the hands of avaricious creditors, build it to a peak of opulence, lose it, regain it, and rebuild it again and yet again, as I shall tell, until by these achievements he gained, in my opinion at least, the right to be called the greatest showman now on earth.

CHAPTER II

SAWDUST IN MY SHOES

My own advent in the circus was both less frustrating and
less dramatic than John's. It happened in 1926, when I was
seventeen, during my summer vacation from Manlius Military
Academy. I went with my mother to stay with Uncle John at
his big house in Alpine, New Jersey. The first evening, he ex-

pressed the opinion that it was time I went to work for the circus. I agreed with him completely.

Uncle John drove me in his Rolls-Royce to Bridgeport to join the train. All the way over he kept talking about my duties. "You don't mind getting up a little early in the morning, do you?" he asked. I gulped—no Ringling, however youthful, likes to get up early—and said, "Not particularly."

"You'd better get used to it," he answered, "because I'm going to send you out with the flying squadron."

At that point I nearly died. The flying squadron was the first section of the four-section train. It carried the cookhouse, menagerie, and layout department. It meant getting up every morning at 3 A.M.

But Uncle John was only teasing me. I was assigned to the fourth section—the last one to reach town. My job was on the front door. I counted tickets and worked on the trunk. This was a big affair, like a theatrical trunk, with compartments and cubbyholes for filing the tickets as they were taken up at the door. The system had not changed since the earliest days of the show. As the collectors took the tickets they passed them on to the counters, who stacked them in bundles of fifty and a hundred. The children's tickets were green, adults' were purple. I got to be a fast counter, but never as quick as my associate, Willy Downing, who was known as Straight-Ahead Willy because he was deaf and never looked around. He could take a bundle of tickets and feel them, discard one or two, and then there would be exactly fifty tickets in that bundle.

I was famous as the fastest man on the front door, but not as a ticket counter. The doors opened for the matinee at one o'clock. I would go through the door at five minutes of one, through the menagerie top, into the Big Top, through the Big Top and into the back yard, into the band top—where my uniform was kept—change, and be back at the front door on the stroke of one.

We had to wear uniforms with no pockets, for the excellent reason that it kept the collectors honest—there was no place to hide the tickets and resell them. The uniforms had a tunic with a tight collar. Sometimes I almost died of the heat, for I had no time to take my civilian suit off and so I just put the uniform on over it. As I said, we Ringlings like to sleep late.

When I was not busy on the door I tried to learn all I could about the circus. The easiest way seemed to be to ask Carl Hathaway, a wonderful circus character who was manager, or George Smith, boss of the front door. When I asked them such questions as how many poles there were and the order of loading, they gave me a foolish answer. I soon found out that this was because they felt that if I really wanted to learn I should go and find out for myself as they had. So I got a little notebook and went all over the lot jotting down statistics. I counted everything in the circus that first season. Uncle John used to laugh benignly at me because, as he said, he did not have the slightest idea about these things. He said, "I have good men who are supposed to know all about that." But I did know, and it stood me in good stead in later years.

That first year, I lived in the staff car because Uncle John wanted to protect me a little. Some of the great characters of the circus lived in that car. There was the treasurer, Charles Hutchinson—Mr. Hutch, to all of us—who had been with Barnum & Bailey's in the old days and was a nephew-in-law of Mr. Bailey. He had a stateroom in the back of the car, where Mrs. Hutchinson lived with him. It was their home.

The rest of us slept in bunks. Mr. Hutch's assistant, Freddie Wolfe, and Johnny Brice, the chief detective, who had been chief of police in Ironton, Ohio. Cap Carol, who was assistant to the assistant treasurer, was a marvelous character who had been with circuses all his life, including the

Sells Brothers Circus in Australia. Frank Cook, the fixer, bunked with us, and Doc Shields. Doc was an excellent doctor who had graduated from Dartmouth and Columbia and could have had a lucrative practice anywhere, but he got sawdust in his shoes and decided to join the circus. And Chick Bell, the superintendent of tickets.

All these men had been with the circus thirty or forty years and here was I, seventeen years old, with eggshell on my nose. The way they treated me was the kindest, most tactful thing possible. They did not make any fuss, but acted as though I, too, had been around forever.

Every night there was a poker game in the car. I played once a week—on payday. It took them only an hour or two to get my money, but we had wonderful times. Johnny Brice liked to drink a bit too much perhaps, but he did his job. In those Prohibition days he laid in a supply of Virginia corn liquor in gallon jugs at the start of the season. He told me it was kerosene, and I believed him until I saw him drink it. On some Sundays there was no performance and we made a long run. It was a great day. We'd have a big breakfast in the afternoon cooked by Cap Carol and Johnny Brice, who were superb chefs. They laid in their supplies the day before. Then Cap Carol would play his mouth organ and guitar simultaneously while Johnny did a buck and wing; and Mr. Hutch sat drinking his own special brand of bourbon, which he never offered to anybody. He was a generous man but not with his bourbon.

Drink was, in real fact, the bane of circus people, and it still is. Most of the wonderful men in that car had the same failing, and at seventeen, I developed a taste for it, too. I had acquired a case of sparkling burgundy in Canada and one Sunday I drank too much of it. As the train pulled into Devils Lake, North Dakota, about one o'clock that afternoon, I came out on the platform ready to rush off to the hotel for a hot bath with all the others—on the train we washed in tin basins. Brother John was outside his car, also ready to sprint into town. As the train slowed down I stepped gaily off the platform without noticing that the steps were not down. I did a double flip that would have won applause in Clown Alley, landing on my back. John yelled at me like a mother walrus fearful that I was hurt. I was afraid he would spoil my fun, so I picked myself up and took off up an alley.

Suddenly I felt terribly dizzy and I sat down in the middle of the street and was sick. Again and again. It seemed as though I never would stop. Each time my new straw hat fell off. Between paroxysms I put it on again, which was a terrible error. Finally I managed to get to the best hotel in town and discovered that John was registered there. He was having a nice quiet Sunday-afternoon poker game in his room with some of his circus friends when his little brother staggered through the door with his clothes in a lamentable condition. I can still see the look of anguished embarrassment with which John greeted me. He frog-marched me to the bathroom, turned on the water, and threw me into the tub, clothes and all.

So, despite Uncle John's effort at protection, I saw the seamy back side of the carefully smiling face that the circus turned to her public. There is a harsh underworld character to life behind the canvas partitions. It is a world of sudden death and slow disintegration; of rackets and outright crookedness; of tawdry passions and bright knives gleaming in flash fights; of hidden brutality toward dumb animals and callous treatment of human beings. A man may go to sleep under one of the great wagons on the lot, and when tear-down time comes, the driver will hitch up, and never seeing him, start off and the great iron-shod wheels will crush him like a broken beetle. If he is still alive he will be given the best attention by the circus, but if he is dead they will leave him in a ditch, for an inquest might delay the whole show for days and the circus must keep her appointments with her public.

She has great attributes as well: deeds of enormous generosity and loyalties beyond the call of duty or even love. There is great beauty: superb aerialists like Alfredo Cadona or Arthur Concello swooping through the air with the grace of barn swallows; equestrian acts like the Christianis, performing their incredible feats with a skill that cannot be taught in a single generation, but is handed down and refined from father to son, mother to daughter, through generations of circus people dedicated to perfecting their art. And courage! They all are brave, from Clyde Beatty, Alfred Court, and Mabel Stark—the scarred veterans of the animal acts, facing their savage actors twice every day including most Sundays —to the high-wire performers working without a net to thrill the public. Even the people who are not taking obvious risks live in danger, for the chance of accident in the enormously complicated operation of the circus, which is literally an army of men and women and hundreds of animals constantly on the move, is very great.

I was fascinated by the intricate logistics of this operation. Every day fifteen hundred people and a thousand animals— many of them savage—from elephants and rhinoceroses, lions, and tigers down to trained fleas, together with the tremendous amount of equipment they required, which included no less than fifty tents besides the Big Top, were moved from town to town. This whole city of canvas was set up, two performances were given, and the whole business was packed up and moved to repeat the operation in the next town the next day. It required more careful advance planning and more efficient timing than the movement of an army corps. Indeed, when Barnum & Bailey was touring Europe in 1899, Kaiser Wilhelm

II of Germany ordered the Imperial General Staff to study the logistics of the circus and apply them to the movement of the German Army. Unfortunately they did it only too well.

Though I saw it done uncounted times, I never got over the wonder of the simple, basic setup and teardown of the circus. In those days the six-pole Big Top seated over twelve thousand people, and you could put a few thousand more on the straw laid down around the arena. We did not like to have the tent this full, for it was uncomfortable and added to the ever hanging danger of fire. But in those little cities in the plains, where farm folks might drive for a hundred miles to see the show, it was almost impossible to tell them they were too late to get in. The expressions on the faces of their kids undid you.

We moved, as I have said, in four trains. The first section was the flying squadron, consisting of the layout department, side shows, menagerie, and cookhouse. The latter was a tent that could seat a thousand people and serve five thousand meals a day. Because the men had to be fed as soon as they arrived, it was the first thing to be put up.

On the second section we carried the Big Top and its rigging and the working personnel of the train and canvas departments. The third section brought the grandstand and the light and wardrobe departments, with attendant personnel. Trucks and baggage stock were on the second section. Ring stock and elephants were part of the fourth section, along with the staff and performers.

The last car of the last section was either the Jomar or the Caledonia, according to whether Uncle John or Uncle Charlie was in command. But it mainly consisted of sleeping cars for the performers and management. I use the word "sleeping cars" advisedly, for they were not Pullmans, but vehicles specially designed to crowd as many people as possible into double (and some triple) decker berths, with some state-rooms for stars and staffs.

The circus owned all its own cars—the only things the rail-road supplied were the engine and the caboose. By having them built overlength we were able to bring the number we needed down from one hundred to eighty. They were all specially tailored for particular uses. For example, the flats on which the giraffes rode were underslung to give more clearance for their long necks, which were bent down in their thickly padded wagons. Other cars had other special features.

To me the greatest wonder of all was raising the Big Top. Great crowds used to come to the lot to see us do it; and in some ways it was a more impressive show than the circus it-self.

First the great center poles, as tall as the masts of a clipper ship and weighing about a ton each, were brought to the lot by the pole wagon, drawn by an eight-horse hitch, and rolled off in approximately the right position. While these were be-ing raised by gangs of men and obedient elephants, the long blue quarter poles and smaller red ones were arranged in position, with the short side poles outlining the perimeter of the tent. Meanwhile the gilly wagon drove around dropping stakes for guy ropes, followed by gangs of men driving them in with heavy sledge hammers in cadenced strokes. Special stakes were driven to hold the main guys, which braced the center poles from outside. These took the greatest stress, for they supported not only the enormous weight of the tent but the rigging for the aerial acts as well. The main guys were steel cables, as were the safeties on the bail rings.

Now the wagons arrived with rolls of canvas as high as a man's head, which were dropped off and spread on the ground. Men swarmed over them lacing the sections together. There was a half-round top at each end. They had a total di-ameter of 210 feet. In between were five center pieces each

60 feet wide. When they were all laced together you had a tent 510 feet long and 210 feet wide.

In those days boss canvasman Happy Jack Snellen had close to a thousand men under him. As you looked across the lot they were swarming all over the place with much less apparent order than an army of ants and far more precision. When the canvas sections had been laced together and the iron-ringed holes tied to the bail rings on the center poles, you could begin to raise it a little. The elephants strained against their padded harnesses, the one-and-one-half-inch manila ropes stretched taut from the blocks, and the center sections lifted slowly off the ground. It was a little like hoisting sail on a great old windjammer. For a fact, much of the circus was rigged like a ship and the words we used came down from the days of sail—"guys" and "falls" and "bail rings."

As the canvas slowly lifted, men got under it to set the big quarter poles. It took about eight men to a pole, for each was thirty-seven and one half feet long with a steel horn at the end which had to be maneuvered into the leather- and steel-bound eyelets in the canvas so that they were partly supported by it. With the elephants pulling the peaks up slowly, the poles slid along the ground until they were in position. These were all related operations, with the tremendous weight of canvas carefully figured out so that center poles, quarter poles, and side poles would never take too much stress and would not snap in two. Finally the peaks reached the top of the poles, all taut and smooth like a well-cut sail, with the flags and pennants flying over them.

As soon as the tent was up, in came the seat wagons. A knockdown grandstand to seat twelve thousand people had an infinite number of component parts. You'd start off with the small A-shaped jacks and then move to progressively larger ones. On top of the jacks went the forty-foot-long stringers, like jagged saw teeth. The stringers supported the hinged planks for the grandstand, which, strangely enough, were called bibles in circus lingo, because they folded together as a Bible folds. On top of these went the chairs—in the reserved-seat stand. Then you had to level off all these things by wedging hundreds of little blocks of wood under them at the right places.

The whole operation was dependent on manual labor done with speed and precision—each piece thrown off the wagons in exactly the right place and immediately raised into position. The Big Top men were mostly Negroes, magnificent, stalwart fellows glistening with sweat, their muscles bulging as they worked in perfect rhythm heaving the heavy beams of wood off the slowly rolling wagons while other gangs lifted them smoothly into position. It was a marvelous sight, and a shame that it is lost forever.

The teardown was nearly as exciting. The loading order had to be as exactly figured as setting up, so that everything would be in place next day. At five-thirty in the afternoon the last person was served in the cookhouse. It was immediately torn down, hauled to the railroad yards, and loaded onto flatcars. As soon as the people were in the Big Top for the evening performance, the menagerie top and side shows were struck and loaded, as was the back yard. So by the time the performance was over, there was nothing left but the Big Top and the paraphernalia required by the different acts.

As the people were leaving at one end of the Big Top, workmen began tearing down the seats at the other, following right on their heels, so that almost as the last person went out, the tent was bare and ready to be struck. The performance usually ended at ten forty-five. Very often, if we had a good crew, the last wagon would be moving off the lot at one o'clock and the last train might be loaded and ready to go by two-thirty.

From all this you may see that the logistics of the circus, until 1938, when my brother John mechanized it, depended entirely on men, horses, and elephants. Though I put them last, these wonderful animals were not least, for they alone were both workers and performers.

One elephant whom I loved well was Modoc. She was a wonderfully intelligent, sly old thing who was most helpful in the teardown, lowering the quarter poles, pushing wagons around, and doing whatever else she was told to do. Then maybe her attendant would doze in an idle moment and Modoc would drift silently off. Her keeper would suddenly come to, and Modoc would be twenty yards away looking over the littered ground for something to eat. She would pick up discarded Crackerjack and popcorn boxes with her trunk and shake them over her mouth to savor the last crumbs of some child's feast.

In the show this same Modoc used to dance all the way down the hippodrome track and stand on her head at the end. She is still with us.

I learned a great deal about elephants during my years on the train. Because of working beside them you became more intimately associated with them than any other animals. One thing I learned was that, though they are used like domestic animals, they are still wild—bred in the jungle—so you can never quite trust them. This is especially true of the males. Unlike most other animals, it is not the female elephant who has a mating season, but the males. Their period is signaled by a small gland beside each eye which exudes a secretion. When a bull is in "must," as this period of mating urge is called, you can't trust him for a second. It does not help to allow them to mate; in fact, it makes them wilder. For from three to six weeks they are insane. This is why we have very few males in the herd.

Another cause of elephant treachery is cruel treatment by some handlers. They use the elephant hook, or ankus, with sadistic pleasure on the tender places behind an elephant's ears. I have frequently taken the hooks away from cruel keepers and fired them. A bull thus treated is extremely dangerous, for though he may appear docile and obedient, there is a very good chance that he is slyly waiting for his moment of revenge. He may bide his time for years, remembering each outrage, and when his moment comes, exact dreadful retribution.

Sometimes even the gentlest of female elephants will have a mental storm. Such a one was Dolly. She was a lovely old lady who had been with the show for many years, right up to the time John and I took over its management. One day in Winter Quarters in Sarasota, a little girl five years old ducked under the rope around the elephant corral. For some inexplicable reason Dolly grabbed the child with her trunk, and holding her thus, knelt on her, killing her instantly.

Of course, we had to destroy Dolly. The newspapers wanted to make a spectacle of her execution, but however much we love publicity, my brother and I did not feel that we should make a reporters' holiday out of Dolly. So we told them it would be the next morning; and planned it for that night.

Dolly knew something was wrong. You could tell by her nervous little tricks that she was worried. In the middle of the night the circus vet, Doc Henderson, and John and I led her out to a desolate field together with her best friend. Elephants usually have an elephant friend next to whom they are stabled throughout their whole lives with the circus.

When we reached this place of scrub palmettos and long coarse grass, Doc Henderson took a hypodermic syringe the size of a grease gun and, introducing it as gently as possible into a vein in Dolly's ear, gave her a massive dose of strychnine. She stood calm and gigantic in the starlight for a few moments. Then crashed down like a falling building.

Loving animals as I do, I got to know all the others as well, too. From the time I was a boy to my last year with the circus, I was always calling on my friends and feeding them. The shy giraffes are surprisingly affectionate. They breed splendidly in captivity, and a baby giraffe is a great attraction to children, and adults, too—a long-legged, soft-eyed little fellow wobbling around with his ridiculous neck all out of proportion.

The cats are always tricky, though charming and affectionate when young. Because they are smaller, young leopards make better pets than lions and tigers—if you like that sort of pet. Doc Henderson and his wife Martha brought up a female leopard on the bottle. Her name was Sweetheart, and even when she grew up she was just like a kitten—when the Hendersons were with her.

The hippopotomuses have always been friends of mine. A hippo's bulk is tremendous—they weigh between two and three tons—but they are practically never vicious. You could stick your hand in their mouths if you felt a little daring. At least I never lost mine.

I remember one whom we had with the circus all my life and longer. He came to us in 1902. He was named August after my uncle Gus Ringling. In winter, August lived in his big pool in Sarasota. Almost every day I would go over to have a talk with him. I would call "August!" in a commanding voice, and he would come over looking for the big forage biscuits I always fed him.

Another, which we got with the Al G. Barnes show, was a wonderful old lady named Lotus. She was so tame that in many a spectacle we had her led around the arena on a leash.

Baby orangutans and gorillas make wonderful pets. Up to the age of two they develop with about the same intelligence as a human child and are as responsive and fun to play with. After that—look out!

I admit I played favorites with the animals. Zebras failed to charm me. I disliked the snapping, barking seals. And snakes left me cold, although they actually like to snuggle up to people because of the warmth from human bodies. One snake charmer whom I knew, Josephine, had a great affection for snakes, which they seemed to return. She would wrap a twelve-foot constrictor or python around her body for a while. Then she would unwrap him and put him back in his box covered up with blankets all nice and warm.

The great snakes will not willingly eat anything but live food. You have to put a living chicken, rabbit, or small pig in their den. Their ingestion is not a pretty sight, although I have forced myself to watch it.

Now, many people think that circus animals live a miserable life: carted from place to place, always on exhibition, or put through silly tricks for the delectation of the crowds, who sometimes seem less intelligent and sensitive than they. My friend Doc Henderson agrees with me that this is not so. In general, the animals soon get used to circus routine and accept it as a normal way of living. In fact, I suspect that many of them, especially the performers, would miss the excitement and applause. The proof of their acceptance of their lot is that they are usually in remarkably good health. Furthermore, they would not be so friendly and affectionate if they were unhappy. At least I like to think so.

So much for the animal friends I made during the years I rode the train. The wonderfully brilliant, lovable artists, who made the show great; those extraordinary people who were kind or cruel, steadfast or psychotic; passionate yet rigorously disciplined; demanding but bountifully generous; and whichever they were, or sometimes all of these things at once, sharing the great uncommon denominator of superlative showmanship—these marvelous friends will walk with us throughout this book.

At the end of my first season, with my inquiring mind and the multitude of notes I had taken, I thought I knew all about the circus. Of course, I did not. For the next thirty-four years—with a few minor interruptions caused by family feuds and a world war—I continued to learn about it. But one thing I knew for sure even then—I had sawdust in my shoes.

Now I am ready to write about my love; write the whole story. Not only the fair face she turns to her admiring public, though I shall try to do justice to her beauty and her splendid vitality, but also the dark and wicked side of her that I know so well. I will tell the story of our circus from the beginning. It is a story of splendid achievement and of the passionate dedication that my family felt toward the beloved institution which they fathered. But I do not propose to spare even my own people in this narrative. Their faults were often as great as their achievements and these, too, will be faithfully chronicled.

There are many strange, great, lovable, or hateful characters in my story, but basically it hinges on the two men who played the leading role in the history of Ringling Brothers— Barnum & Bailey Circus—my uncle John Ringling and my brother John Ringling North. They have many things in common. They both loved the circus and they were both extremely controversial figures. There was a third likeness: Uncle John and his nephew were both nocturnal creatures. Neither liked to get up until afternoon; and they worked or played all night.

As to the controversies, the sharp battles between men and women of the same blood and the murderous conflicts with outsiders, these were made inevitable by their characters and necessities. For certainly Uncle John was, and Brother John is, egotistical, domineering, and eccentric; and dedicated to the circus. Without them our circus would be a very different sort of thing. In fact, it is doubtful if it would exist at all.

Part II
THE SEVEN BROTHERS

CHAPTER III

THE FIRST PARADE

The circus as we know it has always been a family business. I do not speak of its fearful ancestor, the blood baths in the Roman Colosseum, but of the glittering, laughing, exciting spectacle for children-who-never-grow-up which had its beginnings in the small European road shows of the seventeenth and eighteenth centuries. These traveling troupes were almost always composed of members of a single family, with their wives and collateral relations, who had developed some special skills either as equestrians, tightrope performers, acrobats, or tumblers—the aerialists came later.

Even in the present era of big business many individual acts are still performed by big families like the Wallendas, who build a human pyramid on the high wire, or the Christianis, equestrians extraordinary. My brother and I like to think that despite its heterogeneous collection of hundreds of performers, The Greatest Show on Earth is also still a family affair.

Certainly it was in the beginning. Indeed, for a while the five Ringling brothers were all there was to it. However, there was one striking difference between the Ringlings and other circus people. Most of those families have show business in their blood; but there was never a showman in our family until the spring day in 1870 when my five uncles were, by their accounts of it, ring-struck, dazed and dedicated by the sight of a showboat circus. Indeed, their heredity could hardly have been less promising for the parts they were to play.

They stemmed originally from a French Huguenot family named Richelin, who fled from France after Saint Bartholomew's dreadful fete day and settled in the Hanoverian town of Dankelshausen. There they changed their name to Rüngeling and became extremely staid and sober burghers making an honest living and marrying their neighbors' stolid daughters. Perhaps the Rüngelings married too locally. Again and again through the generations the name Bauermann appears as that of the bride. My sister Salomé maintains that this penchant for marrying their first cousins is the cause of our family's notable eccentricities. I have another theory. . . .

My grandfather August Rüngeling learned the trade of

harness maker and carriage trimmer in Germany and, when he was twenty-one years old, departed for America to escape the alarms and confusions of the revolutionary year of 1848. He settled first in Milwaukee and there his father, Frederic Rüngeling, and his mother, Rosina Bauermann Rüngeling, joined him a year or two later. Unhappily Great-grandfather Rüngeling did not long enjoy the freedom of the New World. He died in the cholera epidemic in Milwaukee in 1850.

Early in 1852 Grandfather Rüngeling met and married Marie Salomé Juliar of Milwaukee, Wisconsin, whose parents had left France in 1845. In my opinion it is the Juliar blood which is boiling in our veins when we orbit out of the norm. Certainly my great-grandfather Nicholas Juliar, who was born in 1797 in the Alsatian town of Ostheim on the Rhine, was a formidable character all his days. He stood six feet four, and the turbulence of his nature was as homeric as his physical proportions. Since he was seventeen in the last years of the Napoleonic era, he may have served the Emperor—toward the end of his life he believed he had.

In the 1840s he sold his vineyards on the sunny slopes behind the Rhine, and packing the gold louis in little kegs, set off with his wife, three daughters, and an infant son, my great-uncle Nicholas Juliar, Jr., for America. He put his family aboard a sailing packet at Le Havre and informed his wife that he had certain affairs to attend to in the town. The business was apparently transacted in the wineshops of the port, and when Grandfather Juliar recovered consciousness, he found that the American packet had sailed.

One may imagine the anxiety with which my tiny great-grandmother, surrounded by her sobbing offspring, watched the masts and spires of Le Havre fading in the early mists as the ship bowed and creaked to the Channel seas. One may also share her relief as she saw a swift cutter pursuing the packet and recognized a gigantic figure standing on her bow-sprit bellowing orders for the packet to heave to. But Great-grandfather Juliar was not permitted to share her happiness. He heard of that episode all the rest of his life.

All his long life Great-grandfather indulged in these drink-ing bouts. My uncle John Ringling remembered him when he was in his eighties, a magnificent man still, as straight and tall as one of Napoleon's grenadiers, roaring drunk in the main street of Rice Lake, calling down curses on all Ger-mans, shooting off his ancient flintlock musket, and shouting *"Vive l'empereur!"*

My grandparents had a happy though peripatetic mar-riage. They anglicized their name to Ringling and settled in Chicago, where Albert, the first of their seven sons was born in December 1852. They then moved to Milwaukee, where August was born in 1854. Grandfather Ringling wanted a business of his own. In 1855 he moved to the village of Baraboo, Wisconsin, which became the cradle of our great enterprise. My uncle Otto was born in Baraboo in 1858.

Grandfather announced his new business in a racy, al-most circus-style advertisement in the Baraboo *Republic* of June 23, 1855.

HO, FELLOW CITIZENS! GIVE ATTENTION TO THE ONE HORSE HARNESS SHOP!

He went on to describe his stock of "a saddle or two, a couple of bridles, trunks, valises, whip lashers . . . also fly nets. . . .

"Now if any are desirous to know where these cheap things stay they will crowd their way to the shop of the undersigned nearly opposite the Summer House. A. Ringling."

It appears that business was good at first, for the following year he triumphantly announced:

The ONE HORSE establishment will now, good friends, pass as a DOUBLE HORSE Concern.

However, it seems unlikely that the Ringling boys inherited their business ability from their father. Despite his skill and the rapidly growing lumber industry which created an excellent demand for harness, the following advertisement appeared in the Baraboo *Republic* in 1858:

> A Ringling Announces that in consequence of the Hard Times . . . he is selling out his entire stock of Double and Single Harness, Saddles, etc. At Cost.

In 1860 the Ringlings moved to McGregor, Iowa. There the rest of the famous Ringling team were born: Alfred T., 1862; Charles, 1864; John, 1866; and Henry, 1869.

McGregor was a boom town on the Mississippi probably larger in those days than it is now. For like so many embryo metropolises on the river, it starved and shrank as the steamboat traffic, which was its reason for being, was superseded by the railroads. Grandfather appears to have had his own shop there for a time, and then joined forces with several partners. He also became a founder member of the new Lutheran church.

My grandmother bought a pleasant frame house in McGregor, and there the Ringling boys grew up in an environment almost identical to that of the most famous of all American boys, who lived in a similar river town, called Hannibal, Missouri. Incidentally, Grandfather Ringling's sister was married to Samuel Clemens' first cousin and my mother often visited the Clemens family in Hannibal. The slow barefoot days of summer alternated with the long icy winters. The little schoolhouse might have been the one where Tom and Huck and golden-ringleted Becky scratched with squeaky pencils on their slates and felt the sting of the teacher's hickory stick on their backsides.

However, theirs was not the circumscribed environment of the inland prairie towns. The multifarious life of the great river, which was the main artery of midwestern commerce, poured by on its roiling, muddy current, often pausing at the levee to load cargo or discharge passengers. Even when they did not stop, those splendid white-and-gold steamers with their tall twin stacks trailing tumbling coils of black smoke led the children's thoughts to places beyond the horizon.

Other types of steamers plied the river in those days— showboats and circus boats. And thereby hangs the tale of The Greatest Show On Earth.

Fortunately for Ringling historians, my uncle Alf T. wrote an eyewitness account of the spring day that changed the Ringlings' lives. The event was heralded weeks ahead by big gaudy billboards proclaiming the advent of:

DAN RICE'S
BRILLIANT COMBINATION OF ARENIC
ATTRACTIONS

Dan Rice, who deserved his billing of The King of American Clowns, was one of the first great circus men—he had started his circus in 1848. He was beloved by the crowds and was a friend of the great, among whom were men of such diverse political views as Horace Greeley, Jefferson Davis, Robert E. Lee, and Abraham Lincoln. His showboat circus was no shoddy affair. Though there was only one ring, it was an excellent show. Indeed, it is thought to be the one Tom Sawyer saw.

My uncle Alf T. recorded that he and his brothers got up very early on the appointed morning. It must have been about 4 A.M., for there was no sign of dawn in the sky as the boys—Henry was too young—walked nervously along pitch-black streets made strange by their utter emptiness.

Down by the boat landing a few oil lanterns glimmered in

the thick, dank-smelling mist off the water. Other early-rising boys and men were moving about talking in low tones or skipping stones across the water. In return for permission to make this predawn excursion, the Ringling boys had promised their parents not to mingle with any crowds, so they formed a solid little group by themselves, which was symbolic of the united front they always showed the world. John, aged four, clung to Albert's reassuring hand. He was too young to be there at all, but he was a willful child.

The boys stood listening for the sound of the circus boat's whistle. They could identify every boat on the river by the note of her whistle, but circus boats were easy. Their owners added a set of chromatic whistles to the regular one and announced themselves by sending a steam-fed tune shoreward. This was the origin of the music machine which became symbolic of the circus, the steam calliope.

When the mist had whitened a little and the bellies of the clouds turned gray, the Ringlings saw lights coming around the bend. All the men and boys began to shout and yell, and were suddenly silent again, listening. Let Uncle Alf describe it:

"Far reaching but soft came the melody of a popular air. . . . There were no screeching tones—none of the ear-splitting screams that the calliope of today sends out to rattle against the windows and walls of a city street. The old river calliope made music that was sweet. All its sharpness and its terror were mellowed as it passed over the water, and by the time it reached the shore it was as soft and soothing as a cradle song. . . ."

Grandly the steamer came on, pine torches flaring along her decks. She nosed into the bank with clanging bells and hissing steam. You could read her name on the pilothouse: WILL S. HAYS. Alongside her was a barge loaded with splendid chariots of red and gold, and the tent wagons piled with long poles and great rolls of canvas. These were dragged off first by a windlass; then hitched to six-horse teams and started for the show grounds. The carved and gilded chariots were eased carefully off, as their teams were simultaneously brought off the main boat and hitched up with the precision of a well-drilled battery of horse artillery. Then came the animals—a nose-ringed bear or two, a grumpy camel, the white broad-backed horses of the equestrians, and finally the elephant, testing the gangplank with probing trunk and one great fore-foot. Iron-gray, the color of sky and water, he was monstrously magnified by the mist. Though later the Ringlings owned many larger animals, they all declared that they never saw another elephant that *looked* so big.

Alf T. Ringling states that as he and his brothers walked home for breakfast, they talked together for the first time of having a circus of their own.

The rest of the day was as splendid as its beginning. First the parade, then the performance itself, which was more than anticipation demanded. To the unsophisticated, entertainment-starved children of those small midwestern towns, the color and splendor, the music and lights, the feats of skill, and the uproarious antics of the clowns were beyond any imagining of delight. Even the sleazy, gaudy costumes were trans-figured by their innocent eyes and, for that reason in that time, were truly things of beauty.

The younger boys were completely swept up and out of themselves by the show, lost to time and all reality. But Al watched it with a speculative eye, studying the techniques of the acrobats and jugglers. At eighteen he was strong and agile, and he believed he could duplicate some of their feats.

As is the way of circuses, Dan Rice's show vanished in the night, leaving no trace of its glories but a terrible mess of torn paper, garbage, and old tin cans on the show grounds. However, instead of the emptiness that usually marks the day after such an orgy of delight, the Ringlings were full of enthusiasm. They had decided to put on their own show.

Their first circus was held in a "mammoth pavilion" made of scraps of canvas, old carpets, and moth-eaten army blankets. The company consisted of the Ringlings and a few friends. The admission price was one cent. But such was the eagerness of McGregor's youth to see a show—any show—that a series of performances netted $8.37 (Alf T.'s figures). This was promptly plowed back into the business by the purchase of enough muslin sheeting for a fairly sizable tent.

The Ringlings considered their performance of 1870 kid stuff. In the summer of 1871 they put on a real show. (That year a gentleman named Phineas T. Barnum also went into the circus business.) Apparently the Ringlings must have worked on their circus the best part of the winter and spring and spent most of their earnings on props and ring stock, for it represented quite a respectable entertainment even without the accidental effects that were funnier than the best efforts of Emmett Kelly. Their historian, Alf T. Ringling, left a blow-by-blow description of it.

McGregor was notified of the event by the concatenation of a fife, jew's-harp, bugle, and harmonica, and the booming of an enthusiastic drum. Rushing to porches and store fronts, they saw the parade, headed by a "Democrat wagon" painted in gaudy reds and yellows drawn by a desiccated black mustang pony, with superb harness by A. Ringling and a red, white, and blue sheep's-wool plume nodding from his head. Driving the wagon was Al Ringling, who also played the bugle, while four of his brothers, all wearing plumes like the horse, made up the band. It was followed by a small boy carrying a sign that read:

RINGLING'S BIG CIRCUS

Next in line came Otto Ringling leading a battle-scarred goat known locally as Billy Rainbow, which he had trained to perform certain tricks and reclassified as a "hippo-capra." This in turn was followed by the whole juvenile population of McGregor. Indeed, most of the adults joined the fun, following the Ringlings to the vacant lot where their circular tent was pitched. From its center pole, a young pine tree cut from the nearby woods, floated an American flag, while the sapling quarter poles flew homemade pennants. Over the entrance was a sign:

RING-LING CIRCUS
Admission 5 cents

Over a hundred men, women, and children handed their five cents to Otto at the door and crowded around the little sawdust ring in the middle of the tent. The entertainment started with the grand entry, known professionally as the Spec. Alf T., representing the King of the Sandwich Islands in a Union officer's old dress uniform, a cape made from a crazy quilt, and a gilt-paper crown, led it riding the pony. He was followed by the band and the performers, now dressed in tights made of long winter underwear dyed gaudy colors and meagerly bespangled and decorated with fancy ribbons. Last came Billy Rainbow, led by John Ringling dressed as a clown—he was five years old.

Right at the peak of the spectacle occurred the first of those unpremeditated incidents which convinced the spectators that they were getting their money's worth. As the King of the Sandwich Islands dismounted and bowed to his applauding subjects, Billy Rainbow broke loose from John's feeble hold and with instinctive showmanship butted the seat of the royal pants. The King wept with pain and everyone else in the tent wept with laughter.

From there on the Ringlings had their audience sewed up. Al juggled hats and plates, and the more plates he broke the louder was the applause. Otto Ringling was announced with his performing goat. Under the eye of his real master, Billy Rainbow worked like a veteran.

Display No. 4 was a tumbling act by the entire company. Little Johnny Ringling then sang a clown song, "Root Hog or Die," with the whole company joining in the chorus, and followed it up with some jokes from Dan Rice's show the year before. The next display was an exhibition on trapeze and rings. Then came the crowning performance. While Al acted the ringmaster in a real high silk hat, Charlie Ringling appeared in an equestrian display on the mustang. It was not precisely bareback riding, for the poor beast's razor-sharp spine would have defeated Lucio Christiani himself. Charlie had contrived a riding pad out of half a cellar door and some blankets. It had worked well in practice, but in the hurry of getting it strapped on his steed he had been careless. Every time he leaped onto it, it tilted and spilled him off. Thus, in spite of themselves, the Ringlings followed that old theatrical precept: "Always leave them laughing."

In telling the story of Dan Rice's arrival in McGregor and the first Ringling circus, I have adhered strictly to the facts as set down by my uncle Alf and related to me by my other uncles. But I am not so naïve as to suppose that no exaggerations crept in. Nor should it be otherwise, for without hyperbole circus public relations would be like a Bloody Mary without vodka.

For example, though they always claimed it happened that way, it seems improbable that all my uncles were converted by Dan Rice's lightning like six Sauls on the road to Damascus. This appears especially doubtful in the case of four-year-old Johnny. Yet one cannot be sure, for John Ringling at the last was the most dedicated of all; and he was a precocious child. Like most legends, this one is probably contrary to fact but contains the essence of truth. For that May day did, in fact, determine their lives.

I think that it was Albert Ringling who got the full charge and bellwethered his brothers into a life of showmanship. But they were willing followers, and in the end the disciples out-ran their master. By the time they held their first circus their course was fully charted.

The townspeople of McGregor may have regarded the show as a joke, but to the Ringlings it was a deadly serious business in which they took enormous pride. How proud they were is indicated by the fact that in all the years ahead my shrewdly sentimental uncles numbered their seasons from that first five-cent circus.

CHAPTER IV

RINGLING BROS. CLASSIC
AND COMIC CONCERT CO.

The "hard times" came again for August Ringling in 1872—
a year ahead of the rest of the country.

That autumn the Ringlings moved across the river to Prairie
du Chien in Wisconsin, where my grandfather got a job as a
carriage trimmer in Traner's Carriage Works. He was able to

rent a comfortable house in the village. But bad luck seems
to follow poor businessmen, like a dog after a whistle. The
next fall Traner's factory burned to the ground just as the
great depression of '73 hit the country. It was never rebuilt,
and Grandfather was out of work.

Now the Ringlings reached their lowest ebb. They moved
to a ramshackle house in a coulee, or dry gulch, outside of
town. Naturally it had no plumbing, but a lead pipe mounted
on wooden blocks brought water to the kitchen from a spring
further up in the hills. A narrow strip of land along the road
came with the house, and there those of the boys who were
still at home raised what food they could, with the aid of the
former King of the Sandwich Islands' old mustang pony. In
that house my mother, Ida Lorena Wilhelmina Ringling, was
born on February 2, 1874. She was twenty-one years younger
than her eldest brother, the last child and only girl in the
family. Two other boys and a girl, who all died in infancy,
had been born in between my uncles, but in those unsterile
times, to have eight children survive was an excellent percentage.

After Ida was born, the older boys began to fly the family
coop. Gus was already working as a carriage trimmer in various small Iowan towns. Then Al went off to follow his precarious chosen profession. He had never ceased to practice
his juggling and acrobatics. Now he managed to get jobs in
some "hall shows," as the small troupes of traveling entertainers were called. He appears to have made his head-
quarters at Brodhead, Wisconsin, where he worked as a
carriage trimmer while professionally at liberty. In the summer he came to Prairie du Chien, and while working that thin
piece of land, perfected his most original trick—balancing a
plow on the point of his chin.

Albert Ringling had considerable ability, and what is more,
he had the drive, which in any field is an excellent substitute

for talent. According to an article by J. J. Schicher in the *Wisconsin Magazine of History*, he was so successful that by 1880 he was managing a show. Two ancient Brodheadians remember him living in a large hotel room surrounded by his paraphernalia and practicing his stunts. History does not state how his fellow boarders felt about it. However, one of Uncle Al's specialties was ropewalking, which he practiced out of doors on a rope stretched between two large trees in the town square.

Meanwhile August Ringling was once more on the move, first to Stillwater, Minnesota, and finally back to Baraboo.

Grandfather was surely a glutton for punishment. He had his own shop in Baraboo again in 1876, which was burned up in a fire that leveled an entire block of wooden shops on Oak Street in 1878. Even this did not daunt him. He opened up again at the corner of Third Street and Broadway in the lower floor of a frame house, while the family lived above. In 1880 he won three first prizes at the county fair with a "splendid display of harness," including a "gold- and rubber-mounted double carriage harness . . . the finest ever manufactured in this part of the state."

Sometime during those years Otto went off to find work as a harness maker, while Alf T. and Charles came into their father's shop. But their hearts were definitely not in it. Rather, they liked to practice their musical instruments—Charles played the violin and trombone; Alf blew a loud and melodious cornet.

Meanwhile young Johnny was boiling with that tremendous energy which later made him the most far-ranging of the brothers, both in business and intellectual activities. This does not refer to formal education—he never even finished high school. In fact, my mother used to say that the only way they could keep John in school was to tie him to his desk. Uncle John was never amused by this remark.

When he was twelve years old John Ringling struck out for himself. He ran away from home and set himself up in business in Milwaukee. Long afterward he described to me his first business venture. It was selling a "wonderful" cleaner for pots and pans which he manufactured himself by combining an abrasive powder with a little bluing to give it a distinctive appearance. This he put up in neat little packages. When the police, whom Grandfather had alerted, caught up with John, they found him living in an empty warehouse in Milwaukee, industriously mixing up a batch of Ringling Cleanser. His only furniture consisted of packing crates ingeniously adapted to the roles of table, chairs, and a bed. But business was booming. He was very annoyed at being sent home.

In the next two years John ran away three more times. Somehow he never cared for Baraboo. In fact, as soon as he got enough money he moved away permanently and thereafter referred to residents of his home town as "Baraboobians."

John's final bid for freedom from education came when a small hall show played Baraboo. Uncle John caught up with the show about ten miles from Baraboo at the tiny town of Delton, which has since disappeared without leaving a trace. He asked for a job, giving his age as sixteen, which he looked to be. They promptly hired him as a general handyman. He swept the halls, packed up the paraphernalia, and *took tickets at the door*. His pay was supposed to be three dollars a week.

Uncle John enjoyed the gypsy life immensely, as he ever after did; but he got very tired indeed of never being paid. Occasionally, the manager would throw him a half dollar, but this did little more than add insult to his strong sense of personal injury. Since there seemed no chance of collecting his back wages legally, he decided to do something about it. One night, when the audience was in, he carefully counted the take and found that it came to just about what he figured the show owed him. So he put it in his pocket and left town while the performers were still bringing down the house.

That was in Minnesota. Correctly deciding that he had better get lost, he headed for the great big city of St. Paul, where he bought himself a gold watch and confidently began looking for work. Fortunately, his father found him before his former employer did, and back he went to Baraboo.

The Ringlings' real career was heralded by the merest whisper of publicity. An obscure item in the *Sauk County Democrat* for June 10, 1882, stated, "Albert Ringling is at home for several days' vacation with his parents."

It was no vacation. Uncle Al came to organize a dream— that of having his own show. If August Ringling shook his head it was in silence. Charles and Alf T. were enthusiastic —harness making was never a thing for them. In addition, young Ringling recruited three talented local boys for his little company. Among them was E. M. Kimball, who later made his mark in theatrical history by proxy as the father of the brilliant star of the silent screen, Clara Kimball Young.

With reckless disregard for fact and splendid alliteration, the show was billed as:

Fourth Season, 1882
RINGLING BROS.
CLASSIC AND COMIC CONCERT CO.
A refined and high class entertainment containing
many of the most prominent features of the musical
and comedy world

New Faces   New Acts   New Songs
Wonderful Dancers   Great Specialists
Noted Comedians   Famous Singers
TWO HOURS OF SOLID FUN

As to that questionable "Fourth Season": The Ringlings were not liars; they just liked to stretch truth a little. They justified the statement by counting the five-cent circus as their first season and Albert's three years of managing hall shows as the rest.

The Ringlings spent the rest of the summer of 1882 in frantic preparation. A show was put together and rehearsed. Handbills and tickets were printed; wigs and comedy accessories bought or made at home; trunks purchased and packed. A. M. Young was hired as advance agent to map their route and travel ahead to plaster the towns with gaudy yellow posters. It all cost a great deal of Albert's hard-earned money. Before they put their first show on the road Ringling Brothers were almost flat broke.

On a cold November afternoon the show started from Baraboo with the paraphernalia in a farm wagon and the performers in a three-seat surrey. They drove fourteen miles over the wintry hills to Sauk City, where they took a milk train to Mazomanie, Wisconsin. Their object in taking this roundabout route was to avoid being followed by friends who might come to jeer, not cheer. It was not altogether successful.

When they got to the hotel for breakfast, two young Mazomanians, whom they had once met, greeted them with whoops and hollers. Charles Ringling told how this ill-timed welcome affected them.

"When those two young fellows dashed into our faces with their guileless effervescence, and their carbonic questions made the crowd standing around wise about our newness, we felt like taking the train back to Baraboo. How we could shake hands with the fellows when we felt that they deserved to be murdered, I don't know. We were crushed for all day."

Utterly despondent, the company went through a spiritless rehearsal which was further dampened by their awe of the "grandeur of painted hangings and imitation-marble columns," which were the local theater's stock set.

According to Charles: "At about noon we paraded the streets of the small village with our little band. . . . Alf and one of our hired associates played on cornets, the other played a bass horn . . . and I must have threatened the foundations of the shops with a long and brassy trombone while Al beat the bass drum. . . . As we paraded that first day, each one of us playing for dear life, I was aware of a lump that seemed to come into my throat. . . . From the shopwindows our yellow window hangers boldly proclaimed [that we] would give an entertainment of Mirth and Music in the town hall, and I shuddered at what in my own heart I called 'our awful gall.'"

The historic first performance took place on the evening of Monday, November 27, 1882. It exceeded everybody's worst expectations. According to Charles: "From the very beginning the troupe in its entirety seemed to fly to pieces. Our first number was an introductory overture. We all played in this, ordinarily in a satisfactory manner. . . . [That night] it seemed as if every note from the cornet was a blue one, every tone from the violin a squeak, every blast from the clarinet a shriek, and as if all the different instruments were in a jangle. Oh, it was an awful exhibition of faltering nerve. . . .

"We were a confused and demoralized lot when we left the stage. Our trembling limbs seemed unable to move . . . and we bumped up against one another awkwardly as with bated breath and red faces we shambled off beyond the wings. . . .

"You can imagine how we felt when we had to go out and face the audience singlehanded and alone to perform our specialties. But we did it. Talk about a soldier's feeling before battle! It cannot be a comparison to a real healthy feeling of stage fright. Why, when I came off after my so-called act, my tongue and throat were actually parched from the fever of excitement that was raging within me. . . .

"Now as I look back on that performance, I wonder that it

didn't break up in a riot. . . . The funny part of it was that not one of the fifty-nine people who had come to see the show got up and walked out. They suffered the tortures of our music and bore the weariness which hung upon our jokes with a patience and good nature which I feel grateful for to this day. They even applauded at times. I hope every one of them has prospered since, and may live a long and happy life. Each deserves it after such a sacrifice. . . ."

When the Ringlings counted the house they found they had taken in thirteen dollars. Against this they had the following expenditures:

Livery from Baraboo to Sauk City	$ 8.00
Railroad fare from Sauk City to Mazomanie	2.40
Hotel bill	7.50
Rent of hall	6.00
Salaries	2.00
TOTAL:	$25.90

As the Ringling Brothers left for their next stand at a town with the hopeful name of Spring Green, their working capital was two dollars and fifty cents.

In that vernally named but icy city they got their first break. As soon as the train arrived they hurried to the drugstore which Mr. Young had induced to handle the tickets.

"What is our advance sale?" Al asked, and thought the druggist answered, "Six."

"That's not much," he said despondently.

"I think it's mighty good," the druggist said. "Fact is, sixty dollars is the best we've ever had here."

It is reliably reported that Uncle Al required a restorative. Even when he recovered, he could not understand how the people of Spring Green could be insane enough to buy nearly every seat in the house. The mystery was cleared up by the janitor of the hall, who explained that a local association had announced a dance for that night, but when they tried to hire the hall, it was already taken. The farm boys and their girls had been driving into town all day. When they found the dance was off, they took the next best thing—the Ringlings.

So from the depths of bankruptcy the Ringlings shot to the very peak of prosperity in twenty-four hours. By eight o'clock the house was packed with people; some even roosting on the window sills. The farm folk were out to have a good time; and they had it. As the Ringling orchestra came on stage the audience whistled and cheered, and the timbers shivered to the stomping of cowhide boots. What mattered now an occasional blue note or a slight squeak? The crowd was warm and willing, and the company responded by outdoing themselves, as is always the case when that wonderful rapport which makes the magic of the theater is established between an audience and the performers. Indeed, my uncles said they never played better. Albert was brilliant and sure as he juggled whips, hats, and plates. How the farm boys yelled when he balanced that plow on his chin! The singing and dancing acts were thunderously received. When Alf T. and Charles displayed their versatility by playing eight different instruments, the audience sat in spellbound wonder. Every threadbare joke brought a belly laugh, and the dramatic sketch which closed the show produced an ovation. It was an actor's paradise.

That night set a record but not a precedent. The company rocked along from town to town, scraping bottom all the way. On December 1 and 2 they daringly gave shows in McGregor and Prairie du Chien without being egged off the stage by their former fellow townsmen.

On December 18, at Sanborn, Iowa, John Ringling, aged

fifteen, joined his brothers. He had three comic roles in the show; the first two were a dude and an Irishman. For his final turn he was billed as The Emperor of Dutch Comedians and did a wooden-shoe dance. With his round face and a false bulging stomach he was very funny.

The band needed an alto horn, so Albert ordered John to learn to play it. He went so far as to lock his brother in his room for practice every day until John was able to produce an adequate if not exactly scintillating performance.

By train or in hired wagons and sleigh, the Ringlings followed an erratic course across the bleak Iowan plains playing every night but Sunday. They even gave a show on Christmas night in Flandreau, South Dakota. Then they crossed into Minnesota. Experience made them decide to avoid the larger towns in favor of the little rural communities, which were both less critical and more hungry for entertainment. Their Route Book chronicles the almost forgotten names—Pipestone, Edgerton, Fulda, Jackson, Fairmont, Alden, Austin, Brownsville, Dexter. Next to Dexter is the notation "Snowed in."

There the final curtain almost fell on the Ringling Concert Company. They were operating on so thin a margin that a lost night could mean bankruptcy. Alf T. describes how they dragged their trunks down to the depot through a howling blizzard because the liveryman refused to take his horses out. Their train grunted in hours late pushing a snow plow. It was only twenty miles to ironically named Spring Valley, but the train stuck fast halfway there, and they slept on the plush-covered seats of the chilly cars. The next day the train was hopelessly snowbound, but they succeeded in hiring a sleigh for ten dollars. They had only half that amount between them, but they figured they might get the rest if they ever reached Spring Valley. They did; for the news of their trek spreading through town was better advertising than handbills, and the house was full.

In a mining town they ran into competition from a prize fight and played to six people. This time they had no money to pay their hotel bill, so Jim Hamilton, the proprietor, held their trunks. But the miners felt sorry for them and helped to sneak the trunks out of the hotel in the middle of the night and get them on a barge, in which they crossed the Mississippi River to Wisconsin, leaving Hamilton howling imprecations from the bank.

Then they had a few good nights and sent Hamilton a money order for his bill. How extraordinary such honesty was considered is shown by the receipt he sent them.

> Received of Ringling Bro. this day and date 7 dolars witch I neaver thot Ide get, but witch I am sorey I dident trust them for because they are honest even tho they are acters whitch you cant say of all of them. But I have been skined so many times by men who say nice words, that I have to be careful.
>
> If you eaver come this way agan Ide trust you but I was awful mad when I thot you had skip for good.
>
> JIM HAMILTON.

About this time Otto Ringling joined them, replacing A. M. Young as advance man. And now the five original partner-brothers were all together.

Through that frozen, desolate countryside the tour continued. In some respects their life was more rigorous than that of the pioneers who had but lately preceded them. For the first settlers were at least properly clothed, housed in snug cabins, and equipped to live off the country swarming with game; whereas the Ringlings were nightly on the road, half frozen in their thin citified clothes, and dependent for their food on the fickle favor of the public, which was a considerably less reliable provider than a Winchester .44.

When they had time to sleep at all, it was in flea-bag hotels where the top price for a room was a dollar and fifty cents and not worth it. In this connection, Uncle John used to tell the tale of arriving late at one such hostelry and hauling the proprietor out of bed, whose unsavory appearance and gamy smell foretold the conditions ahead. He came to the front desk and reached for the key with his right hand, vigorously scratching his exposed armpit with his left. "Here's number four for you two," he said. With his left hand he hooked a second key off a nail while scratching his left armpit. "You two gentlemen bunk in number five."

Then with both hands energetically scratching his belly, he remarked with undue optimism, "Have a good sleep, gentlemen."

The initial tour closed in Viroqua, Wisconsin, on February 27, 1883, and they all went back to Baraboo, no richer, but considerably wiser. However, they started out again on March 12, and played throughout April. One more brief foray, which lasted a week in May, ended the season.

What the Ringlings did throughout the summer is not recorded. They certainly did not live on their profits. Nor did they work in the harness shop; for August Ringling had upped stakes again to locate in Rice Lake, Wisconsin. He hoped to find a market for his handmade harness by moving westward to this frontier town, which was so deep in the forest that my mother remembered being frightened by a great black bear when she was picking berries.

Whatever occupation the brothers found, it was only a stop-gap. Neither storm, nor sleet, nor gloom of public apathy could stay them from their self-appointed course. On August 30, 1883, they started out again with a more elaborate show. Otto, Alf T., Charles, and John headed it—Albert was traveling with another troupe, which had made him an offer he could not afford to turn down. In addition, there were eight hired performers, including a married couple, and a brand-new portable organ. One thing the Ringlings had learned on their previous tours was that the word "classic" held no appeal for their public. What the people of those small western towns wanted, and needed desperately, was entertainment, so this season the show was billed as:

RINGLING BROS. GRAND CARNIVAL OF FUN

They headed straight for the lumber towns, where the axmen and loggers had pay in their pockets and no place to spend it. They did very well—at first.

On September 22 they played Rice Lake and held a family reunion. Their deep German sentimentality and strong family ties had survived transplanting to the New World as it was to survive the harder pressures of great wealth and diverse interests. Though I appeared thirty years and thirty million dollars later, I can still remember the tremendous family gatherings at Christmas in Baraboo, when all the uncles came home with their wives and children to celebrate with an enormous meal and joyous expressions of their deep affection for one another. So one can easily imagine what a *gemütlich* time they had that night in Rice Lake, with their parents, and their baby sister, and Henry, who grew to be six feet three and weigh three hundred pounds. One can also envisage the meal that Grandmamma cooked for them of rich, heavy German dishes, and how wonderful it tasted after the slops that were served on the fly-specked tables of hotel dining rooms.

As the Carnival of Fun moved on into Minnesota the weather hardened, and the hired performers became a good deal less enthusiastic.

The trouble came to a climax early in November. For that date the Route Book has the brief notation: "On November 2'd all people were discharged, and on Nov. 3'd at Starbuck, Minn., made parade. Alf Ringling, Cornet; John Ringling,

Alto; Chas. Ringling, Baritone [Trombone]; Otto Ringling, Bass Drum. [Otto was tone deaf.]"

Fortunately Alf T. Ringling provided a considerably more detailed account of the crisis. According to him, the management held a conference at which one of the brothers remarked, "Next season let's go it by ourselves."

It was Alf T. who said, "I'd make next season begin tomorrow."

The next day happened to be payday. The company was much gratified and slightly surprised to get their full pay that night after the show. Then they all went to bed in the hotel across from the railway station. As soon as the Ringlings were reasonably sure that their employees were asleep, they sneaked out and borrowed the baggage truck from the railway station. Then they woke the proprietor and told him that they were leaving and wanted their trunks. His alarmed protest was silenced by being paid in full for everybody through breakfast on the morrow.

Only one hitch occurred. One of the trunks had been left in the hotel parlor. Since every room was taken, the proprietor had put a cot in it and rented it to a most respectable widow. Naturally nervous about inhabiting the same hotel as a troupe of actors, she had locked her door and paid no attention to polite rapping. At this point Uncle John showed that gift of improvisation which took him so far. He banged urgently on the door with his cane and said in a commanding voice, "Quick, madam! I can still save you."

The door opened a crack. Uncle John inserted his stick. His brothers rushed in to get the trunk. Over to the station on the luggage truck, and they were off bag and baggage.

When Otto met them there in Starbuck the next day, he asked, "Where are all the others?"

"Shook," said John.

It is further recorded in the Route Book that with Otto out ahead, Alf T., Charles, and John played the show alone until Al joined them at Lincoln, Nebraska, on January 6, 1884. Apparently they did very well, for by that time they were able to see the shimmering mirage of a Big Top of their own. There is a picture of the five brothers parading in this final flowering of the Carnival of Fun. They have abandoned the uniformed-band idea and are fashionably dressed in Prince Albert coats with gleaming high silk hats. Albert and Charles already have grown the glossy black walrus mustaches which became a trade-mark of the Ringling brothers. On his travels Al had acquired two valuable assets. One was the friendship of a grand old circus man who was down on his luck; the other was a wife.

Her name was Louise Morris, and she was a woman of many parts, among them a dauntless disposition and the ability to charm snakes. The senior Ringlings were somewhat less enthusiastic about their first daughter-in-law than her merit deserved. This is implied in a pathetically polite letter from her, written the following year while her husband was off with the Carnival of Fun.

> Baraboo, December 21, 1884
>
> Dear Mr. and Mrs. Ringling:
>
> I suppose I should say Father and Mother but it seems kind of strange to say that. But it has been long anuff ago to not be strange by now.
>
> Al wrote to me saying you want to now why I never wrote to you. I wrote last if I am not mistaken and I supposed you knew all about Al and I being married as I think Al wrote it to you last winter just after we was married. It was ages ago the 19th of this month. . . .
>
> Well I just think there is no better man than Al. We all got along spendid last summer and had a nice time and I am very anchuss to see him here again as I am very lonesome here all alone this winter. I am

doing some dress making but don't have mutch to do
not like I used to have. But I am trying to help all I can
so Al can keep even with the rest of the Boys. . . .

Well Ida how do you do and how are you getting
along with your music as I see by the Boys' letters
that you have a new organ?

I will close at this time hoping to here from you soon.

I remain yours with respect,

LOU RINGLING
Love to you All.

Despite her deficiencies in grammar and spelling, Louise
Ringling was a beautiful young lady. A contemporary photograph shows that she had a willowy, wasp-waisted figure, dark
hair and eyes, and a small heart-shaped face with finely
modeled features. In the picture she is wearing a handsome
afternoon gown of satin and lace adorned with all the frills
and furbelows of Victorian high fashion. The contrasting
sash, draped over the full skirt, is a live boa constrictor.

In her anxiety to help Al "keep even with the rest of the
boys" she outdid even them. She and Al had a small house in
Baraboo, where all five brothers lived when they were at
home, eating gigantic meals which Aunt Lou cooked. When
they got the wagon-show circus she made most of the costumes, cooked for all hands, and acted as adviser and house
mother to the female performers, and was the star equestrienne. When necessity arose she even did some snake charming.

Later, when Al Ringling was equestrian director of the
hundred-car railroad show, Aunt Lou always traveled on the
train with him. Throughout the years he relied on her.

As to the friendship Al had made, that also fostered great
events.

CHAPTER V

THE WAGON SHOW

Al Ringling's new friend and mentor was Yankee Robinson, an old man on the last downward slope from the pinnacle of the circus world. Like most of its citizens, he had had a whip-sawed career. His first big success, in 1854, was a traveling tent show which gave a circus in the afternoon and *Uncle Tom's Cabin* at night. *Uncle Tom* was dropped, and it became all circus for its tour of the South; but in 1859 a South Carolina mob took offense at Yankee's nickname, and he took off with whiskers streaming while they destroyed his whole equipage. Prudently remaining in the North, he recouped during the 1860s, and in 1869 his huge wagon show grossed more than any American circus had until then.

Overconfident expansion brought bankruptcy in 1876; and when Albert Ringling met him, he was operating a small hall show. My uncle John once told me that all he could remember about Yankee Robinson was his magnificent spread of white whiskers and his passion for oysters. These delicacies were very hard to come by in the inland states, and whenever he happened upon a supply, the old gentleman prepared to enjoy himself. He would sit down before a great pile of oysters and carefully place a brass spittoon beside him. Then he would begin to eat, and when he could cram no more oysters down his throat, like the old Roman he was in spirit, he would vomit into his spittoon; and start afresh.

Tired of the halls and longing, as all of us do, to return to the tented arena, Robinson eagerly agreed to throw in with the Ringling gamble. He brought no capital but his experience. However, he clothed our show with the authority of his tattered fame.

The first definite proof that the Ringling dream was assuming concrete form comes in a letter from Montello, Wisconsin, dated April 9, 1884:

> Dear Parents, Bro and Sis:
> It froze today. Will be in Baraboo Saturday. We bought a team in Waukon, Iowa. We have one wagon in Baraboo, another horse in Iowa. Have all our mail sent to Baraboo.

Hoping this finds you in good health as it does us.
Yours
RINGLING BROTHERS
The name of our show is Yankee Robinson's Great
Show and Ringling Brothers Carnival of Comedy.

This letter is in the round, immature handwriting of John
Ringling, which remained round and immature until he died
at the age of seventy. The most interesting aspect of it is that
Uncle John, writing to his own family, signed it "Ringling
Brothers." That indicates how proud were the brothers of
their partnership, and how completely they regarded themselves as a single entity in which any one of them could speak
for all.

Not that they did not have hot arguments among themselves. My mother said that sometimes when they were all at
Grandmother's house discussing business they bellowed and
roared and swore at each other, eyes flashing, fists clenched
as though they would assassinate one another at any moment.
My tiny grandmother could always control them through
their love and respect for her. Above all, no hint of disagree-
ment ever leaked outside their private discussions through
all the long years, until one by one they died.

My cousin Richard Ringling, looking backward at the great
circus empire which they built from so small a start, once
said to me, "Perhaps it wasn't that the uncles were so smart,
but just that there were so God-damned many of them." He
should have added, "All working with complete loyalty and
a single purpose."

The Carnival of Fun closed and returned to Baraboo on
April 12, 1889, after a highly successful season. The Ringlings
had a thousand dollars in the bank and a little over a month
to get their circus together. With so small a stake they had
to do almost everything themselves. They ordered their Big
Top (90 by 45 feet) and a smaller one for the side show

from a tentmaker, but according to Alf T., they cut the poles for it themselves in a tamarack swamp near Baraboo. They had bought three spring wagons to convey the personnel and management across country. Over these they put covered-wagon tops of sheeting painted vermilion, with lithographed pictures of wild animals—of which they had none—and the name of the show in gold letters. Its billing had been changed to the more imposing title of:

YANKEE ROBINSON and RINGLING BROS.
GREAT DOUBLE SHOW
Circus and Caravan

While this work was going forward, local carpenters were building knockdown benches under their direction, and Louise Ringling was industriously sewing costumes.

To move the show they had, in addition to the spring wagons, several farm carts and a big dray for the tent poles. Whether they actually owned three or five horses is obscure, but most of the animals which hauled the wagons were hired from local farmers, who drove their own teams. As finally constituted, the caravan consisted of twenty-two horses and nine wagons, not counting the "Privilege Wagons," as the personnel vehicles were called in the Route Book. One of these was sent ahead as a "Flying Squadron."

Meanwhile, throughout the last part of the carnival tour, they and Yankee Robinson had been negotiating for a small group of performers. As the time drew near for the grand opening, telegrams arrived from various parts of the Midwest requesting the Ringlings to wire railroad fare so that their indigent employees could get to Baraboo. These extra demands cleaned out the last of their bank account. On the opening day the Ringlings were, as usual, stony broke.

The Ringling circus opened at Baraboo on Monday, May 19, 1884. Luck smiled on them from sunny skies and a gentle south wind full of the promise of summer. Shortly before the performance, the five-Ringling band, beefed up by two of the new performers, made a parade with Yankee Robinson marching ahead. At the corner of Third Street and Broadway he halted the procession and addressed the crowd in the bull-fiddle tones of a barker and the lachrymose verbiage of a professional tear jerker.

"Ladeees and Gentlemen," he bellowed. "I am an old man. For forty-years I have rested my head on a stranger's pillow. I have traveled every state in the Union. . . . Soon I will pass to the arena of life that knows no ending. And when I do, I want to die in harness . . . with my name associated with that of the Ringling brothers. For I can tell you [here his voice is reported to have sunk to a confidential note of prophecy], I can tell you that the Ringling brothers are the future showmen of America. They are the *coming men!*"

The dear, mendacious old gaffer, ballyhooing a forlorn hope, would undoubtedly have dropped dead if he had suddenly foreseen how right he was.

Amid friendly applause, for the Ringlings were popular in Baraboo before success somehow soured their relations with their fellow townsmen, the parade moved on to the lot where the two tents stood with proudly waving pennants. Robinson led them into the Big Top and then took his station near the door, urging on the customers and exchanging jokes with them, while Otto sold tickets from the tailboard of a privilege wagon.

The tent could hold six hundred people around a ring made of red turkey cloth staked out in a circle. Six hundred "Baraboobians" paid their twenty-five cents admission. As they crowded up on the new seats, a section collapsed, dumping a jumbled mass of men, women, and children on the muddy ground. Yankee Robinson gave the brothers their money's worth right there. He shot over to the scene of

catastrophe, cracking jokes like a string of firecrackers, helping people up, soothing children, putting everybody back in
a genial humor. For such services and the use of his name,
his compensation was one third of the after-show concert's
receipts.

According to Alf T., the main show could not have been
much more sophisticated than the original five-cent circus.
The entire company, including the five Ringlings, the hired
performers, roustabouts, teamsters, and Louise Ringling,
numbered twenty-one persons. There was not even one horse
in the ring. As Alf T. observed, the animals which the show
owned "were fitter for a glue factory than an equestrian act."
The displays consisted of tumbling, horizontal-bar acts, a
contortionist, and juggling and balancing acts, interspersed
with some of the comedy bits from the Carnival of Fun. John
Ringling was the only clown.

To wring the last possible dime out of the customers, the
brothers sold tickets to the after-show concert, and Yankee
Robinson advised everybody to be sure to see the side show,
the feature of which was an educated pig, whose proprietor
paid half his take for the privilege of traveling with the show.

As soon as the customers cleared the Big Top, the weary
showmen began loading the wagons for the trek to Sauk City.
Because of confusion and lack of practice, it took longer than
it took to load the hundred-car train in the days of glory. It
was nearly midnight when the caravan started up the narrow
dirt road across the Wisconsin hills. The Ringlings in a spring
wagon led the way, followed by the four-horse hitch of the
dray, stacked with the long tent poles bending almost to the
ground behind it, with the rolls of canvas piled on top. The
heavily loaded farm carts followed, each with its swinging
lantern slung between the wheels to guide the next in line.
The horses moved at a dead walk. Their hoofs were muffled by
the thick white dust, and there was hardly a sound but the

sleepy creak of harness and wooden wheels turning slowly.

Sleepy indeed. Hardly a person was awake in that whole company except the brothers in the lead wagon. After such an exhausting and exciting day, weariness and the soft night air overcame them one by one no matter how hard the seats or cramped their position. Uncle John told me that the thing he remembered best about his days with the wagon show was his desperate craving for sleep, for it seemed that they never had time to lie down at all.

It must have taken them five or six hours to make the fourteen miles to Sauk City, for when they passed its first outlying farms the sun bounced over the horizon. The town was astir to greet them, and it was time to begin putting up the tents.

They gave two performances in Sauk City that day, and moved on to Black Earth, Wisconsin. Two performances there, and on again. Mount Horeb came next, and Mount Vernon; then, on Saturday, New Glarus. On Sunday they rested.

That was the routine of the wagon show—when conditions were good. The Ringlings did not mind, for ambition and inner compulsion drove them, and every quarter that Otto collected for the cashbox enabled them to see their goal more clearly ahead. Yankee Robinson was a good old trouper who took things as they came, and Louise Ringling a grand young one, who thought only of her Al. In fact, she later became their first equestrienne, in addition to snake charming, and in one crisis she drove a four-horse hitch, pulling two wild-animal cages over the muddy roads for four days.

However, the farmer-teamsters soon got tired and homesick. A loyal canvasman reported to Otto Ringling that a group of them were thinking of pulling out with their teams. Otto countered this dire threat by spreading a rumor that a troupe of giants named the Ananias Brothers were about to join the show. According to backstage gossip, they were eight feet tall and very generous with their tips. Anybody who deserted now would miss a good thing.

Of course, the mythical Ananias Brothers never showed up, and Otto's strategem only postponed trouble. Every time it rained, or the wind blew, or the wagons stuck in the mud, two or three farmer boys headed for home with their horses. Then the Ringlings would have to beat the countryside for some character with a team of horses and a desire to see the world. Somehow the show continued to meet its daily engagements.

One loss they could not replace. In August, Yankee Robinson must have had a premonition. His unfailing good humor and cracker-barrel wit had not failed, but his frail frame had. Learning that his son was playing in a hall show in Jefferson, Iowa, he took a leave of absence to see the boy. He died suddenly on the train to Jefferson.

For the first time in forty years of showmanship, he was billed under his right name in the Route Book: "Fayette Ludovic Robinson died at Jefferson, Iowa, about August 25, 1884." So Yankee Robinson got his wish.

That first year the Ringling circus showed a profit, though a small one. The ambitious brothers had hardly closed it for the winter when they took to the road again with the Carnival of Fun. In the latter part of the season they were joined by talented young James Richardson, who was billed as Monsieur Dialo. They liked him so much that they engaged him for the circus as well. The Carnival of Fun played almost continuously until May 6, 1885. The Ringlings allowed themselves all of twelve days to catch their breath.

They opened the circus on May 18, at Baraboo. It had grown, as the billing shows:

RINGLING BROS. GREAT DOUBLE SHOWS CIRCUS, CARAVAN, TRAINED ANIMAL EXPOSITION

The trained animal was, of course, that educated pig, but during the winter they had acquired a discouraged hyena in a secondhand cage, who was billed as:

HIDEOUS HYENA—STRIATA GIGANTIUM
The Mammoth, Marauding, Man-eating Monstrosity, the prowling, grave-robbing Demon of all Created Things, who while the World Sleeps, sneaks stealthily under cover of Darkness to the Cemetery and with Ghoulish Glee robs the Tomb.
His Hideous Laughter paralyzes with Terror the Bravest Hearts. He leaves behind him a trail of blood; and the Wails of the Dying are Music to his Ear.

It took fifteen wagons to transport the 1885 show and they had a round top eighty feet in diameter.

After it closed, the Carnival of Fun again went barnstorming, as it did each year until 1889. Indeed, its profits swelled the proportions of the circus, whose growth is recorded each year in the Route Books: In 1886 it is "Ringling Bros. Great Double Shows and Congress of Wild and Trained Animals," with a ninety-foot round top and eighteen wagons as well as "2 cages, Ticket and Band Wagon." The menagerie included "Hyena, Bear, Monkeys, Eagle."

A note states: "Bought the donkey and Shetland pony, January, and Minnie at Winnebago City, Minn., June 23. The first trick act with the show." The roster of professional entertainers had also grown to twenty-three, not counting roustabouts.

In the course of that season the Ringlings fought what was probably their first successful engagement in the circus wars that flared up in every town where two rival shows happened to meet either accidentally or on purpose. In a letter to James Van Orden, president of the Bank of Baraboo, Otto Ringling described it with an early American exuberance which now seems to have disappeared, even from the circus scene:

> Vinton, Iowa
> August 23, 1886
>
> Dear Sir:
>
> This will notify you that we have sent our draft to Chicago for $1000.
>
> Today we have fought and won a bloody battle between Ringling Brothers and the Renier Brothers' Great European Railroad Show. We got to the Courthouse Square [first] for our billboards and a great number of small boards [3½ by 8 feet]. We had every available place in town. Besides we literally covered the town, in fact we painted the town red and we won easily.
>
> We again fight them on Wednesday at Vale. Then we may not get off so victoriously. They have put up a board 500 feet long [there]. We do not want to fight them since as a railroad show they have a big advantage over us. But they laughed at us and were inclined to belittle us, and thought that all they would have to do was to tell people they were coming and we would run away to the backwoods. Now they will be as anxious to avoid us as we are to avoid them.
>
> Very sincerely,
> RINGLING BROTHERS.

The show practically doubled again in 1887. It was now "Ringling Bros. United Monster Shows, Great Double Circus, Royal European Menagerie, Museum, Caravan and Congress of Trained Animals." It owned sixty horses and the menagerie consisted of "1 Elk, Bear, 2 Lions, 1 Kangaroo, Hyena [that good old faithful friend], Birds, Monkeys, Deer, 4 Shetland Ponies, 1 Camel—Bought one on the road—it died." All the new wagons, cages, chariots, and bank wagon were built by their cousins the Moeller brothers, who continued to furnish these gaudy but sturdy vehicles for thirty years.

In September 1886 Henry Ringling, a strapping giant of sixteen years, had joined his brothers, though not as a partner. Unhappily, even this early in life Henry had a "weakness" which he may or may not have inherited from his grandfather Juliar.

When the big new show of 1887 went out, it was decided to send Henry out ahead to map the parade routes through the towns they were to play. In order that he might fittingly represent the dignity and grandeur of the United Monster Shows, his brothers bought him a stylish phaeton drawn by a pair of beautiful trotters.

The first day, looking very elegant in a fawn-colored double-breasted coat and tan derby, Henry dashed into Pardeeville, Wisconsin. Had the show followed the route he laid out, it would have been the longest parade in history. For he kept right on going on a glorious bender that lasted six weeks. When his money gave out he sold the horses and carriage. Then his fine clothes went. My uncles found him, drunk and destitute, in a small Iowa town.

It is typical of their family solidarity that they kept Uncle Henry on with the show. But not as an advance man. He was put in charge of the front door, where he kept an eye on the ticket takers and the uncles kept an eye on him.

Despite their gargantuan eating, drinking, and wenching, none of the Ringlings but Henry were victims of their vices, and in the end he mastered his. But before he did, this tremendous uncle of mine, the biggest of all the brothers, looked over the abyss. He was more conscious than anyone of his failure, more contemptuous of himself. At the age of twenty-nine, he saw himself as a huge sodden hulk. In a fit of despair he tried to destroy himself.

His brothers found him at the moment he was about to cut his throat with a straight razor. What they did or said, whether Uncle Henry took a cure, or if the view from the brink was sufficient, I do not know. But this I do know—from that time forward Uncle Henry never took another drink. Eventually, when Otto died, he was made a full partner in our enterprise and played his proper part in the management.

But in one sense he never recovered. Unlike his gusty, jovial brothers, he was morose and withdrawn. As a boy I remember him very well, storming down the main street of Baraboo, a gigantic Atlas with a world of care on his shoulders, passing his own sister on the street with never a glance or nod.

"What is a terrace without peacocks?" The Earl of Beaconsfield was rhetorically inquiring a world or so away from the western prairies. "What is a circus without elephants?" would have been a more pertinent query for my uncles. In due time they got terraces with peacocks; in 1888 they got elephants for their circus. The two "Gigantic Pachyderms" were named Babylon and Fannie, and they cost over two thousand dollars apiece at a sheriff's sale of a bankrupt circus. Two camels, Sampson and Queen, also joined the circus, as well as a "Zebu" and an emu. The new Big Top was 148 by 100 feet. There was also a menagerie top, three horse tops, and—unparalleled luxury—a dressing-room tent. Ringling Brothers had a real circus now, and they put the price of admission up to fifty cents (twenty-five cents for children). This was the standard charge for all full-grown circuses and remained the same for twenty or thirty years.

But they were terribly overexpanded. No one would go into the circus business who was not a raging optimist, and the Ringlings were no exception to this rule. They were in hock to their eyebrows to Mr. Van Orden and the Bank of Baraboo when the show opened in its home town on May 5, 1888.

It was miserably different sort of weather from their first fine opening day. The dams of heaven were running over on the sodden earth—rains continued for nearly as long as the Deluge. According to the Route Book, "We did not see the sun for four weeks." The Ringlings were, in fact, like a family of Noahs with no ark.

One can imagine them setting out on that muddy trail, a mile-long caravan of misery; lions coughing and wheezing in their leaky cages; camels stalking and balking; Babylon and Fannie squashing massive feet into treacherous slime with elephantine resignation; red-and-gold chariots black with mud; and a hundred or so human beings, wet, cold, and in a state of utter exhaustion, trying to give two gay shows a day to empty tents.

In fact, we do not have to imagine it, for Otto Ringling described it in an understandably incoherent letter to Mr. Van Orden:

Waukon, Iowa, May 15, 1888
To the Bank of Baraboo
Gentlemen:

We have had the worst experience in business since we started the past ten days. It has been raining and the roads have been in terrible condition. We were stuck in the clay hills between Ontario, Hillsboro and Cazenovia during the worst part of the storm, and now looking back cannot realize how we ever got out without being far behind our appointed schedule. During the past week commencing at Reedsburg we showed only one half of the time. Our wagons totally bogged down near Hillsboro and then we hired all the farmers we could find along the road and their teams to draw them on into town. Of course our expenses were much more than usual and besides that it has been raining all the time and we only showed 6 times instead of 12 all week.

This week so far continued rain has put the farmers

behind in their work and it will necessarily make business dull for a short time. After considering everything carefully, we have decided that it will be better for us to cut down the show to 25¢ and reduce our expenses to a low notch and be entirely safe.

In order to do this we must pay off all the people we do not want next Saturday and ship what stuff we do not want to carry back to Baraboo. If you could loan us enough to do this effectively and before we suffer any more losses, we will give you any security you may ask for, houses or notes. . . . You can rest assured that we will meet our obligations all right, but we do not feel like borrowing money of you and still continue the 50¢ admission when we can cut our expenses right down and have a sure thing at 25¢.

If you can loan us $1,000 we will come out all right. Please telegraph it to Caledonia the 17th of May. If you will favor us in this manner we will give you a bill of sale of everything we have, the big elephant which will sell for $2,000 any time, a bill of sale on the house or anything you may choose. . . .

> Very respectfully,
> RINGLING BROS.

Then comes the postscript in which the brothers' despair reaches back to us through the years.

You cannot form any idea of the strain on us with everything at stake in the rain and mud all day and night for over a week. After Reedsburg it was almost unbearable, those clay hills were almost impassable. The wagons would sink down to the hubs and the poor horses could not budge them. We had to hire farmers at their own figure to help us with their horses and we had to put all our men to work with shovels to get the clay away from the wheels. Our repair bills besides were enormous. Wagons continually pulled to pieces, springs broken, etc.

That letter would have melted a man of stone, which Mr. Van Orden was locally considered to be. It melted him—of course, Babylon really was worth two thousand dollars, so he was not risking much.

A letter from Plainview, Minnesota, on May 26, 1888, says:

> Received money at Caledonia O.K. Thank you very much for the kind favor shown us and we hope it will be in our power to show you our appreciation. We have been in the rain ever since we left Baraboo. We have not used any of the money you sent us yet. Are trying our *utmost not* to.

However, they were not out of the woods. On June 14, Otto writes:

> I will give you one instance of what we have been through. The distance from Blooming Prairie to New Richland, Minn., is 30 miles. We left Blooming Prairie Friday night after the show and reached New Richland Saturday afternoon at 4 o'clock, after building two bridges which had been washed out. Nothing to eat all day. We opened the doors at 5 o'clock. Our main show took in $22.00. It ended at 6:45. We opened the doors again at 7:30 PM to a fair night house. Everybody tired out. Left the next morning at 8 o'clock for Wells, 20 miles through swamps and lowlands. Got 18 miles at dusk Sunday PM. Had to camp out. Got to Wells Monday morning 11:30 and gave two performances to fair business.
>
> That was 10 days ago. Have been doing good business since then. Fair weather now and we think we can come in next fall with a reasonably fair profit. During 4 weeks of Hell you could have seen a cold, muddy disheartened gang of people if you had been with our show. . . . It was our first experience in a losing business and coupled with the terrible work and uncertainty of being able to get the show through the mud was disheartening. But now the sun shines again.
>
> Very respectfully,
> RINGLING BROTHERS

The Ringlings wrote in the Route Book, "We left the rain and mud on June 5th." It was exactly one month from the day they had started from Baraboo. The financial skies cleared as well, and drafts began to go back to Mr. Van Orden. However, the brothers soon had their first experience of the violent tragedies of circus life. On June 23 their good friend and star performer, "Mons. Dialo [James Richardson] was shot and killed at Webster City by Thomas Baskett, who was sentenced to 15 years at Anamosa."

Poor M. Dialo paid the price of knight-errantry. Thomas Baskett, a bellicose saloonkeeper of Webster, had gotten into an argument with a fellow townsman, Roll Brewer, whom he followed into the show grounds and beat up in a brutal fashion. When Brewer's daughter tried to help her father, Baskett knocked her down and began to kick her. Several showmen, among them Dialo, tried to interfere. In the ensuing brawl, Baskett whipped out a pistol and shot Dialo in the abdomen. James Richardson died twenty-four hours later.

The circus did not miss a performance. The show must go on or go broke.

As they moved back into Iowa in July, the sun shone steadily and the crop of green dollars rivaled the tall rows of corn.

> Winterset, Iowa, July 7, 1888
> Mr. J. Van Orden
> Bank of Baraboo
>
> Dear Sir:
> Please find enclosed draft on Chicago for $1000. We resumed 50¢ admission last Saturday. . . . We have made $3,000 in one week and one day. A few weeks like this will make up for the spring. At any rate we are even with you and will get back to Baraboo with enough to feed the elephant. How is the hay crop

around Baraboo? Crops in this country are immense. The fields look almost tropical.

Respectfully,

RINGLING BROTHERS.

N.B. We didn't touch the 1,000 dollars you sent us, but we got down to 122 dollars cash on hand besides your remittance. That was the low water mark.

CHAPTER VI

"THE SUNDAY-SCHOOL CIRCUS"

Eighteen eighty-nine was the last year of the wagon show. Despite the terribly discouraging start of the season of 1888, the Ringlings had come home with far more than enough to feed the elephant. In their then personally frugal, business-wise extravagant way they poured all their money back into expanding the circus. In order to compete with the really big-time shows, they advertised, in addition to the "United Monster Circus, Museum, Menagerie and Universal World Exposition," something that they called a "Roman Hippodrome."

This was in direct imitation of Barnum & Bailey's chariot races around an arena. Furthermore, it must have been an even greater exaggeration of fact than usual; for two years later the Route Book rather naïvely states, "Put in a real Hippodrome for 1891." However, one may be reasonably sure that their customers got their fifty cents' worth, for they flocked to see the show in droves.

The start from Baraboo was particularly auspicious. The weather was perfect, and my grandfather and grandmother came all the way from Rice Lake to see *all* of their seven sons go out with their circus. For Gus had at last joined his brothers. All this time he had been quietly earning his living by his father's trade in Minneapolis, but now they persuaded him to join them and share the family bonanza.

Gus was, perhaps, the gentlest of the brothers. He had a dreamy, poetic face and a way with animals. When Mother was a little girl in Rice Lake, he brought a bear cub home from the forest and built a little shelter for it in the back yard. It lived there for a long time.

He loved the woods and had wonderful hunting dogs, which he trained himself. My mother's favorite was Tippy, which Gus had taught to go out to the wood box in the back yard, nose up the lid, take out a log, and carrying it back to the kitchen, lay it beside the big wood-burning stove.

The brothers made Gus advertising manager of the circus.

Another Ringling joined the circus that year, Mrs. Charles Ringling. The autumn before, Uncle Charlie had married nineteen-year-old Edith Conway, whose father was the

Methodist minister in Baraboo. Like Al's wife, Louise, Edith Ringling turned into a good trouper, though she had been teaching school until Charlie married her. She always traveled with the show, and like Louise, worked hard at repairing costumes and sometimes took tickets at the door.

One of her first experiences with the circus would have been enough to cure most girls of sawdust fever. She was sitting outside the menagerie tent one day when Fannie the elephant got irritated by something her keeper had done and decided to take it out on Edith. She lumbered up and took a swipe at the young bride with her trunk, knocking Edith fifteen feet through the air and smashing the chair to kindling. While the keeper hooked Fannie's ear with his ankus, one of the old circus hands dashed over to pick Edith up, saying, "Daughter, daughter! Are you hurt?" Just as he reached her he fell over in a dead faint. Edith scrambled to her feet without assistance. She just took it as an occupational hazard.

Apparently the tour of 1889 was unusually serene. Only one tragedy is recorded. Worn by the passing of many a season and surely having given the brothers far more than their money's worth, the "Mammoth, Man-Eating, Monstrous" hyena wearily turned up its toes and died.

Serenity means prosperity in any business, but particularly in the circus, which is so vulnerable to mischance. At the end of the season the Ringlings had an enormous profit. They used part of it to build a wide-verandaed frame house in Baraboo, where their father and mother could settle down at last. With the remainder they prepared to enter the big time in a big way.

Take a look at them at this turning point in their lives, for they would never be quite the same again; yet, in another sense, they remained unchanged, but now able to expand their personalities, each in his different way.

At first glance they seem as alike as seven Siamese twins. For this was the era when they introduced on their letterheads and advertising the famous picture of the heads of the five partner-brothers all with seemingly identical profiles and those magnificent mustaches—the irreverent called them The Mustache Boys. With deliberate conformity Gus and Henry also grew mustaches. But this was as far as conformity went. Though bound together by their strong family ties and their common interest in their circus, they had sharply different personalities.

To begin with, their physical resemblance was nothing like as great as their identical facial adornment made it appear. They ranged in height from Charlie's neat five feet eight to Henry's elephantine six feet three. Their faces, unmasked, were equally disparate. Al's was thin and eager, at least in his youth. Gus had the visionary expression of a poet. Alf T. appeared to be determinedly businesslike, whereas Charles looked like the well-groomed sportsman of the Gay Nineties. Otto's face wore a banker's solid look. John, the only one with curly hair, had the round-faced, round-eyed humorous expression which had set the farmers laughing in the prairie village hall, whereas Henry, though also round-faced, was beetle-browed and slightly sinister.

Except for their common fondness for huge, rich meals, which eventually put considerable poundage on all of them and doubtless shortened their lives, their personal tastes and hobbies were as different as could be. When money gave them freedom of choice each went his separate way in private life, though they remained indissolubly bound together in the partnership.

Even in the business they specialized, though they all had such an intimate knowledge of circus management that in a pinch any brother could substitute for any other. Albert Ringling, who was known to the whole back yard as Uncle

Al, was the equestrian director, which is circus talk for the producer and director of the whole show. I suppose the title comes from the fact that the early European circuses were often built around the equestrian act and therefore the equestrian director was the head man in the tent. Uncle Al not only staged the show and dreamed up the great spectacles of later years; he also paced the performance from the ringside, keeping it fast and furious with sharp blasts of his whistle, which signaled the start and finish of each display.

Since he loved horses, his title was peculiarly appropriate, and during his lifetime equestrian displays were sure to be a main attraction, culminating in 1899 with his famous sixty-one-horse finale, in which sixty-one liberty horses were actually in the arena at one time. In order to accommodate so many, they were raised on stages making a pyramid of horseflesh, at the top of which was a single magnificent white Arabian.

Uncle Charles (Mr. Charles) was the physical man in charge of the tremendous logistics of moving the army of people and animals over thousands of miles through six months of one-night stands. He commanded the train and was, in effect, the general manager. Though other people usually held that title, he was the head man. He kept what the brothers called his Book of Wonders. This was a notebook in which he was constantly jotting things down throughout the tour. At the end of the season he would present the Book of Wonders to the partners and managers. It contained a complete summary of all the things that would have to be done during the winter, including purchases, repairs, additional work horses, ring stock, and animals as well as new ideas for improving the physical aspect of the show.

Otto Ringling was nicknamed The King, because he held the life-and-death power of the purse. His management of the finances was both sound and imaginative. To give an idea of his foresight, in 1903 he proposed to the brothers that since in metropolitan areas vacant land suitable for accommodating fifty-odd tents was getting scarce, they should buy fifteen-acre plots close to every large city in America. His brothers by that time were more interested in spending their money on pink marble palaces or pseudo-Norman castles of their own, so they vetoed the proposal. Imagine what their holdings would have been worth now had they followed his advice!

Alf T. Ringling was in charge of public relations. This, of course, included all the means and media which stimulated an overwhelming desire to see the circus in everybody within one hundred miles or so of any town where the show was playing. He was so successful that railroads used to run special trains from all parts of a county on circus day, and in a town like Concordia, Kansas, of 7500 inhabitants, the circus would play to a total of 16,000 people in one performance. Another function of circus public relations was running down the opposition shows. How my uncle Alf T. did this will be told in the account of the great circus wars of the 1890s.

As soon as they put the show on rails, John Ringling was given charge of routing. This was a very intricate job, essential to the success of a season. When the great four-train hundred-car show was on the road, it meant planning the exact time of each section every day in co-operation with dozens of railroads and hundreds of branch lines. Uncle John's prodigious memory became practically a railroad guide to the United States. For example, if you wondered in his presence how best you could get from Altoona, Pennsylvania, to North Yakima, Washington, he would instantly come up with train times, junction points, and connections. One of his favorite tricks was to let you name a railroad and timetable, and then stick a nail file into the *Consolidated Rail-*

way Guide, as thick as the New York telephone book, and come within a page or two.

In later years Uncle John also did most of the discovering and negotiating of new European acts for the show.

Thus the five brothers worked when they were all alive. Gus out ahead with the advance car and Henry at the front door completed the Ringling team.

The Ringling brothers' first railroad show opened in Baraboo on Saturday, May 2, 1890. The train consisted of two advertising cars—one of which was sent ahead—one performers' sleeper, one elephant car, five stockcars, and eight flatcars—eighteen cars in all. These transported two tableau wagons, two band wagons, fifteen cages (four open dens included) and one hundred and seven horses, three elephants, three camels, four lions, two cub lions, a hippopotamus, and assorted other wild creatures, besides fifty-four performers. However magnificent it was compared with the little wagon show that had started hopefully out from Baraboo six years before, it was still only a one-ring show, peanut-sized compared with the great railroad shows it was about to challenge.

For by this time the circus in America had reached a high state of development. Phineas T. Barnum, the greatest showman of them all, had hurled himself into the circus business with a tremendous splash in 1871, when my uncles were holding their five-cent circus. By 1873, eleven years before the Ringling wagon show started, Barnum's *Advance Courier* could describe his circus—more or less truthfully—as a "Colossal World's Fair by Railroad—20 Great Shows consolidated; 100,000 curiosities, 5 Railroad Trains 4 miles long, 4 bands, 12 golden chariots; 100 vans in a procession 3 miles long."

The lead article, written by Barnum himself in the finest flowering of circus style, begins, "Although the fire of December 24, 1872, totally destroyed my museum building [in New York] and magnificent collection of rare animals . . . I have emerged again from the cinders and smoke with an unimpaired constitution, unabated energies and a more earnest determination than ever to gratify the demands of the amusement-seeking public.

"Hence, before the sparks ceased rising from my burning museum, I subsidized the powers of electricity to such an extent as to enable me to start again by April, 1873, with a Museum Menagerie, Caravan, Ornithological Cabinet, . . . Polytechnic Institute [whatever that was] Coliseum of Classic and Equestrian Equitation, Aquarium for Marine Monsters . . . combined with Dan Costello's Mammoth Double Hippodrome, Monsieur d'Atalier's Equestrian and Arenic Exposition, making, in fact, the largest and most elaborate and exhaustive combination of traveling exhibitions ever seen on earth. *The Greatest Show on Earth.*"

Nor will I argue with Phineas T.—it was just that.

By 1890, when our railroad show first went out, Barnum had added a tremendous spectacle play—"Imre Kiralfy's Grand, Romantic, Historical Spectacle—Nero and the Destruction of Rome, including thrilling Roman Chariot Races in the Circus Maximus."

All for fifty cents!

This was pretty tough competition. In addition, other great shows of the time, all older and larger than Ringling Brothers, included Sell Brothers' fifty-cage, four-ring circus with a forty-five-car train; the Great Wallace Railroad Shows; John Robinson's Ten Big Shows, and the Buffalo Bill Wild West Show, which though not a true circus was very real competition.

By means of John Ringling's skillful routing to small neglected towns, our circus managed to avoid direct clashes with the others that first year, except in five or six towns.

They came triumphantly back to Baraboo with a load of boodle.

Again they greatly enlarged their show. In 1891 it became "Ringling Bros. World's Greatest Railroad Shows, Real Roman Hippodrome, 3 Ring Circus and Elevated Stages, Millionaire Menagerie, Museum and Aquarium and Spectacular Tournament Production of Caesar's Triumphal Entry into Rome."

It sounds as though they were breathing down Mr. Barnum's neck; but enthusiasm must have prevailed over truth, since the whole show moved on a twenty-two-car train.

And again the luck was with them; such wonderful luck that it seemed as though the gods of the arena were repenting the dreadful trials they had put the brothers through in 1888. The Route Book for 1891 records, "The canvas was only loaded wet 3 times during the entire season."

There was, however, a curious footnote which demonstrates that circus people had to be good fighters as well as good performers. The unsavory reputation of the circuses of that era sometimes exploded in fierce riots between town and show, even when that hostility was undeserved. This happened. "At Bolivia, Mo., on Sept. 26th, a very fierce battle was fought between the show and the people of the town and vicinity. Many of the local bad men were badly injured. The show got out after a very exciting experience without suffering any injury."

The affray at Bolivia points up a problem that my uncles faced as their first brightly painted train steamed out of Baraboo into the big time. That was the question of circus ethics. Most of the shows operated on the principle of taking the suckers for all they were worth. This was based on Barnum's theory that the suckers enjoyed it. In his case there may have been some justification for the thought.

William Lyon Phelps, an ardent circus fan who was my beloved mentor at Yale, described how this worked in our circus program for 1939. In his article Professor Phelps reminisced about the circus of his childhood. He had seen The Greatest Show on Earth when Barnum was alive.

"During the performance, P. T. Barnum dressed in formal black clothes and looking like a clergyman was introduced to the audience as one of the benefactors of mankind, which I do not think was an exaggeration. He was broad and fat and unctuous, and in the language of Dickens, he seemed to be one vast substantial smile.

"Barnum was the Shakespeare of advertisers and has never been surpassed. His knowledge of what the public wanted was infallible. He knew they loved to be swindled so long as the swindle was understood to be a glorious joke on both sides. At one of his circuses he had a big sign inside the main tent:

TO THE EGRESS

"Hundreds of people followed that sign thinking they were on the way to some African monstrosity, but soon found they were outdoors and had to pay fifty cents to get back. Instead of being wild with rage they were delighted and when the word was explained to them, they said, 'Isn't that just like Barnum!'

"On another occasion in New Haven one of the side shows, which I believe had an admission charge of twenty-five cents, announced:

CHERRY COLORED CAT

"Now people supposed that a cherry colored cat was unique. They trooped in there by hundreds and all they saw was a perfectly ordinary black cat. When they looked at this and demanded an explanation the attendant said, 'Well you know some cherries are black.'

"Instead of being angry the crowd looked at each other with foolish grins and exclaimed, 'Sold again!' They even went back to the main tent and told every stranger, 'Have you seen the cherry colored cat? It's the most marvelous exhibition ever given.' So that each person who had been deceived got five other persons to swell the coffers of the management."

Barnum's flimflamming was fun. But the philosophy behind it set a low moral tone which corrupted the whole circus scene. Anything was all right to part the suckers from their money.

For example, ticket sellers were paid no salary; indeed, they often paid the management for the job. They made their living by shortchanging the public, at which they were better magicians than any "professor" in the show itself. I used to watch for crooked ticket sellers myself when I was a boy around the circus. One of their favorite tricks was obviously to overpay a customer who had changed a big bill, counting out as much as five or ten dollars too much. In his cupidity the customer would grab his change and rush off not noticing that the seller had counted one bill two or three times. When we'd grab a crooked ticket seller he would protest that he was not really doing wrong, because the customer was trying to cheat him.

In addition to this racket, all sorts of shady businesses swelled the coffers of some of the shows. Crooked gamblers, shell-game operators, and confidence men rented concessions from the management just like legitimate vendors. Some circuses even hired professional pickpockets, who circulated in the carefree crowds and split their take with the management. A clever assist was often provided by the management by having a side-show talker (barker) dramatically announce to a well-thronged midway that local police had informed the circus authorities of the presence of well-known pickpockets in the city who had come to prey upon the circus crowds. When the grateful yokels so warned patted their hip pockets or caressed their breast pockets or fondly fingered their stickpins and gold watch fobs, the very dips they had been warned against would be observing their actions in preparation for later lifting their blocks (watches), pokes (purses), etc.

As a result, a vast organization of sinister rackets grew up in the shadow of the tents. A rabble of petty criminals attached themselves to circuses, with or without the owners' knowledge. Cheating and trickery flowered into organized crime. Even armed robbery and murder were not unknown.

Very early in their careers the Ringlings decided to have an honest show. This decision was partly due to their financial integrity. For despite the amoral attitude of most of them toward the minor vices, they all had an almost puritanical financial integrity—as witness Jim Hamilton. Their other reason was that they believed honesty was really better business; that if they acquired a reputation for giving entertainment at a fair price and protecting their patrons, they would prosper accordingly. Other managers and even their own employees laughed at them and said you could not run a circus that way. But they did it, and they certainly prospered.

Of course, it was a never ending battle. As long as there are ticket sellers and a gullible public there will always be a risk. In fact, as late as 1955, my brother John and I had to take drastic measures to clear out gambling and other rackets which had attached themselves like barnacles to our circus. As in 1890, we were told it could not be done. But we did it!

One thing which enabled my uncles to clean up their show was that there were "so damn many of them." They were all over the lot constantly on the alert, and with Henry watching over the front door like an angry grizzly bear, the ticket sellers were pretty careful.

However, as the show got bigger, the task of keeping it clean was too much for the brothers, and they retained the great William J. Burns detective agency to guard their patrons. A little later they went even further. Realizing that shady practices in any circus redounded to the discredit of all, including their own, they secretly sent Burns detectives to certain other shows to seek out and arrest crooks operating with them. A great many were brought to book. The owners were not a bit grateful. They irately assailed the Ringlings as meddlers and ironically christened their show The Sunday-School Circus. But George Ade, who was also a circus fan, gave the Ringlings his accolade: "They found the business in the hands of vagabonds and put it into the hands of gentlemen."

CHAPTER VII

BILLS, BANNERS, AND BLOODY HEADS

No mortals may long enjoy the favor of the gods, they say. This goes double in circus business. After three tremendously fortunate seasons, the Ringlings' luck broke in 1892.

The two things we dread most are fire and train wrecks. The Ringling show had three train wrecks that year. The first and worst came two weeks out of Baraboo in the rain near Washington, Kansas, on May 17. In the tremendous crash four of the slatted wooden stockcars were reduced to matchwood, and twenty-six screaming horses were killed or had to be destroyed. The human toll included two men killed and four seriously injured. But there was no time to stand and mourn. The Route Book laconically states, "Show missed one stand [Washington, May 17th] and showed Concordia, May 18th, with side wall only. Short of stock—bought 18 [horses] at Concordia, and received carload of 20 at Wichita, May 21st, from Chicago."

The other two wrecks occurred at places named Centralia. On September 18, at Centralia, Missouri—"six cages demolished and lost the day. No further damage except marring the sleeping cars." On the way back to Baraboo, at Centralia, Illinois—"Rear end collision. No damage beyond a few broken irons on the cars."

However, railroad inefficiency was not all that dogged them. They dared the big cities of Milwaukee, Omaha, Kansas City, and Topeka, where they ran head on into the great Barnum & Bailey show. In other towns they noted, "Smaller opposition—several stands, Wallace Show; three stands, John Robinson Show."

In addition, the weather turned on them. "This is the worst spring we have ever seen—30 days rain. [Had they forgotten 1888 so soon?] Season on the whole, however, was very big."

So began the Ringlings' bitter battles for a place in the circus sun. If, as I describe them, I seem to dwell more on our wins than losses, remember that most of the stories were told to me by my uncles and that old soldiers only remember their victories. In common fairness, however, it must be added that the Ringlings ended by owning virtually all of their opponents.

Our most bitter opposition in the early days came from the

four Sells brothers. Their territory, like ours at the time, was primarily west of the Alleghenies. During the season of 1894, when we invaded Texas for the first time, they deliberately tried to day-and-date us all over a state they thought they owned. At one town, where they couldn't arrange their schedule to conflict with ours, they subsidized a free balloon ascension as a counterattraction. On that occasion Uncle John went out to see how many people had been drawn away from the Ringling show. There were so few that he sent Lew Sells the following telegram:

> An old man, a young boy, a hound dog and I watched your balloon ascension. It didn't go up.
> JOHN RINGLING

Uncle John thought it was very funny; but his older brothers gave him a sharp dressing down. They did not consider it a nice or dignified thing to do.

In fact, these circus wars were commercial rivalries which seldom embittered the relations of the principals. As lawyers storm at each other in court and then have lunch together, so the circus owners called each other liars, fakes, and cheaters in their publicity and greeted each other as old friends when they met.

For example, one time when we were having opposition from the Buffalo Bill Wild West Show somebody arrived in Baraboo with a message from Colonel Cody: "Tell John Ringling he'd better stay out of my way or he'll bitterly regret it."

Uncle John said, "Give Colonel Cody my compliments and tell him I'm not very worried. In fact, the next time I see him I'm going to throw him down and scalp him."

When they actually did meet in a bar in Philadelphia, the only argument was who should blow whom to drinks.

My uncles regarded Lew Sells as a fine old gentleman, which he was. In his own circus he was referred to as Uncle

Lew, just as Albert Ringling was called Uncle Al. When I was a boy working with the circus during my summer vacations, we employed a side-show announcer named Pete Stanton, who had formerly worked for Sells Brothers. He told many amusing stories about Lew. For instance, at that time, even as now and probably as long as circuses continue, mothers would lie to get their small fry into the show without paying adult prices. (Children under twelve were half price, babes in arms free.) Lew Sells would place himself by the main entrance to his tent, and as the mothers staggered up toting husky boys four or five years old, he would shout out, "Let them menfolks walk!"

When the tent was not well filled, Sells would sit himself next to someone in the blue seats (general admission). After a bit he'd say, "We can't see a darn thing from here. Let's go buy reserved seats." He would lead his new friend to an inside-ticket seller and then slip away to work his wiles on another customer.

Another good story concerns the time Sells paid a high price for a superb black panther, of which he was very proud. One morning when they were setting up for the matinee the panther got loose just as Lew Sells walked into the menagerie tent. He saw the crowd of trainers and roustabouts trying to force the dangerous animal back into its cage with crowbars, pitchforks, and poles. Lew was terribly worried that an accident might happen—to his panther. "Be very careful not to injure that beast," he shouted. "It's a very valuable animal and I want you to be very careful down there. Get him back in his cage, but on no account injure him."

At that moment a black streak soared in a beautiful thirty-foot spring over the heads of the encompassing crowd and started up the tent with sinuous bounds. Going even faster, Sells headed for the exit yelling over his shoulder, "Shoot the son of a bitch."

Despite the amenities exchanged by the owners, the circus wars were bitterly fought. They were, indeed, matters of financial life and death. The principal weapons were show bills. The advance men would literally plaster a town with circus posters and banners, trying to hire every available billboard, barn side, and store window before the opposition got to town. Then they would have to guard their bills from being torn down or covered over. Our victories were not always bloodless. Uncle Charlie told me of one occasion when he was on the advance car. He and one of his billposters put up a very important display. Then they lay in ambush behind the billboard waiting for the opposition to try to pull it down. Sure enough, one of Sells' men came along, pointed like a bird dog as he saw the Ringling display, and started for it with a scraper. Uncle Charlie hopped out from behind the board and laid him out with a tack hammer.

On another occasion one of nature's own creatures took the part of the opposition. This time Uncle John was out in advance, riding an ordinary day coach on a very hot night. He was terribly tired and trying to sleep. He put a newspaper over his head to shut out the light. It almost suffocated him. Just as he took it off, the train stopped in an open cutting, where a skunk basked on the lingering heat of sun-warmed earth. Irritated at being disturbed, the creature took careful aim through the open window of the train and let poor Uncle John have it right in the face.

My uncle told me that it was the most horrible experience of his life. As he staggered to his feet, dripping with that asphyxiating effluvia, and started blindly for the washroom, there was a riot in the car. All the passengers were screaming hysterically at him to keep off and diving under their seats to get away from him. He finally succeeded in getting his spare suit out of his bag and changing in the washroom. He threw his old suit out of the train window and cleaned up as best he could. Even then he was popular neither with his fellow passengers nor himself.

Another weapon of these hot and cold wars was the inventory bill, or "rat sheet." This was a poster put up by one show to expose the claims of another. They were not only libelous but downright defamatory, though nobody that I know of ever sued for libel. A typical inventory bill directed against us would read something like this:

WHY WASTE YOUR MONEY ON A BUNCH OF FAKES, WHEN SELLS BROTHERS CIRCUS GIVES YOU TWICE AS MUCH FOR THE SAME PRICE?

The Ringlings are cheap crooks who try to inflate their Pitiful Third-Rate Show by extravagant FALSE claims, as shown below:

RINGLINGS' CLAIMS	THE TRUTH
The Ringlings call themselves the "World's Greatest Show."	They have a 22-car train. We travel in 45 cars.
They claim that Zip is the largest elephant in captivity.	Zip is really a runt. We have ten elephants that are bigger.
They advertise a Roman Hippodrome and Caesar's triumphal entry into Rome.	Their hippodrome consists of two battered two-horse chariots drawn by spavined nags that can't get out of a walk. Caesar would have blushed with shame if he could have seen their cheap depiction of his triumph.
Millionaire Menagerie	It is a collection of two sick lions, three small elephants, and a few other miserable creatures which would not bring $500 on the auction block, where they soon will be.

Museum and Aquarium

The Museum contains some Indian Arrowheads. The Aquarium is the size of a goldfish bowl and about as interesting.

This is a fair sample of the Deceit practiced on the public by these Notorious Swindlers. The public are not *Fooled.* Instead they come in DROVES TO
SELLS BROTHERS
ENORMOUS UNITED SHOWS

The most vicious and peculiar inventory bill that ever attacked our show was put up by the crooks and gamblers whom my uncles had thrown out. It read:

When Thieves Fall Out, Honest Men Get Their Due.
WARNING!
Neighbors, unchain your dogs! Get out your shotguns! Keep your children at home! Lock all doors and windows!

THE MARAUDERS ARE COMING
You will know them by their Greasy Appearance! They are Thieves, Liars and Scoundrels. They have no Show worthy of the name. . . . We give you this warning because we are also thieves, but we have fallen out with the greasy pack and now tell THE TRUTH.

As can be seen, these inventory bills lied recklessly; they diminished the truth as greatly as the posters exaggerated it. Oddly enough this form of negative advertising persisted among smaller circuses right up to modern times. I have at hand an inventory bill of 1937, in which Clyde Beatty berates poor little Cole Brothers Circus and warns the residents of Rochester, New York, not to waste their money on it.

Sells Brothers gave the Ringlings a very tough time in 1894. They fought us not only in Texas but in Iowa and Minnesota as well. There they even reduced their price of admission to a losing twenty-five cents and the Ringlings were forced to meet that price. In the South both circuses maintained the regular fifty-cent admission.

The Ringlings survived this attempt to put them out of business and came home to Baraboo with sufficient profit to enlarge their show to forty-four cars in 1895.

Having tested their mettle and emerged victorious, those optimistic uncles of mine decided on two tremendous gambles. First they would raid the very heart of enemy territory; challenging not only Sells Brothers but the great Barnum & Bailey show itself. And take on Buffalo Bill as well.

As if this were not enough, they took, perhaps, an even longer chance by opening their show in Chicago *indoors*. Over sixty years later, when my brother John decided to abandon the Big Top and show only in coliseums, the traditionalists howled that the circus would never be the same. It is interesting to note that back in 1895 Ringling Brothers faced the same die-hard caterwaulings. An article in the *Circus Annual* begins:

"There are a great many people who believe that a circus cannot be a real circus unless it be seen under canvas, with dirt rings and the sawdust smells that go with it, in imaginary descriptions at least. Doubtless there is some truth in this belief, if it means to compare the modern up-to-date show with the small traveling concerns of the past that would be completely lost in an amphitheatre." Pretty pompous, considering that only eleven years had passed since the Ringlings had proudly set out with the very smallest "traveling concern" on the road.

Tattersall's, which the Ringlings had chosen for their great experiment, had the general contours and all the charm of a carbarn. It was an enormously long drab building with a curved glass roof supported by ugly steel girders. The rectangular arena was surrounded by rows of backless wooden benches where cattle and horse buyers customarily sat through public auctions. My uncles spent a fortune to change all that. Here is their description, overblown perhaps, of the metamorphosis they accomplished.

"The grim old walls, . . . steel roof girders, homely wood-work . . . had been transformed into a veritable fairyland by the magic touch of money. . . . Everything was spick and span. The grimy rafters were literally buried beneath masses of flags of every nation, banners and bunting of every color of the rainbow. The aisles and corridors had been transformed into floral gardens [with] potted plants and blooming flow-ers. . . . The seats were gone, too, and in their place modern, comfortable folding open chairs, and in front of them a com-plete circle of private boxes . . . richly draped and furnished with artistic chairs of unique design.

"Overhead, amidst the sea of bunting, depended a myriad of ropes, trapezes, and other aerial paraphernalia, each indi-vidual piece of which was as white as pipe clay and strong arms could make it. The dirt rings were not there, either, but instead rings of wood with earth floors, perfect and complete. Neatly uniformed ushers seated [the audience] and all the hurry, jostle, push and annoyance of their old-fashioned, ideal boyhood circus had vanished. . . ."

The traditionalists must have been further disturbed by the fact that they could actually see the show at night perform-ances. For bright, though crude, electric lighting had re-placed the smoky reflector oil lanterns and glaring acetylene lamps which had made the interior of the tent a bewildering, though picturesque, chiaroscuro of shifting shadows.

Into this brilliant amphitheater the Ringlings threw a show that really deserved the magniloquent adjectives of their perfervid publicity writers. Three days before the opening, the show moved in a three-mile-long torch light parade proudly led by Al Ringling on horseback, through the narrow pack-jammed streets of Chicago—the first such in its history. There were a fifty-five-piece band; several hundred horses ridden by performers or drawing the red-and-gold chariots; and the cages containing lions and tigers, panthers and pumas, a hippopotamus, a rhinoceros, and an infinite variety of other wildlife. Open glass-walled dens displayed snake charmers working boa constrictors or animal trainers cozily caged with their charges. Of course, there was a whole herd of elephants, dozens of clowns, and bringing up the rear, a perfectly deafening calliope.

The show itself consisted of over twenty displays exhibiting every familiar feature of the circus we love, from the band concert led by the famous cornetist Signor A. Liberatti (one seems to hear the echo of a familiar modern musical name) through the great equestrians, aerialists, performing elephants, and on and on to the finale of four-horse-chariot races driven by girls in flowing classic draperies. Special attractions were Phillion's Aerial Globe display, in which that talented fellow performed on a high spiral tower standing on a rolling globe; and the nine Landaures in their Living Statue act. These ladies and gentlemen, dressed in nothing but very tight tights covered with white paint, assumed the attitudes of famous pieces of classic sculpture. It was a highly popular display, since it permitted the sex-starved midwestern audience to enjoy the appearance of nudity under the guise of appreciation of Art with a capital A.

The most sensational act—a great deal more dangerous than Zacchini's modern cannon act—was an insane character, calling himself Speedy, diving eighty feet from the dome of the roof into a small tank of water three and a half feet deep.

To quote the *Circus Annual* once more: "The verdict of Chicago pronounced it the largest as well as the best show ever given there. . . . The Circus became a fad; it was the thing to do and the thing to see. . . . Hundreds of thousands saw it; thousands were turned away."

In plain fact, the Ringlings had finally caught up with their splendid boasts.

Fresh from this success the show moved on to St. Louis and, in June, to Boston, where, though it showed in a tent, special grandstands with private boxes were erected and lavishly furnished as in Chicago. In spite of following both Barnum & Bailey and Buffalo Bill, the Ringlings scored another triumph.

This upset the opposition no end. All three of the other great shows, Barnum & Bailey, Sells Brothers, and Buffalo Bill, combined to fight them, led by James A. Bailey.

Now I think I should speak a little of our chief opponent, although his story is well known. Bailey reached the top of the circus world by bluff backed by ability, for he was second only to Barnum himself in imaginative showmanship. His real name was James A. McGinnis. When he was about twelve years old he ran away from home and talked himself into a job with the Cooper and Bailey circus, where he made himself so valuable that, when Mr. Bailey died a few years later, he was in a position to ask for a partnership. Mr. Cooper agreed that he deserved it, but is reported to have said, "We don't want to change the name of the show. You can be a partner if you change your name."

So McGinnis became James Anthony Bailey. By the time he was twenty-six he had gained control of the show. In 1880 he outsmarted his great rival Barnum on a deal over a baby elephant, which so impressed the supreme flimflammer that he offered Bailey a partnership. This combination of talented necromancers produced The Greatest Show on Earth, which was without a serious rival for fifteen golden years, until the Ringlings brashly challenged it. When Phineas T. Barnum

died in 1891 in his eighty-first year, Bailey stood alone at the
pinnacle of the circus world.

But he knew that you did not stay there without fighting,
and in 1895 he went after the Ringlings. His first move was to
buy into partnership with Colonel Cody. While his own circus kept clear, he used Buffalo Bill's cowboys and Indians to
harass the Ringlings at almost every stand in the East. My
uncles retorted with the unparalleled effrontery of playing
Bridgeport right in the shadow of Barnum & Bailey's huge
winter quarters.

This did nothing to reduce Mr. Bailey's blood pressure. He
already owned the Forepaugh Circus and in 1896 he bought
a half interest in Sells Brothers Circus, which he sent out to do
battle with the Ringlings under the name of the Forepaugh-
Sells Circus.

That year the Ringlings tried to keep out of trouble
by avoiding the East, but Bailey sent Forepaugh-Sells raiding
after them through the West. The two shows clashed directly
at no less than forty-five stands during a hectic season in
which the battling billposters painted virtually every town in
the Midwest red, not only with flaming posters but with their
blood.

That was the ruggedest campaign. By 1897 both Mr.
Bailey and the Ringlings realized that nobody wins a spite
fight. In that heyday of the circus there was plenty of room
for two great circuses and several small ones. By tacit agreement they arranged their schedules to avoid each other. There
was only one direct clash, when Barnum & Bailey and the
Ringlings hit Minneapolis at the same time. Apparently
Bailey's billposters won a battle but not the war, for the
Ringling Route Book records, "At Minneapolis, Minn., we
were shut out of billboards—used no large boards or walls—
only banners, small boards and newspapers strong. Turned
people away each performance."

That day in Minneapolis was the last great scene of carnage. In a sense the Ringlings won the ultimate victory by default. Whether from prudence, weariness, or a desire to gather new laurels in fresh fields, Mr. Bailey took The Greatest Show on Earth to Europe in 1898. It remained abroad for five years, and if laurels were indeed his goal, he reaped a great harvest of them. As they liked to phrase it those royalty-loving days, all the crowned heads of Europe came to look and remained to applaud. More important from a financial point of view, the uncrowned heads turned out in multitudes. The tour was a spectacular success.

While he was away, Bailey left Forepaugh-Sells to hold the eastern seaboard for him. If he really expected those boys to do a man's work, it was a serious miscalculation. Perhaps, in the flush of his European triumphs, he did not really care. In any event, during those years the Ringlings established themselves as the pre-eminent figures of the American circus—a position that was never afterward successfully challenged.

CHAPTER VIII

HEYDAY

At the end of the century the American people were moving out of their homespun phase. Those who could afford it were going to Europe in search of the culture and amenities of an older civilization, while those who could not, nevertheless aspired to a more sophisticated mode of life. The adjective "elegant," instead of being synonymous with "pretentious," as it now is, was an accolade. The Ringling brothers felt the popular pulse, as good showmen always do, and went in for elegance in their circus; and in their private lives as well.

This trend was apparent in the lavish way they furnished Tattersall's in 1895. In 1897 they added a number of things to the circus which were designed to appeal to this taste. The first was their famous mounted band, thirty brilliantly uniformed bandsmen mounted on pure-white horses. The glitter of their highly polished brass instruments was equaled only by the golden sparkle of their red-plumed helmets as they maneuvered their steeds and simultaneously tootled their horns in the parade or arena with military precision.

The Ringlings' second concession to culture was a truly original contribution to circus lore, known as the Bell Wagon. It consisted of a twelve-bell carillon mounted on an ornately decorated chariot drawn by eight matched bays. A musician, perched on a gilded rumble seat, caused it to discourse melodious chimes as it rumbled along.

The Bell Wagon was dreamed up by Charles and Alf T. Ringling, whose love of music contributed much to the high standard of the music which accompanied the show. Though certainly not great musicians, they composed many pleasing tunes for the circus of that era, just as my brother John does now. Since they could not write music, they played the airs for the musical director, George Ganweiler, who wrote them down and scored them.

Like all our magnificent chariots of that time, the Bell Wagon was built by our cousins, the Moeller brothers. Under its fanciful decorations they concealed a rugged frame. The biggest bronze bell weighed nearly a ton, with the others in proportion. Since the wagon would be parked on muddy circus lots, where under its weight the iron-shod wheels would sink so deep that a fifty-horse hitch might be needed to wrench it free, it had to be constructed so that, speaking quite literally, wild horses could not pull it apart.

Another touch of elegance with which the Ringlings adorned the 1897 show was the English Derby Day Pageant with its concourse of beautiful carriages of the time: coaches, victorias, landaus, phaetons, tallyhos, two-wheeled dogcarts, and other "nobby private equipages" drawn by high-steppers hitched in fours, in pairs, and in tandem, in which rode fashionably dressed gentlemen and ladies of the company.

A number of great equestrian acts were with the circus that year, among them the Rooneys. A member of the family, Charlie Rooney, who was also with the Barnum show for a while, came back to us as boss of the ring stock when he got too old to do stunts. Later still he retired to live in Baraboo.

He was a wonderful horseman, and he used to take care of my first pony for me.

So Charlie Rooney became a friend of my youth and sometimes a terrifying one. He was a disastrous drinker and when he got d.t.s he would not recognize me. I would go out to the stable expecting to see my old, kindly Charlie. Instead he was a wild man, seeing snakes and monkeys climbing the beams and running along the rafters. Perhaps he mistook me for one of those hallucinatory monkeys, for he would take off after me with a terribly purposeful look in his eye. And I would take off too.

But at their time of greatness, the Rooneys, especially Lizzie and John, were as fine as any equestrians in the world, and they, too, contributed to the beauty and elegance of the circus.

As a gesture toward the imperial splendors then touching the American imagination, the parade included elephants dragging siege guns, just as in Rudyard Kipling and as they did, in fact, with the British Army in India. According to Kipling, the elephants were too intelligent to take the guns

A solid Ringling front to the world: Albert, Alf T., August, Charles, Otto, John, Grandmother, Grandfather, Mother, Henry. (*Lawrence Studio*)

The five who built the circus, and their mustache cups.

The Ringlings always took part; LEFT: Uncle John was known in 1882 as "The Emperor of Dutch Comedians." BELOW: Brother John at seventeen rode in the parade as a hussar. (*Lawrence Studio*)

Of all the Ringling wives, Uncle John's Mable was the most beautiful.
(*Lawrence Studio*)

In Uncle Al's "château" in Baraboo, where we Norths grew up.

BELOW: At three Brother John was an angel; RIGHT: At three I was a wild Indian. (*Lawrence Studio*)

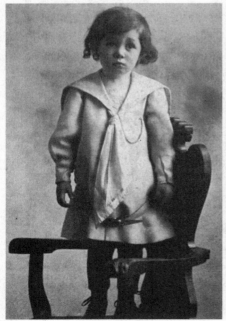

The Norths were seldom so serene: BACK: Mother and John; FRONT: myself and Salomé. (*Lawrence Studio*)

ABOVE: Uncle John and Aunt Mable, with Jacob and Tel, at the "modest" first home in Sarasota. BELOW: Their fantastic home, Ca' d'Zan (House of John), with its art collection, was worth millions.

Symphonia, Uncle Charles' yacht, was even bigger than Uncle John's.

Saloon of Uncle John's *Zalophus*. She sank with Jimmy Walker aboard.

Even when we were grown, Mother would caution us as we took off on the great circus train: "Be careful of those tracks! Please be careful in the railroad yards. Watch those trains, they're dangerous!" *(Steinmetz)*

into actual battle—I have always had great respect for elephants.

For a fact, an Indian durbar at the peak of Victorian pomp and circumstance could hardly have had the impact on its viewers of the arrival of the circus at a small American city of this period of our history. Half the adults and all the small boys would be up in the gray dawn, and the column of smoke from the engine of the first section of the circus train led them to the railway tracks as inevitably as Moses' pillar of cloud led the Israelites to the Promised Land. An eyewitness account of its arrival gives a vivid picture of it.

"The engine drags its line of gaudy yellow stockcars and flats with heavily laden wagons carrying canvas, stakes, stable tents, etc., slowly over the Main Street crossing to the sidings. The 'runs' [wooden troughlike planks] are quickly placed in position against the flats. Roustabouts and razorbacks swarm off the sleeping cars. The gigantic pole wagon comes slowly down the runs and its ten-horse team hauls it to the show grounds. Two-, four- and ten-horse teams come out of the stockcars with clocklike regularity, each arriving at the runs in the nick of time to pick up the proper wagon.

"Meanwhile another long train and another and another arrive in the yards. With the same precision their contents are transported to the show grounds, which becomes a city of tents as exactly situated as a military encampment."

Our anonymous eyewitness goes on to cite the tremendous effect of the parade on the people: "The sidewalks, curbs, gutters and streets are a packed, surging mass of humanity when the first of the chariots appears around the corner. The enlivening strains of the superb band starts the enthusiasm, . . . a round of applause which develops into a salvo of greeting as den after den of the grand menagerie passes in review; the side-show band in glaring uniforms of red, richly emblazoned and heavy with gold; the famous English Derby-

Day section . . . ponderous war elephants hauling cannon . . . the children's section with allegories of Mother Goose and dainty cages displaying baby animals. The Arabian Caravan; the representatives of the standing armies of the nations of the world—all these as well as each of the thirty separate sections of the grand spectacular street pageant, bewilder the eyes of the throng with their very magnificence— a mile and a half of marvels."

The accent was indeed on splendor. But do not suppose that the circus was going sissy then any more than it is now. There were plenty of "death-defying feats," low-comedy clowns, and such side shows as Lionette the Lion-faced Girl, human skeletons, fat girls, bearded ladies, and three-legged men, to appeal to the earthiest instincts of the crowd. In fact, it had something for every taste, which is exactly what a circus should have.

In general, however, the trend toward splendor, continued during the five years when freed from the competition of Barnum & Bailey, the Ringling Circus waxed and grew great. Of course, they took the whole of America as their province. In 1901 the circus ranged from Boston, Massachusetts, to San Diego, California; and from Montreal, Canada, to Yazoo City, Mississippi.

During each of those years the uncles added to the beauty and grandeur of the show. In 1899 Uncle Al staged the famous sixty-one-horse spectacle. More and more of the great European acts were scouted and imported by Uncle John, giving finish and style to the performance. The chariots, although always gaudy, were artistically improved until some of them became genuinely valuable examples of the wood carver's art. And, of course, the spectacles that opened and ended the show not only became ever more lavish but also better staged and more historically accurate.

Though all this striving after splendor and style may sound

somewhat farcical and phony, it did in fact meet a public need, and it gained an appreciative response. For this reason I feel that my uncles and other showmen like them contributed something of real value to American life by introducing scenes of comparatively sophisticated magnificence and beauty to a public that, especially in the small western cities, hungered desperately for the things which they had read of but never seen.

In 1903 James A. Bailey brought the Barnum show home from Europe with a fanfare worthy of Phineas T. Many splendid things had been added, among them the Two-Hemispheres Band Wagon drawn by the famous forty-horse hitch of matched English bays. Another importation was Ella and Fred Bradna. She was the finest equestrienne in the world. Dressed in a beautiful sequined evening gown with its skirt slit to the waist, she performed an astonishing series of equestrian acrobatics, including a bareback ballet dance which ended with a somersault from the galloping horse to the ground. Her husband, Fred Bradna, was a militarily slim man of aristocratic birth and impeccable dress, who was a great ringmaster and, later, a fine equestrian director.

In addition to these and many other European novelties, Bailey had some splendid new chariots made in America, the most beautiful being the tableau wagon America. It was a massive vehicle of red, blue, and gold, decorated by carved medallion heads representing the different countries of the two Americas liberally interspersed with shields of the United States.

As The Greatest Show on Earth landed from a small fleet of chartered ocean liners in New York, it looked as though the stage were set for the battle of the new century between the titans of the circus world. It never came off.

There were two reasons for this. The first was that the

Ringlings were by now so strongly entrenched in the favor of the American people as to be almost impregnable. The second was that Mr. Bailey was growing old and weary. Had it been otherwise, who knows what might have happened, but like Napoleon at Waterloo, he was not the man he once had been.

After testing his strength against us in the season of 1903, Bailey offered my uncles a treaty of peace, which they sensibly accepted. In that agreement Bailey sold them a half interest in the Forepaugh-Sells Circus, which was sent out under the management of Henry Ringling, who had proved his ability by managing the John Robinson Circus, which the Ringlings had leased in 1898. All three circuses were carefully routed to avoid any conflict of dates.

This arrangement prevailed until 1906. In the spring of that year, while Mr. Bailey was directing the three days of chaotic rehearsals in which he customarily threw a new show together at Madison Square Garden, he was suddenly stricken with erysipelas. The fine old gentleman was carried unconscious to his home in Mount Vernon, where he died within forty-eight hours.

Control of the Barnum show was inherited by his widow, who sent it out that year under the joint management of George O. Starr and her nephew-in-law Charles Hutchinson, whom I later knew and loved as Mr. Hutch.

The season was a disaster. Without the generalship of Mr. Bailey everything went wrong. In addition, rainy weather pursued them and the final catastrophe was a tornado which hit the show at Iowa City, Iowa, blowing every tent, from the Big Top to the smallest dressing tent, into shredded canvas. Although in true circus tradition they dug themselves out, scraped off the mud, and gave a performance in the open air the following day, it was a terrible blow.

Sometime during that fatal season, Mrs. Bailey telegraphed

Henry Ringling offering him the position of manager. He put it up to the conclave of the brothers, who told him to refuse. Perhaps they were already contemplating a more drastic move.

Nineteen hundred seven was a panic year. Barnum & Bailey, now under the management of W. W. Cole and Hutchinson, continued to lose money. Its stock fell to eighty-five cents a share. John Ringling began to buy it.

John was the most ambitious of the Ringling brothers and the most daring. His was the spirit of the great industrial empire builders of the day; and he saw a chance to gain a monopoly of the circus business. Pride, too, may have entered into it. Even when Barnum & Bailey was in Europe, the Ringlings never had played the greatest city in America, for Bailey controlled Madison Square Garden, the only suitable arena in New York.

That summer, stocks were crashing in Wall Street and banks were failing all over the country. (Incidentally, the Ringlings more than repaid their debt to the Bank of Baraboo. It was on the point of collapse when they shipped sackfuls of greenbacks and silver dollars, direct from their ticket windows, to restore its credit.) In the midst of panic, John Ringling began secretly negotiating with Mrs. Bailey for the purchase of Barnum & Bailey. The poor lady was fearful of losing her whole patrimony and agreed on a reasonable—a very reasonable—price. Then John laid his deal before his brothers.

No one quite knows what went on in that momentous conference, though it appears that most of them were against taking a chance in such dangerous times. But Otto, who always thought big, was for it; and they respected his judgment.

So the deal was approved and consummated. The Ringlings bought The Greatest Show on Earth for $410,000. In 1908, while Charles and Albert ran the Ringling Circus, John, assisted by Alf T. and Otto, commanded the Barnum train. Its profits in that one season were greater than the price they had paid for it.

Part III
JOHN RINGLING AND THE NORTHS

CHAPTER IX

THE APOTHEOSIS OF JOHN RINGLING

In their private lives the Ringling brothers, each according to his taste, began reaching out for a more spacious life. This was only natural, since most of the brothers had married by now and were raising families. Gus, who had married Anna Herley, had three daughters, Mattie, Lorene, and Alice. Alf

T. was married to Della Andrews of Baraboo and had a son, Richard. Charles and Edith had a boy and girl named Robert and Hester.

In 1902 Henry married Ida Palmer, also a Baraboo girl. Their son, named after his father, was always known as Little Henry, even after he grew to be six feet two and a half and weighed well over two hundred pounds, though he never attained the gargantuan proportions of his father. Al and Louise had no children and Otto never married. He always lived with the Alf T.'s when in Baraboo.

The first luxury the brothers bought themselves was a splendid private car in place of the old sleeping-dining car they had first used. This was not really a luxury at all, but a necessity, since they and their wives, especially Al and Charles, spent a great part of their lives on the circus train. It was at about this time that Charles began his collection of exquisite old violins, many of which he carried with him on the train. He loved to play duets with Edith, who accompanied him on a reed organ or a piano.

The brothers often took their children along on the train, just as later they took John and me. That the younger generation had a keen sense of the *most important thing* is shown by two letters written to my grandmother from circus trains. The first one is in a round baby hand on note paper adorned by a photograph of a round-eyed little girl with long corkscrew curls. It is dated Spokane, Washington, August 15, 1903.

> Dear Grandma
> I am with the show now but I am coming home soon in about a week. We are all quite well and the weather has been fine and business is good with the circus. . . .
> Love to all
> Hester Ringling

The second one, written from Canada the same year, is from an even younger Ringling:

Dear Grandma

Yesterday it was hot and today is very cold. I feel fine and get my lessons every day. There is the tiniest pony colt with the show I ever saw. His name is Meagher.

How are you and do you ride every day? The cars are by the lot. Business is good.

Your loving grandson
Richard

Soon the brothers began building big pleasant houses in Baraboo. Gus did not long enjoy his, for he died in 1907, the first of the brothers to go. Charles', Alf T.'s, and Henry's homes were spacious columned pseudo-colonial houses. A little later Al outdid them all by building the great castle-château in which John and Salomé and I grew up. As I said, when Uncle Al died in 1916, the conclave of surviving uncles made a settlement with Aunt Lou which gave them the ownership of the house, and they told my mother to go and live in it. The fact that Aunt Lou had removed the furniture and left the place as bare as a Roman ruin had escaped their notice. When my distraught mother called this to their attention they promptly supplied the deficiency with van loads of massive furniture in the latest style.

The other brothers developed their hobbies. Alf T. had his music. In addition to collecting violins, Charles became an avid fisherman and sportsman. Otto amassed a library of fine books, every one of which he read. Unfortunately, his hobby for food led him to eat more than any one person should— he would eat a large sirloin steak for breakfast—which undoubtedly contributed to his early death. Henry, too, was fond of reading, and was, perhaps, the most home-loving of them all.

In these ways all the brothers but one opened the windows of life, though remaining based in Baraboo. The seventh brother sought much wider horizons. John Ringling was the sport of the family, using that word in both its colloquial and its biological meaning. He got out of Baraboo just as quickly as he could; and he ranged very much further afield, geographically, financially, and artistically than his brothers. This restlessness is exemplified by the fact that he was the only brother who ever ran away from home. He kept on running all his life. However, he was not running away from things, but toward them.

As early as 1890 he went to live in a hotel in Chicago, only returning to Baraboo for circus business or family gatherings. He must have been a very gay young man; indeed, he basically ever remained so even when weighted with years and troubles. This is one of the stories he told me about the early days in Chicago:

"We had great fun tishing the girls," he said. "Do you know what that is?"

Of course, I said, "No."

"Well," he said, "it was what I used to do when I was a young man around Chicago. We were just getting started with the circus and didn't have too much money, but we liked to have a good time and this was a way to help out a meager bank roll. We would go to the sporting houses and the girls would come in. Now, it was the custom in those days, in the higher types of places, that there would be no discussion about payment. Anything like that would spoil the temporary romance.

"You would probably order a bottle of wine and sit around talking about anything but money. The girls all wore high silk stockings with round garters, and after you had warmed up a bit the big spenders would just bring out a fat roll of bills, and pulling back the garter a little, slip the roll down a girl's stocking. This made the girl happy and you had a fine time.

"Now, I didn't have such important rolls at that time, so I

would prepare a bit. I'd take a twenty dollar bill and wrap
it around a big wad of tissue paper, so it looked like a big,
splendid thing. When the time came I would shove it down
the girl's stocking and she would never know until afterward
the nature of the gift. Your uncle Charlie and I used to call it
'tishing the girls.'"

Later, when Uncle John was fairly rich, he lived at the
famous Palmer House in Chicago, but he had not changed
his ways. The hotel was very strict about propriety, and the
house detective, a man named Bismark, was most conscien-
tious. For years Uncle John and Bismark fought a battle of
wits. He would sneak a girl into his room without being seen,
but somehow Bismark would sense that she was there and
come barging in to spoil all the fun.

Finally my uncle discovered how the detective did it. He
would come along the corridor after the room key had been
taken up and the occupant was supposedly in bed, and lean
a wooden match upright against the door. If it was not still
standing there the next time he came around, he knew some
unauthorized person had gone in.

After he solved the mystery, Uncle John defeated Bismark
for quite a while. When the girl was safely in his room, he
would pull the door almost to. Then he would lie down and
slip his fingers through the crack and carefully balance a
matchstick against the door, which he then closed very
gently. When Bismark made his rounds there was proof that
the propriety of the Palmer House was intact.

Incidentally, Uncle John had one rigid rule of conduct in
the matter of women. He never went with any of the girls in
the show, though some of his brothers did. I am not sure
whether this was because he felt it was undignified and bad
for discipline, or whether he thought that his position as
owner gave him too great an advantage and that it was unsporting, like shooting a sitting bird. In any event, he never

broke this rule, and Brother John, who modeled himself in many ways on his beloved uncle, keeps the same code.

In the nineties Uncle John began making his annual trips to Europe to collect new acts for the circus. In his inquiring, untaught way he loved beauty, and the great pictures he saw abroad stirred him as nothing of an aesthetic nature ever had before. He decided he would like to have some that he could enjoy at home, and he began to buy, indiscriminately at first, but never rashly.

Once, many years later, I was going through the warehouses at Sarasota, where the treasures he had brought home from Europe were stored waiting for the completion of the museum which he intended to present to the state of Florida. Uncle John loved to go through the storage rooms and look at his great pictures. He would tell me which ones he wanted to see and exactly where they were. I would haul them out and he would sit on a crate in the bare, vaultlike room drinking in their beauty by the hour.

On this occasion I unearthed a perfectly frightful late-nineteenth-century picture. It was a painting of a nude female statue in a garden setting. The lady was holding some cherries in her hands. She made me think of Venus rising from a bed of concrete. Uncle John sat looking at it, not exactly proudly, but nostalgically. "That is the first picture I ever bought," he said.

For all I know, it is still in the cellar of the museum, for he never sold a picture in his life.

John Ringling did not long make such mistakes. As his interest in pictures grew, he studied art with the terrific intensity which he applied to any field in which he became active. He devoured books on the subject by the authoritative critics and spent hours and days in the great European museums training his eye to form and color and technique.

For the most part, this was because he liked what he was

doing; he seldom did anything he did not like. But there was also his fear of being flummoxed by the art dealers. For John Ringling had a most suspicious nature, and his misgivings were indubitably justified at a time when many unscrupulous dealers regarded the whole year as the open season for wide-eyed American millionaires. Furthermore, he enjoyed horse trading as much as David Harum; and how could a man best another without expert knowledge of the matter in hand?

By the time he finished educating himself, Uncle John, if not a great connoisseur, had a very respectable knowledge of the subject, which, coupled with his innate taste and shrewd instinct for detecting a phony, whether in works of art or human beings, made him a formidable bargainer.

Part of his method was to conceal his knowledge behind a bucolic manner. Arthur Newton of the Newton Galleries in New York likes to tell the story of the time in the 1920s when he spent days of hard trading with John Ringling over the purchase of several minor works of the eighteenth-century English school. While Ringling was viewing these pictures, a fine Sassoferrato was hanging in another room. Ringling hardly glanced at it as he went past. However, after offers and counteroffers had been made and the deal seemed stalled, my uncle sent for Mr. Newton. When he came into the beautifully furnished New York office, where Ringling sat in suitable grandeur behind a huge flat-topped desk, he was greeted by the words "You had better sit down, Mr. Newton, while you listen to this offer."

Newton perched himself nervously and gripped the carved arms of his chair. "Now I tell you what I'll do, Mr. Newton," Uncle John said with affected rusticity. "I'll give you two thousand dollars for the lot, provided you throw in the Sarsaparilla."

It was exactly the minimum Newton would take and the deal was made.

Another of Uncle John's techniques was to go to the great auctions at Christie's in London accompanied by Newton or some other expert. He knew that the other dealers would try to bid him up, so he would have Newton bid on the pictures he really wanted, while he ostentatiously bid for pictures he did not particularly like.

Now, I do not want to imply that my uncle never got stuck, for he assuredly did. Some of the pictures he thought great bargains had been impugned by the experts, though Uncle John never believed these gentlemen if he did not choose to. But the fact remains that his do-it-yourself art education enabled him to amass a collection of old masters—he never bought modern pictures—which at the time of his death was appraised at close to $15,000,000, about five times what he paid for it. His collection put the John and Mable Ringling Museum in the first rank among the galleries of the world.

While John Ringling was cultivating artistic discrimination, he also acquired a good deal of social polish. Though he had no affectations, except his occasional affectation of vulgarity, he was far too sensitive not to perceive the merits of good usage. One of the first things to go was that barbershop mustache. His store-bought clothes were replaced by the products of Saville Row or equally well-cut and even more expensive garments by Mr. Bell of New York. Good horses were an inherited love of all the Ringlings. After all, such products of the harness maker's craft as "a gold- and rubber-mounted double harness" needed a blooded animal to show it off properly. As the age of the automobile came in, impatient Uncle John transferred his affection to them, though Uncle Al did not. However, Uncle John was equally fastidious about internal-combustion locomotion; he never owned anything but Rolls-Royces and Pierce-Arrows.

The one vulgar taste he kept was food. Though he could

enjoy a European dinner with vintage wines, what he liked
best was Old Curio scotch and hash—any kind of hash. He
could put away tremendous quantities of hash. I remember
an occasion when a Chinese valet who had left Uncle John's
employ came to his Venetian palace in Sarasota to see him
and ask for his old job back.

"But I have a good man now, Willy," Uncle John said. "I
don't need a valet, I need a cook."

"I can cook, Mr. Lingling," said Willy, who had the oriental
block against the letter r.

"You kept your secret well," Uncle John observed. "Can you
make good hash?"

Willy beamed. "Mr. Lingling," he said, "I can make sleven-
teen kinds of hash."

He got the job.

So far I have discussed the frivolous side of John Ringling's
emerging character. But anyone who supposed that this was
his measure—and some did—was apt, in the words of the old
song, to find "his head tucked underneath his arm."

During the time of Ringling Brothers' great expansion he
gradually assumed the leadership of the partnership. Though
in theory each partner remained equal with an equal voice,
in practice Uncle John played the dominant role. There were
several reasons why he was able to do this. For one thing,
the others were immersed in the technical problems of their
respective departments of the circus, while John, freewheeling
between Europe and America, did not get bogged down in
details. Coming back from his trips with a fresh point of view,
he was able to see what military men call the big picture. And
his imagination showed him the way to profit by it.

While his brothers were generally content to progress
slowly, John's tremendous drive and soaring ambition made
him impatient with conservative policies. His was an all-or-
nothing spirit, ready to go out on a long financial limb to

grasp glittering opportunity. Because he was also the most ruthless and egotistical of the brothers, he forced them to go along with him. And because he was the most farsighted, with the possible exception of Otto, his gambles paid golden dividends for many years, until in the days of depression, when opportunity shriveled and all bets were off, he came close to lonely ruin.

Nor were John Ringling's ventures confined to circus business. As he traveled around the country on the circus train, his eyes were always searching for opportunity. He loved money more than anything except pictures, and he never missed a chance of making some. He might see a theater in some small city that was doing badly and could be turned into a profitable movie house; or a streetcar line that needed a little capital; or even a steam laundry whose owner wanted to retire. It did not matter to Uncle John what the line was as long as there was money in it. As a result, he owned businesses all over the United States.

Another of John Ringling's extracurricular activities was building short-line railroads. Since he routed the circus, he was as familiar with rail systems of the United States as a spider with its web. Although the great railroad-building days were over and the transportation system almost complete, Uncle John occasionally would discover a missing link that might be forged with profit. One such line, built about 1911, was the fifty-five-mile connection between Mark Twain's home town, Hannibal, Missouri, and Bowling Green, which Uncle John proudly named the St. Louis and Hannibal, though it went nowhere near the Missouri metropolis. It operated profitably until the 1930s, when it was scrapped.

Another short line was in Montana. Before starting this railroad, Uncle John took the precaution of buying about 70,000 acres of adjoining real estate. He then built a twenty-mile line from White Sulphur Springs, Montana, to Broken

Jaw, whose grateful inhabitants rechristened their town Ringling—a great loss of picturesque nomenclature, but very gratifying to Uncle John. With his usual recklessness of geographical exactitude he called it the White Sulphur Springs and Yellowstone Park. It is still running, with my brother John as president, while my cousin Paul Ringling ranches the remaining 20,000 acres of the original landholding.

My uncle's fondness for calling his railroads by high-sounding names was probably a reflection of circus-style exaggeration. One of his most grandiose gestures in this direction was the twenty-mile railroad he built between East-land and Breakwater, Texas, which he called the Eastland, Wichita Falls and Gulf. The family were teasing him about this pretentious title when Uncle Charlie came to his rescue by saying, "It may be only twenty miles long, but it's just as wide as anybody's railroad."

The most profitable of all John Ringling's gambles in railroading was not due to his acumen, but to pure happenstance. Perhaps this is not quite correct, for Uncle John always put himself in the path of Opportunity and that capricious dame did not even have to knock once; she had but to droop her left eyelid.

In 1913 one of her favorite haunts was still the old Waldorf bar. At five o'clock every weekday afternoon tycoons and tycoonlets gathered under the potted palms in its somber magnificence to discuss past triumphs and future amalgamations; and to refresh themselves with old bourbon or those newfangled martinis. There might sit Otto Kahn, Frank Vanderlip of the National City Bank, and George F. Baker of the First National, a trio of Morgan partners, a couple of Vanderbilts, Charles M. Schwab, Payne Whitney, Cornelius Kelley of Anaconda, and, with ears quivering and his mind working like a still uninvented electronic computer, that brilliant young opportunist, Bernard M. Baruch.

Into that utopian gathering where every man was a king—oil king, steel king, copper king—came one afternoon an ambitious but relatively unknown gentleman from Oklahoma who was looking for money. His name was Jake Harmon, and he hoped to get financing for a railroad which he expected would open up the cattle country of his native state.

Mr. Harmon sat alone at a little table. He knew that almost every man in the room was a Who, but he had no idea who was who. Among the men crowding the famous long bar, he noticed an impressive individual dressed in superbly tailored clothes. He was a big man, getting a little stout, and he carried himself with an air of authority. But Harmon noticed that his face was round and merry and his manner was simple and friendly.

"Who is that?" Harmon asked a waiter.

"John Ringling, the circus king," was the reply.

Harmon told my uncle that he decided that he was the most amiable looking king in the room. He got up and shoved his way to the bar. In doing so, he knocked over Uncle John's drink. Jake Harmon pretended to be terribly embarrassed by his clumsiness. Playing Uncle John's own game of exaggerated rusticity, he begged him to show his forgiveness by letting him buy a drink. Uncle John was practically always willing to let somebody else buy the drinks.

Jake Harmon's guardian angel could hardly have led him to pick a better man. John Ringling's short-line railroads were doing very well. He lent an attentive ear to Harmon's sales talk and was induced to go to Ardmore, Oklahoma, with him to look the ground over. The upshot of the trip was that Uncle John bought a townsite in the cattle country near a farm owned by a certain Mr. Heald. He called his town Ringling and helped Harmon to finance a twenty-three-mile railroad from Ardmore to Ringling, which he named the Oklahoma, New Mexico and Pacific.

Now, the law of averages always operates in the long run. The red and the black come up the same number of times if you give them long enough; and no run of luck lasts forever. But there seems to be another law of chance which ordains that a great gambler's luck is either very, very good or incredibly bad. There are no little swings, no median range. These were the years when Uncle John's luck was very, very good.

Just as the railroad was nearing completion, a wildcat oil well on Mr. Heald's farm came in with a stupendous roar that blew the derrick into the next county. Before they got it capped John Ringling had the circus lawyer John M. Kelly down there buying up oil leases. Kelly stood in the bar of the local hotel and bought them from speculators and farmers, and from the Indians. My uncle used to say, "If Kelly had not had to go to the men's room, I would have owned the whole Healdton field. While he was there some good parcels got away."

This, of course, was circus talk, but he wound up with about eight thousand acres, and the Healdton field became for a while the largest oil producer in the world.

Jake Harmon became one of the richest men in the state and aspired to be governor of Oklahoma. However, the luck turned against him. Mr. Harmon had the misfortune to be murdered by his sweetheart.

Uncle John did very well indeed. He took approximately $7,000,000 out of his holdings in the Healdton field. My brother John and I still own 60 per cent of the eight thousand acres, having purchased them from John Ringling's estate. Some of the wells are still producing.

CHAPTER X

THE BROKEN WHEEL

No matter how widely John Ringling's interests ranged he never neglected the circus. After his great coup in purchasing Barnum & Bailey, which resulted in a virtual monopoly of the field—a sort of circus trust—he devoted most of his energies to that show. In 1908, the first year it was under Ringling

management, Uncle John routed both shows. Though he
hated detail work, routing the trains was a game to him like
doing an enormously intricate crossword puzzle. His card-
index memory and relentless accumulation of facts enabled
him to know exactly which towns in any state were to be
avoided because of depressed conditions, local strikes, or crop
failure, and which had bumper crops of greenbacks to be
harvested. His routing of the two trains was a tour de force.

The following year, 1909, the brothers' council decided
that Ringling Brothers should open in Madison Square
Garden in New York and Barnum & Bailey in Chicago.
Whether Uncle John approved of this decision or not, I cannot say. He may have gone along with it because of family
pride—after all, the Ringling show had never played New
York. In any case, it was a mistake. New Yorkers thought that
Barnum & Bailey was the only circus worth seeing, and
Chicagoans were equally loyal to Ringling Brothers. Both
cities felt cheated and neither show did well. The experiment
was not repeated.

Though he routed both shows, Uncle John took a prime
interest in his new acquisition; for one thing, he had to prove
himself right. That first year, 1908, he rode the Barnum train
almost all the way. While Otto Ringling tightened up management procedures, John oversaw the performance. Ed Shipp,
who had been Uncle Al's assistant on the Ringling Brothers
show, became equestrian director of Barnum & Bailey, but
John Ringling was really in command. He added to the
splendor and precision of the performance, which had
deteriorated during the interregnum, and made notes as to
the acts he should seek in Europe to strengthen the show.

His first move was to give Ella Bradna and Fred Derrick
the center ring with nothing else going on to distract
audience attention. They had developed a remarkable equestrian act. May Wirth, who came to us from Australia in 1912,

may have excelled Ella Bradna. She easily accomplished feats few men could do—the forward somersault, back somersault with her back to the horse's head, and somersault from one horse to another. But Fred and Ella as a team were without a peer in the style, elegance, and beauty of their performance. Fred Derrick dressed for his act like an ambassador to the Court of St. James's, except that his tail coat and knee breeches were made of white satin. Ella wore a low-cut white bodice embroidered with sequins. Her long graceful legs were displayed in white tights. She wore long white kid gloves and carried an ostrich-feather fan.

She opened the act standing astride two white horses Roman style and lifting Derrick to her shoulders. From there he somersaulted to the ground and began an incredible series of leaps and pirouettes off and on the horse, never once missing. After that Ella did her famous fork leaps and bareback toe dance. They came together again at the finale in a dazzling series of equestrian acrobatics in unison.

In 1915 Uncle John made Ella's husband, Fred Bradna, equestrian director of the Barnum show, a post he held with Barnum, and later with the Combined Shows, for over thirty years. He and Ella were unique in their zany, quixotic self-characterizations of their Bohemian heritage. Fred was the son of a solid banking-brewing dynasty from Strasbourg in Alsace. He was a lieutenant in a crack cavalry regiment in the German Army when the small circus in which Ella was the star equestrienne came to Dieuze, where his regiment was stationed. He resigned his commission and chucked his career and his family to marry her. They were together until his death sixty-four years later.

Though Fred traded his uhlan's uniform for the silk hat, tail coat, and patent-leather boots of an equestrian director, he never for a moment lost his air of command. He ran the circus like a Prussian drillmaster. He was a perfectionist who would not tolerate the slightest letdown in even one of hundreds of performers. Woe to the actor who gave a slipshod performance.

Though Fred was small and slight, he was capable of towering rages and could curse majestically in at least nine languages. I remember one season when he used all nine simultaneously at every performance. The object of his wrath was Papa Leers, whose daughter Lucita was an outstanding acrobat. At the end of her act she did a full split on the roman rings and lowered two ends of a rope to the ground, where Papa was waiting for his moment of glory. The climax of the act was the spectacle of a lovely muscular girl with the weight of a fully grown man dangling from her torso while in the impossible position of a full split on the roman rings high above the center ring.

But Papa ruined it every time by hamming up his part to attract attention to himself. Though each day Bradna threatened to grind him into *pâté de maison* and eat him spread thin on slices of pumpernickel, Papa persisted. Lucita never quite split in two; Papa never became a sandwich spread; and Fred never forgave him.

Everyone in the circus knew that Ella was several years older than Fred, but that gallant gentleman always insisted that he was ten years older than she. In spite of Uncle John's sensitivity to the true ring of a well-turned dollar, he too remained a sentimentalist about Ella. Long after she had passed her prime and could no longer pretend to her former excellence as an equestrienne, he kept her in the center ring with "The Act Beautiful." This was a weird sort of display that she and Fred dreamed up, in which Ella made her entrance in a golden chariot drawn by a white winged horse, with large dogs running under the chassis and little ones treadmilling on top of the wheels, and a supporting cast of twelve beautiful girls and a flock of pigeons dyed to match the colors of the costumes.

It required a whole railroad car to transport the animals and equipment, but Uncle John paid and smiled benignly and nostalgically upon the fading queen of bygone years as twice daily she got herself inextricably involved with that fantastic collection of people, birds, horses, and dogs. The latter ranged from a huge Siberian husky named Zero to a whole pack of peanut-brained Russian wolfhounds and yapping Pomeranians.

By the time my brother John took over the management, changing conditions made "The Act Beautiful" impossible, but the indestructible Ella was still young in spirit, so he continued to feature Mme. Bradna in the center ring on a reduced scale of magnificence. Zero, the wolfhounds, Pomeranians, and pigeons had long since passed to the place where the cookhouse flag is always up and every day is payday, but "Mein" Eagle, Ella's favorite Arabian stallion, was as durable as she. Until 1942 these two defied the clock and, in a decorous exhibition of manège, brought to us who knew and loved them a daily remembrance of what circus life should be—a combination of gaiety and pathos.

In 1913, when Europe was quivering in anticipation of the First World War, the Bradnas became very homesick. Uncle John sent them to Hungary, ostensibly to sign up the Kŏnyŏt family, whom he had scouted the year before, but actually so that they could have a final reunion with their families. Like most of Uncle John's generous gestures, this profited him as well, for Bradna secured the fourteen Kŏnyŏts, who were so multitalented that they performed in six different specialty acts. They were immensely valuable when the war shut off the supply of European performers.

Another great family troupe that Uncle John imported was

the Hannefords of Ireland. They, too, were equestrians—commanded by a magnificent matriarch, Mrs. Elizabeth Hanneford, who acted as their ringmaster clad in a long evening gown ablaze with jewels and a headdress of ostrich plumes. The star of the family of six was Poodles (Richard) Hanneford. In calculated contrast to his mother's coruscating ostentation, he staggered into the ring, apparently drunk and disorderly and dressed in rags which would have made Emmett Kelly seem a model of sartorial splendor. Clinging in simulated helplessness around a horse's neck, he had a series of hilarious mishaps which involved such skillful equestrian acrobatics as have seldom been equaled. In later years Poodles performed some of these same feats in a derby hat and a ragged coonskin coat that trailed on the floor.

My brother John has often been accused of corrupting the simon-pure atmosphere of the "real" circus by introducing the beautiful production numbers designed by such theatrical artists as Charles Le Maire, Miles White, and Max Weldy. It may be news to his critics that the circus was "corrupted" when he was still in grade school. In 1914 John Ringling staged a ballet danced by eighty trained ballerinas, and this at a time when most Americans regarded the ballet as an exotic and alien form of art.

For that matter, the merging of theater and circus was evident in the spectacle plays which Barnum first introduced and which Alf T. brought to a sophisticated peak of perfection in such productions as "Joan of Arc" and "Cinderella." To stage the latter, a large section of seats was removed and replaced by scenery representing a medieval castle, including a broad, practical staircase down which Cinderella fled from the ball. Even Billy Rose's imagination never vaulted to such extravagant heights as this Ringling Brothers "spec," which required a cast of 1370 performers, 735 horses, and "five herds of elephants." They would have astonished Cinder-

ella, who must have thought that her Fairy Godmother was
drunk with power.

Despite his ruthlessness in financial matters, John Ringling
was attentive to the safety of his people. He objected to the
brutality of wild-animal acts and there were few in our
circus while he was running it. He also disliked uselessly
dangerous stunts, though he was obliged to have these to
appeal to the thrill-seeking audience, who still retained some
of the same instincts which animated the crowds in the Roman
Colosseum. He had one of the most dangerous acts ever staged
in the Barnum show just before World War I. Ernest Gadbin,
a mad German acrobat who appropriately billed himself as
Desperado, did a swan dive from a height of eighty feet,
landing on his chest on a sort of toboggan slide made slippery
with a layer of corn meal. He landed going more than a mile
a minute, shot down the slide and up its curving end to soar
off into a net.

Such acts were gradually toned down, but, of course, you
could never completely eliminate risk in running a circus,
and Uncle John did not expect to. He just tried to make it as
safe as possible.

An example of this is described by Fred Bradna in his book
The Big Top. It was in 1928 and the circus was located on
a muddy lot in Washington, D.C. That year the Wallendas
had joined the show. The climax of their act came when four
members of the family, in human-pyramid formation, rode a
bicycle across a tight wire stretched across the very top of
the tent with no net beneath them. The wire had to support
about a thousand pounds of people and equipment. If it
sagged during the perilous trip, the Wallendas were in bad
trouble. Once, when a storm hit the Big Top, the Wallendas'
wire loosened. As the bicycle went over, Karl Wallenda, who
was riding it, grabbed the wire and caught Helen by the neck
with a scissors grip of his legs as she went past. He held her

until a hand net was rushed under them. Meanwhile Herman Wallenda caught his brother Joseph in the same fashion and went hand over hand along the wire to the platform.

In Washington, John Ringling was dissatisfied with the way the Wallendas' wire was rigged, and so was Karl. They tried various means of mooring it, without success. Finally, about midnight, Fred Bradna suggested putting two heavy poles *outside* the Big Top and bracing the wire to them with a series of stays. "But where are you going to get poles at this time of night?" he asked.

"Take me to a telephone," said Uncle John.

Within an hour an emergency squad from the Chesapeake and Potomac Telephone Company was driving two telephone poles into the ground.

Though his working hours drove people crazy and his distaste for detail made him prone to rely too much on his subordinates, Uncle John was both an imaginative policy maker and a magnificent field commander. He was at his best in an emergency, and there were plenty of them to test his quality. In those days the tents were waterproofed with paraffin, which made them horribly combustible. One season both Barnum's and Ringling Brothers' Big Tops burned up within a few weeks of each other. Luckily no one was badly hurt. The audience dropped between the seats and crawled out under the bottom of the tent. We were not always so fortunate. . . .

Despite his distaste for Baraboo and his far-ranging travels, abroad and on the circus train, Uncle John had the same strong fraternal feeling which kept the family so closely united. As I have said, Christmas was the time when they all got together at my grandparents' home. As long as his father and mother lived, Uncle John always came home for Christmas. Only once, in 1907, he did not quite make it.

When my grandmother heard that her son was unable to reach Baraboo until mid-January, she simply postponed Christmas. In this connection, we have a check for fifty dollars drawn to her order by Otto Ringling and dated December 24, 1907. She even refused to cash it until John came home. The check was never cashed.

Grandmother decreed that Christmas should fall on January 16, 1908. That evening all seven of her surviving children, their wives and offspring, gathered as always in her home. My brother John was there; I was not yet born. As always, they had a roaring wonderful reunion with plenty of rousing arguments and homeric gustatory exploits. That night my grandmother died in her sleep. One may be sure she was very happy.

On April 4, 1911, Otto became the first of the partner-brothers to go. Though he died in New York with the Barnum show, Otto was brought home to Baraboo to be buried from Uncle Al's great house, which was directly across the street from the little frame dwelling where he was born. There was no circus that day. Barnum & Bailey in New York and Ringling Brothers in Chicago canceled all performances. All the brothers came to Baraboo, and special cars from Chicago and New York brought people from the two shows to pay their respects to "The King." Perhaps the most touching tribute was a floral piece in the shape of a wheel from a Roman chariot, with one of its five spokes broken as a token that one of the five founders had gone.

Though John Ringling began to play a leading role in the councils of the brothers as early as the turn of the century, his final position as absolute czar of the circus world was due to his powers of survival. Until 1932 Ringling Brothers was not a corporation, but a simple partnership. As one by one the partner-brothers died, the survivors made a settlement with their heirs and carried on.

Since Otto had no descendants, they divided his share among themselves, giving some of it to Henry Ringling and making him a partner in Otto's place. However, Henry, though hard-working and competent, could not fill Otto's shoes. "The King" had the most financial acumen of them all. The inevitable result was that Uncle John became more dominant than ever, taking Otto's place as arbiter of Ringling Brothers' finances.

CHAPTER XI

THE NORTHS

So far I have spoken of things of which I had no direct knowledge, but the time is past due for my appearance, as I was
born in 1909. In order not to confuse the narrative, I have
hardly even mentioned my mother. However, since her children later played a not insignificant part in the history of

our circus, it is time she was introduced. Her upbringing—
and ours—was very different from that of her brothers and
exemplifies the changes that money brought to the Ringlings'
way of life.

Ida Ringling was only sixteen when our show first went on
rails, and therefore her brothers were able to give her ad-
vantages they had never had. Of course, she lived with her
father and mother in the house my uncles had given them in
Baraboo and was graduated from Baraboo High School in due
time. At that time she was very lovely, a tall girl with olive
skin and dark auburn hair which was so long she could sit on
it, a highly thought-of accomplishment for young ladies of
that era.

Her life was extremely sheltered. No young woman of today would stand for the restrictions which an old-fashioned
German father and mother and seven sedulous older brothers
imposed on her. Even when she was a grown woman they
would never allow her to come home from dances or evening
parties with one of her beaux. Either her father or one of
the brothers would always call for her. She found it very
embarrassing but could do nothing with them. On one occasion, when the party she was at broke up early, she walked
home a block and a half with a young doctor. Her parents
and brothers treated her as though she were a fallen woman.

On another occasion, when her brother Alf T. took her to
call on some old friends in Baraboo, she decorously crossed
her ankles—not her knees—in the parlor. When he brought
her home, Uncle Alfred was livid with rage at her unseemly
conduct, and not only her father and mother but every one of
her brothers and their wives spoke to her severely.

In fact, all her life Ida's menfolk bossed her. It was not
that she lacked spunk; but they were all so utterly immovable
in their ideas of right and wrong and propriety—for women.
And, of course, there were "so damn many of them."

Like Alf T. and Charles, Ida was very musical, and her brothers gave her every opportunity to develop her talent. That new organ which Louise Ringling mentions Grandmother getting was bought for Ida. And as soon as they could, her brothers gave her a piano. When she had exhausted the extremely limited tutelage of the best piano teachers in Baraboo, she was sent to the Chicago Musical College, run by Professor Florenz Ziegfeld, the father of the famous Florenz Ziegfeld, Jr. In Chicago, Mother also studied with Professor Emil Liebling, who was recognized as one of the best piano teachers in America.

Ida became a very fine musician, but her accomplishments were only for the enjoyment of her family and friends. She never played professionally—the brothers would not allow it.

Naturally, Ida was not allowed to live alone in a big bad city like Chicago. Her brothers arranged for her to stay with an Italian family named Allegrhetti, of whom she became very fond. Already an expert in German and Alsatian cookery, she learned to make wonderful Italian dishes from them. In fact, she was as much a virtuoso at the cookstove as on the piano—and equally temperamental. In later years it was absolutely impossible for us to keep a cook. Mother was always out in the kitchen giving orders, and finally taking over herself because she thought she could do much better than the professionals. She could.

In all her life Ida Ringling defied her family only once—when she married my father.

Henry Whitestone North was an engineer on the Chicago and Northwestern Railroad. However, his ancestry was considerably more distinguished than that of the Ringlings. He came from one of those aristocratic English families who had acquired land in Ireland during the British conquests of that unfortunate island. The family place in Galway was Northbrook, a small eighteenth-century manor house set in wide lawns, shaded by great oaks and copper beeches. The stables were far more impressive than the residence, as became the fox-hunting Norths. Built around three sides of a flagstone court, they were made of red-hued field stone with slate roofs the color of mist off the western sea. The fields of Northbrook spread over some 600 Irish acres, equivalent to 1500 of ours, and were watered by a small clear stream which ran under a massive single-arch stone bridge. My brother and I recently bought Northbrook back.

My great-grandfather was Captain William North of the British Army. Many people know their great-grandfathers. But so long is the span of generations in the North family that mine was commanding a company of infantry at Gibraltar during the Napoleonic wars and there my grandfather was born in 1812. This foreshortens history for me. He married a Spanish lady, about whom I know only that her name was Letizia.

Samuel Wade North, my grandfather, being a younger son, came to America about the same time as the Ringlings. After pausing in Montreal to abstract a pretty seventeen-year-old Irish girl named Mary Fahey from her convent and marry her, he settled in Onalaska, a village near Lacrosse, Wisconsin.

There he lived the life of a displaced Irish gentleman. Down the main street of that little frontier town, among trappers in fringed buckskin, farmers in overalls, and Indians in blankets and feathers, he would stroll wearing formal gray-striped trousers, a cutaway coat, and a high silk hat. He never, never did a stroke of work.

It is hard to imagine anyone living in a land of such vast opportunities and bustling enterprise that it was difficult to make a move without making a fortune, and not doing anything at all. My father remembered being lined up, when he was a very small boy, with his two older brothers by my grandfather, who told them, "You must remember that a gentleman never works."

Unfortunately, he neglected to provide his sons with the means of following this precept. But he did give them a knowledge of Greek and Latin and other impedimenta of a classical education far beyond the capacity of a one-room schoolhouse.

I remember my father very well, though I was only eleven when he died of a heart ailment. He inherited a Spanish cast of features from his grandmother Letizia, with thick dark hair and an olive skin. He was a short, powerfully built man with enormous strength in his arms—a natural athlete. As a youth, he was catcher for the Lacrosse, Wisconsin, baseball team. In those days they wore no gloves, but the catcher used a hunk of raw meat to protect his left hand.

Harry North came to live in Baraboo about 1891, because it was a division point on the Chicago and Northwestern. He was in his early thirties at the time, with all the devil-may-care gaiety and charm which even the English acquire after a few generations in Ireland. My mother met him soon after she graduated from high school, and they appear to have fallen in love for keeps. But their courtship was hardly as rapid as the ignition of love. It lasted for ten years.

The delay was due to parental and fraternal objections to Harry North. Ida's family had nothing against him personally; in fact, they liked him immensely, as did everyone who knew him; but there was an insuperable objection rooted in his past. Harry North had been divorced.

It is difficult now to recall the terrible stigma attached in the nineties to those who, whether at fault or not, had broken the bonds of matrimony. But it existed even in the most sophisticated society. Imagine, then, the horror with which Ida's naïve, strait-laced family regarded the prospect of their sheltered darling's marriage to a man under so dark a cloud.

The struggle between love and filial duty continued unabated all those years. However medieval their attitude toward women, the Ringlings could not prevent the young people meeting frequently. For Harry North was very popular in Baraboo and was invited to many parties that Ida also attended. One of the great amusements of that sweet time was amateur theatricals, and they both took part in these. But it must have been a difficult and heartbreaking period for them both, and a stringent test of the strength of their love and the constancy of their characters.

In the end, prejudice appeared to triumph over love. Under extreme pressure Ida gave up Harry North and became engaged to a young man of her family's choice. The invitations were out; the house was full of wedding presents; when, like Lochinvar on an iron horse, my father swept my mother off and married her in Chicago.

That was in 1902. For a whole year no member of the Ringling family spoke to my mother. She lived in Baraboo because of her husband's job; and she suffered the misery and shame of being cut dead on its familiar streets by those she loved most next to him. Only when her first son was born and christened John Ringling North did her parents and brothers forgive her. The family circle opened to enclose her and hers in its protective shield against the world.

My brother John was born in 1903. Four years later came my sister, who was named Mary Salomé Ringling North, after our grandmother. And I, Henry Whitestone Ringling North, was born in 1909.

The Baraboo where we grew up was still quite close to pioneer times. Not too many years before, the streets had been full of Indians, and even in my memory the Winnebagos and Chippewas came back every year for their spring encampments. They pitched their tepees just outside of town and held a sort of fair to sell beadwork moccasins and baskets. They were exciting, picturesque, and smelly, though perhaps not in that order.

Old Indian John, who lived in a shack outside of town, was a friend of mine. His face was etched with wrinkles like an engraver's copper plate, and he said he was a hundred years old. Mother hired him in Prohibition days to make some wine for us, which was his specialty. When Mother went down to the cellar to see how he was doing, she found him chewing tobacco and casually spitting into the great mash of grapes.

"Now you'll have to throw it all away," she said sadly.

"No, ma'am," said Indian John. "It will work off."

Very good wine it was, too. My cousin Henry Ringling and I sampled it by sticking a rubber hose into the kegs and sucking hard. That was my first hang-over.

Having forgiven my mother, the uncles set about spoiling her children. They were experts in this pleasant art, having had a great deal of practice with our numerous older cousins. I have already given some description of the wonderful times they gave us.

In those days the Moeller brothers were still building our wagons. My cousin Heinrich, or Henry, Moeller, though many years older than I, was a great friend of mine. Some of the happiest times of my childhood were spent in his black-smith-wagon shop, where I took my ponies to be shod. He was the one who used to ride out to the cemetery with me in later years on my periodic returns to Baraboo. I'd say, "Come on, Henry, let's go to the cemetery." And he would always reply with a ritual joke: "O.K., Buddy, I'll go, but you'll have to promise not to leave me there."

However, he had no horror of it. When his brother and partner Corwin died, Henry had a tombstone made. To save future expense he had his own name carved on it as well as Corwin's, leaving his date of death blank. To my great delight it wasn't filled in for many years and Henry lived to be ninety.

Once Henry saved me from being expelled from Baraboo High School. The principal, Mr. Kingsford, though a fine man and a splendid educator, had a violent temper. One day it flared at a small boy named Calflish. Mr. Kingsford threw him down on the floor and began belaboring him. It was more than I could stand, so I tapped his shoulder and, calling him by his nickname to enrage him further, I said, "Hey, Ding! If you want to fight, why don't you pick on somebody your own size?"

Mr. Kingsford dropped the little Calflish boy and took off after me. But I was fast in those days. Not being able to catch me, Mr. Kingsford expelled me.

I went to Cousin Henry with my troubles. He took me by the arm and led me back to school and into Mr. Kingsford's office. And Henry said, "Mr. Kingsford, my cousin Buddy says you've discharged him from school. He told me the circumstances leading up to it. I don't think you're right, Mr. Kingsford. I think you'd better let Buddy back in school."

Mr. Kingsford looked at my cousin Henry, who might have posed for Longfellow's blacksmith with his big brawny arms. He stood looking at those arms; and finally he said, "Buddy can come back to school."

Another cousin Henry was a close pal of mine; this was Henry Ringling, Jr., "Little Henry." He was a sickly child, though, as I have said, he grew to be a perfectly enormous man. Henry was just as imbued with love of the circus as we were, and after Brother John put away childish things and went with the real circus, it was Henry who helped to stage our annual children's show in Baraboo.

To show you how crazy Henry was about the circus: when he was about twelve years old and at summer camp at Culver Military Academy, he heard that the Ringling Circus was going to be at Portage, near Baraboo, and that we were all going to see the show. He ran away from camp and beat his way home, hooking rides on trains when his money ran out. We found him early in the morning asleep on our porch with his white sailor suit looking as though he had ridden in a coal car. The consensus of the family was that anybody who cared that much about the circus ought to be allowed to go, so Mother cleaned him up and took him along.

He and I disappeared as soon as we reached the show grounds to call on our friends. Uncle Charles finally found us playing craps with some roustabouts under a lion's cage— we had won most of their money. Nothing much happened to us, but the roustabouts caught hell, which seems hardly just.

As I said, I knew almost all the circus people, either from riding the train with Uncle Charles or from meeting them at Winter Quarters. Most of them went off for part of the winter to do their acts in indoor shows, such as Shrine circuses; but there were always a few who remained in Baraboo. And in the spring they came drifting back, so that the place was swarming and hustling with all the activity of getting the show on the road, until the great day came when the long gaudy trains pulled out on their way to Chicago. Everybody in town was lined up along the railway tracks yelling and cheering; and people on the trains yelling back, and clowns doing funny tricks, just because they felt like it; and the lions and tigers, catching the excitement, roaring and screaming in their cages. It was a great day. But when it was over, the town seemed empty and dead and you had a gone feeling in the pit of your stomach.

One spring the trains went out, and they never came back. This was in 1918, when Uncles John and Charlie decided to consolidate the two shows at the Barnum winter quarters in Bridgeport. Bridgeport was more convenient from every point of view than Baraboo. The move made good sense, but their fellow townsmen never forgave them. For without the circus Baraboo was dead.

CHAPTER XII

"THE BIG ONE"

In 1903, at thirty-seven years of age, John Ringling had
finally married. His bride Mable Burton of Columbus, Ohio,
was in her twenties. She and her sister were dancers in one
of the great specs of the circus. Though John Ringling would
never trifle with the performers, he could and did fall completely in love with one. Marriage was different.

Of all the Ringling wives, Aunt Mable was by far the most beautiful. In describing her, one is forced to fall back on all the old-fashioned adjectives out of Victorian novels. She had a lovely, piquant little face with delicate features and large brown eyes that always seemed to have laughter close behind them, just as her lips always seemed to be on the point of smiling. Her dark hair was piled in a Gibson-girl pompadour. She had the figure known as willowy and was able to wear the long elaborate gowns of the Edwardian era with beauty and distinction.

Aunt Mable was, in fact, exactly the right wife for Uncle John, and their marriage came as close to perfection as any union between mortals may, which is astounding in view of John Ringling's character. Not that he was completely faithful to her. When he was with her he was a devoted husband, showing her the gentle consideration which could come only from deep affection. She usually accompanied him on the circus train, but when he was on it alone or off on his business trips, he was apt to relapse into his bachelor ways.

With far more wisdom than most women, Aunt Mable realized that her husband was too old and gay a dog to learn new tricks of behavior. She treated his infidelities as though they had never happened. So, of course, they did not exist for her. In this she was far more intelligent than Aunt Edith, who soured her happiness with constant worry about what Uncle Charlie might be up to.

When they were first married the John Ringlings lived in an apartment-hotel on Dearborn Avenue in Chicago. It was there that Uncle John bought his first Pierce-Arrow—a clear sign in those distant days of opulence and distinction. By 1910 my uncle had moved to New York, where for many years he resided in a handsome apartment at 636 Fifth Avenue. I have two outstanding boyhood memories of it. One is of an exciting parade, viewed from the windows of the Fifth Avenue side, celebrating the state visit of King Albert of the Belgians right after World War I. The other is of the wonderful ice-cream desserts that were the creation of some nearby confectioner, and my uncle's and my chief delectation at every dinner—Uncle John often said that he wasn't finicky in the slightest degree about dessert, as long as it was always ice cream. I can see him still, sitting erect and dignified in the back seat of his chauffeur-driven Rolls consuming with obvious relish and childish delight a huge ice-cream cone which he had sent me to procure in the course of an afternoon's drive.

Uncle John also bought a country place at Alphine, New Jersey, with a huge field-stone house and hundreds of acres of lawns and meadows, great trees, and little lakes. We Norths often stayed with them there, and it was from that house that I started with Uncle John officially to begin my career with the circus.

The John Ringlings went to Sarasota, Florida, in 1909 and fell in love with it at first sight. At that time it had less than a thousand inhabitants, a very small town on the Gulf of Mexico, with a huge harbor protected by the long, uninhabited outer keys. A few discriminating wealthy people had recognized its charm, however, and built winter cottages along the bay front. Uncle John bought one of these, about three miles north of town, from Charles Thompson. It was a spacious frame house with the gabled roof and columned verandas that made the dwellings of that period such comfortable, happy places to live in. With it the Ringlings acquired about a thousand feet of water front and a long wooden dock. The house looked over the bay toward the dark green tangled wilderness of Longboat Key. To the northwest you could see the open Gulf.

With his strong family feeling, Uncle John wanted his relatives around him. In 1912 he persuaded Uncle Charlie to buy a similar place adjoining his. The next year Uncle Al came to Sarasota for a few months, and Uncle Alfred rented the Ralph Capleses' big bungalow next door to Uncle John. Uncle Henry, who liked to be different, moved to Eustis, Florida, some one hundred miles away.

In 1913 we Norths also came to Sarasota. At this time my father was a semi-invalid who could no longer withstand the bleak Wisconsin winters. The year before, we had gone to Biloxi, Mississippi. Incidentally, it was there that I first gave promise of a little literary bent and a large tendency to say the wrong thing. My mother introduced me to a southern lady named Mrs. Brown, who had come to call. I acknowledged the introduction by saying:

> "Mrs. Brown
> Came to town
> Riding on a billy goat
> Upside down."

I meant no harm; I was very fond of billy goats.

There were no proper houses for rent in Sarasota, so Uncle Charlie got us half of a double bungalow on what, I believe, was then Fourth Street. The John Burkets lived in the other half. It was the beginning of a friendship that has lasted until the present time.

So Uncle John brought all the Ringlings together again, a long way from Wisconsin. It may seem strange, but Florida reminded them of their childhood in the northern woods because of the great pine forests which existed there. Now they have mostly been cut down or burned off to make room for jungles of modern housing, but forty years ago there were long, solid, fragrant stretches of pine.

The Sarasota I knew, before the Florida boom, was half fishing village, half western cow town. The level, grassy plains inland provided fine pasturage for animals, and the great cattle industry which now makes Florida one of the leading beef-raising states was just getting started. The herds were still the runty native cattle, scarcely larger than Shetland ponies. They looked very strange to a boy from Wisconsin's lush valleys.

On Saturday nights the cowboys rode in from the ranches and turned Sarasota into a reasonable facsimile of a TV serial. As the raw corn liquor took hold there were shootings and knifings on Main Street. The sheriff was a very busy man.

I remember Sheriff Hodges well because he was the most important man in town (at least on weekends) and a character right out of Owen Wister. In fact, I hoped to grow up to be like him. I can see him now with his drooping mustache and black slouch hat, riding a big western-bred horse, with a shotgun in his saddle holster and a pair of handcuffs clinking ready on a hook behind his saddle.

The sheriff was also fire chief. When a blaze broke out, he fired off his shotgun to sound the alarm and galloped to the shed where they kept the hose wagon. At the signal the volunteer firemen dropped everything and hurried to rally round him. So did everybody else in town. So you see, life was not dull in Sarasota.

During those years when Father was so ill, we children spent a great deal of time at Uncle Charlie's place. Though Aunt Edith was well into middle age, she was one of the nicest companions I ever had, for she had a wonderful faculty for making young people enjoy themselves. Sometimes in the early morning, when the tide was out, we would walk 'way out on the glistening sand flats collecting the curious, beautiful shells for which the Gulf coast is famous. Quite often Uncle Charlie would go along, and he, too, was a good companion. He invented imaginative games for us to play—one day I would be Captain Kidd and the next, George Washington.

When I was about ten Aunt Edith taught me to shoot her favorite gun, a fine little 28-gauge Parker Double Barrel. A little later I used to go hunting with an old Negro named Cummins, who worked on the Charles Ringling place. He used an ancient 10-gauge shotgun held together by copper wire, a regular blunderbuss that sounded like a cannon and belched great clouds of black powder smoke. I must shamefully admit our victims were meadow larks as often as quail.

One of Cummins' jobs was to take care of the chickens. In summer, when Uncle Charlie and Aunt Edith were away with the circus, my uncle kept getting monumental bills for chicken feed. He could not understand how so few could eat so much. When he got home a little detective work uncovered a still in the pinewoods back of the house, where Cummins was turning the corn into moonshine.

Another colorful retainer of whom we were all very fond was Julius, who worked for Uncle John. I suppose everybody looks big to a little boy, but Julius must have been a gigantic man by any standard. He got into a fight one Saturday night in town and the police were called in. Julius refused to surrender, and my friend Sheriff Hodges shot him three times. Julius ran at least a block with three forty-five-caliber slugs in him before he toppled over dead. And there was great sadness at Uncle John's.

I did not see much of Uncle John in those days except at family parties. I remember meeting him on the street one day and his asking me, "Why do you always go to Uncle Charlie's? Why don't you visit me more often?"

I could not think of the right answer, but the truth was that, though he liked having us around, Uncle John's schedule did not coincide with that of a little boy.

A few years later, when I was thirteen or fourteen, I used to skin out the window of our bungalow at night and set off to see life on Main Street. Sometimes I'd meet Uncle John on the street around midnight. He would never express any surprise at seeing me out at that hour; perhaps he felt none. He would likely say, "Buddy, would you like to borrow the Pierce-Arrow tomorrow?"

Of course, I would answer, "Yes, Uncle John," and he would say, "Come up and get it!"

When we first moved to Sarasota, John and Salomé and I went to Miss Pierce's private school, which she ran for the children of winter visitors. It consisted of a one-room wooden building, in which she taught children of all ages—I believe I was the youngest. Miss Pierce taught us reading, writing, arithmetic, history, literature, and French. I was very fond of her despite the fact that I was very bad in school and spent most of the time behind the wood box.

At school we met the children of the winter visitors. It was a small but rather distinguished colony, which received the final accolade when Mrs. Potter Palmer, leader of Chicago's Four Hundred, or whatever the magic number was in that city, built The Oaks near Sarasota. She also went in for real estate in a large way, buying over a hundred thousand acres of inland fields and pine forests. Her aunt by marriage, Mrs. Benjamin Honoré, also built a rather elaborate residence, called The Acacias. When Mrs. Honoré died, her niece Mrs. Frederic Dent Grant, daughter-in-law of the President, inherited it. Mrs. Grant's daughter, Julia Grant, had married Russian Prince Michael Cautacuzene. In 1918, when the Cautacuzenes got out of Russia just ahead of a Bolshevik posse, they came to live at The Acacias.

The princess had lost most of her possessions in Russia, but not her grand manner. She decreed that my sister and I were among the few children eligible to play with the little Cautacuzenes. It was always a big deal. Mother would dress us in our very best clothes and we would be taken to the big solemn house, where we would play decorously with the little prince and princesses. Then we would be served a nursery tea and sent home in the limousine. It seemed pretty dull after our freewheeling life. We were glad our uncles were only circus kings.

It took a very sad occasion to bring all the brothers back to Baraboo once more. On New Year's Day 1916, Al Ringling died. He was the real founder and anchor man of our enterprise, balancing the Concert Company, like the plow, on his chin, and equestrian director of the show from that first performance of the circus in Baraboo until the summer before he died. While his brothers branched out into finance and social life, he remained a working circus man.

In fact, his illness dated from one of those fires which have played such a tragic role in circus history. In Cleveland the cars had been run on a siding near a lumberyard. The yard caught fire and the blaze spread to the circus train. Though the equipment and animals had luckily been unloaded, many of the cars were destroyed. As equestrian director, Uncle Al was determined that the show would meet the next day's engagement. He worked all that day and night; dragooning the railroad to divert other cars to him, double-loading those that remained, and, somehow, fitting the other equipment and cages into the cars borrowed from the railroad. Then he directed two shows the following day.

The excitement and a forty-hour stretch of work was too much for him. He developed a heart condition which culminated in the fatal attack on New Year's Day.

Al Ringling had the sweetest disposition of all the brothers; he was the one whom the circus people really loved. When the news reached Winter Quarters, clowns and cooks, hostlers and equestrians, wept for "Uncle Al."

He was buried from his great house in Baraboo, with all his remaining brothers and their wives and, of course, my

mother and father present, as well as circus people from all
parts of the country. His fellow townsmen were there, also
deeply affected. For they knew that Al was the only Ringling
who really loved his home town. Alf T. had built a magnificent
place in New Jersey. Charles was settled in Evanston and
Sarasota, while Henry spent comparatively little time in
Baraboo.

But Al had built his life in Baraboo and spent his money
there. Only the year before he died, he gave a further proof
of his affection for the little city. He built a small exquisite
opera house, which he intended to present to Baraboo. It was
an almost perfect copy of the theater Marie Antoinette built
at Versailles. His last public appearance was his attendance
at the opening, on November 17, 1915. Unluckily for Baraboo,
he died before he signed a deed of gift.

After Uncle Al's death the conclave of uncles took over his
affairs, as they always did at the death of a brother. As I have
said, they handed down their ukase that my mother should
live in Uncle Al's mansion. They also decided not to present
the theater to Baraboo.

This was typical of their highhanded ways. Their reason
was that the city fathers were taxing circus property in what
they considered an extortionate manner. By their reckoning
they had contributed far more to Baraboo than Baraboo to
them. Their indignation, righteous or otherwise, ran high.
Here was one way to get back at the townspeople. The
theater just went back into the family pot. Had gentle Uncle
Al been at the conference, the result would have been far
different.

That was the last great avuncular conclave. The Ringling
brothers were not very old—Uncle John was just fifty—but
the scythe swung fast among them. Henry was already facing
death; he died in Baraboo in 1918, aged forty-nine. Uncle

Alfred died in 1919. He lived just long enough to see the first performance of Ringling Brothers–Barnum & Bailey Combined Shows—The Big One, as circus people called it—at Madison Square Garden in 1919.

The decision to combine the shows had been taken by John and Charles Ringling the year before, in 1918. That was the summer when the First World War reached its crisis of slaughter and national effort; and its climax of victory. The brothers had managed to keep both shows on the road despite wartime shortages of labor, material, and transportation. This presented a tremendous problem and would have been impossible without government co-operation. But then, as in another war, the authorities took cognizance of the circus as a national institution and a morale builder.

However, wartime stringencies had little to do with the decision to combine the shows. Two other factors were controlling. The first was the canny conclusion of Charles and John that the American people would no longer support two circus colossi. With the coming of the movies and the automobile, the farm communities were no longer so isolated; their tremendous hunger for entertainment was appeased if not yet sated. They would still go to the circus—all America loved the circus—but it was no longer the single great event of the year, no longer an absolute must. Also, with the new mobility they could travel farther, and therefore one combined show playing the large centers of population could take care of them.

The second factor was the question of management. There were no longer "so damn many of them." One or more of the partner-brothers had always been on the trains to make instant decisions, quell revolts, or meet emergencies with the full authority and confidence of all the others behind him.

What then of the younger generation, who might have been

expected to be waiting like heirs apparent to grasp the
scepters their elders let fall? They were not there.

The seven brothers between them had only three sons.
Little Henry was a big good-natured fellow whose mother
had deliberately alienated him from circus life. And besides,
he was only twelve when his father died.

Uncle Charlie's son, Robert Ringling, had made a fine
career for himself in a different, though allied, world. In fact,
he had two careers in unusual juxtaposition. The lesser one
was as a sportsman—a daring and successful owner-driver of
very fast racing boats. By profession he was an opera singer.

I can personally testify that Robert had one of the most
beautiful baritone voices I have ever heard. This opinion is
confirmed by the fact that during his fruitful years Robert
sang in half the great opera houses of Europe and also with
the famous Chicago Civic Opera Company.

It must be admitted that Uncle John could not stand him.
I remember one evening when Robert came to Ca' d'Zan with
his music, prepared to give us a marvelously enjoyable
evening, and Uncle John naughtily said, "I have a treat for
you, Robert."

He called in his valet, Taylor Gordon, who was studying
voice on the side, and Manny (as we called him) sang for
hours while Bob listened as gracefully as possible.

Shortly after his musical evening Manny asked my uncle
John for the loan of a thousand dollars so that he could
seriously pursue his studies. I would like to report that my
uncle promptly granted the loan which started Manny on
his road to fame and world acclaim, but that would be only
half the truth. What actually happened was that Uncle John
recognized Manny's preoccupation with his music by firing
him for paying more attention to the perfection of his
cadenzas than to the pressing of my uncle's suits and the
shining of his shoes.

Little more than a year after his dismissal Manny stopped my uncle in the foyer of the Palace Theatre on Broadway and proudly called his attention to the lobby posters which announced that Taylor Gordon was to make his debut that same night as a headliner. With relish he also presented his former employer with two complimentary tickets, and Uncle John and Aunt Mable attended happily. Manny went on to become a highly successful concert singer.

Richard, Uncle Alfred's only son, was a very different sort of person. He was the best companion, the wittiest, the most imaginative, and the worst spoiled of all my cousins. He once told me that at the age of twelve his father took him to task for smoking and drinking too much. He promised Uncle Alfred that he would take only one drink and smoke one cigar a day. He kept his word, but he made the drink in an oversize beer stein and had specially procured cigars that were a foot long. That is Richard's own story; perhaps he exaggerated it, for after all, he too belonged to the circus.

Rick was indeed enterprising; he was also so unstable that it ruined all his enterprises. That and the fact that he was a two-bottle man—two bottles of whisky a day did little to sharpen his judgment. His biggest investment was in Montana ranch land. But he at one hilarious period of his too short career owned a billiard parlor on Broadway. He loved the life along the Main Stem and was always surrounded by a cast of Broadway characters straight out of Damon Runyon —prize fighters, theater people, racing men, and gamblers, though he was no gambler, except in business. Shortly before he died Rick realized the heavy price he was paying for overindulgence and went on the wagon. Unfortunately, it was too late, as his health had already been irreparably damaged.

Rick was a circus fan, but he never worked in the Ringling show. He told Uncle Alfred that he wanted to work up as his father and his illustrious uncles had, with his own show.

In other words, he wanted to start at the top. Uncle Alfred was willing to give his only son anything he wanted. He set him up with a truck circus. It was small but completely equipped from excellent acts to a little menagerie. It had everything but managerial ability. Rick took it out as the R. T. Richard Circus. In half a season it went into bankruptcy.

So the trucks and the new tent and the cages of animals rolled sadly back to Alf T.'s country estate. Until they could be disposed of, the lions and tigers were housed in the big stables, where their ululations shattered the peace of the well-groomed New Jersey countryside. Guests who wandered down to those formal brick stables with their coach house and box stalls, courtyard and belvedere with a gilt trotting-horse weather vane, were considerably startled by a sign that read:

WILD ANIMALS
BEWARE!

Richard was the only one of the boys who inherited a financial interest in the circus. Alf T. left him his share of the partnership by will—a full third. Theoretically, this gave Rick a voice in the management. Practically, it did nothing of the sort. Uncle John and Uncle Charlie simply ignored him. This may have been reasonable in view of his record. But they would probably have done so even if he had been a second Barnum.

So much for the second generation in 1919, for I was only ten and Brother John sixteen; and no one could know that he was destined to be the true heir. I have said that Richard was the only boy who inherited a financial interest in the circus. This is true, for John and I *bought* our shares many years later. The only thing that Brother John inherited was the most valuable of all—the Ringling touch.

It was easy for Charles and John Ringling to decide to combine the shows. Doing it was as intricate and explosive an exercise in diplomacy as a European peace conference. When the Ringling show was ordered to winter in Bridgeport instead of Baraboo, the performers became uneasy. Tensions built up which exploded in panic when the combination was announced. Everyone was frantic about his job or possible loss of prestige through the competition of other similar acts. Nor were the uncles unmindful of these human problems.

During the strain of operating under wartime conditions the show people had been extraordinarily loyal to them. Both circuses were short of everything. With no new acts coming from Europe and foreign performers being called back to serve in their respective armies, there were simply not enough to go around. Everybody had to double in brass. In the Barnum show, for example, the Kŏnyöts appeared six times under their own name and five times as the Spelvins. Great equestrians risked their necks riding as jockeys in the hippodrome races; and acrobats learned to walk the tightwire. Finally, because the labor shortage was even more acute— 80 canvasmen instead of 250—everybody pitched in to move the show. Equestrian director Fred Bradna would be out at 6 A.M. swinging a sledge to drive stakes for the Big Top; aerialists and clowns manhandled the poles, seats, and canvas; great women stars loaded wardrobe trunks on the wagons. Now, as the war suddenly ended and two shows were telescoped into one, there was too much of everything. And the extra people had to be taken care of.

Part of the problem was solved by natural attrition. Performers drifted off and were not replaced. Others hastily got new jobs on their own. A few retired on their savings, or were pensioned. There was room for most of the rest in the greatly enlarged Combined Show—if they would work together and accept some downgrading. An act that had been guaranteed the center ring might have to go in a wing. There was the rub!

Since Uncle Charles had been more intimately associated with the Ringling show, and Uncle John with Barnum & Bailey, each had his favorite people whom he wished to put in the top spots. The most touchy question was who would be equestrian director of the Combined Show. Charles promised the post to John Agee, who had succeeded Uncle Al in the Ringling show. John gave a similar promise to Fred Bradna. It looked as though an immovable force had met an irresistible object.

Bradna and Agee were in a dither. The two Ringlings were worried. They both knew that although Agee was an excellent equestrian director, Bradna was an inspired one. However, Agee had Charles' promise and my uncle was a man of his word. Finally John Ringling came up with a face-saving suggestion. "A great show like this needs two equestrian directors," he said. "Let's make Agee equestrian director, and Bradna *general* equestrian director."

So it was done. John Agee did not like it much, but honor was satisfied.

One of Uncle John's favorites with the Barnum show was an enormous girl named Katy. She lay down flat on her back in the ring. Her assistant put a plank over her stomach and then led a hefty work horse over the plank. One season Katy was pregnant, but she continued the act until the last month. A few days after the baby was born, Uncle John dropped in to see the show and did not believe his eyes. There was Katy with the horse walking over her. He insisted on keeping Katy.

The two brothers spent most of the winter of 1918–19 in Bridgeport, planning, programming, and placating. There were 168 different acts to be fitted into the performance. When the Combined Show opened in New York on March

29, 1919, it was a tremendous and harmonious aggregation of talent, noise, and glitter. There was not room for all of it in Madison Square Garden. Some of the side shows and lesser acts had to wait until it went on the road under the enormous new six-pole Big Top. Nor did it reach its full effulgence in that first year. Throughout the twenties new acts were added and the best of the old ones retained. At its zenith, about 1928, it was in very truth The Greatest Show on Earth. There had never been anything like it before; and I am willing to prophesy that there will never be again.

CHAPTER XIII

IN THE BACK YARD

I have already spoken of some of the great artists of the circus during the twenties, especially the Bradnas and the Hannefords. There were even greater ones with us during those years of glory. When I was a little boy May Wirth was queen of the back yard. In his book, Fred Bradna unequivocally states that she was the greatest equestrienne of all time; a true and generous tribute, since May was a rival of Fred's beloved Ella. It is doubtful if there will ever be another like her, for the family discipline that made her great is out of fashion.

When May came to Barnum & Bailey from Australia in 1912, she was sixteen years old, a small, softly rounded girl with lovely, pure features. She wore her hair tied little-girl fashion with a big bow of pink ribbon. May had been an equestrienne under her mother's tutelage since she was five years old and was a star at thirteen. Perhaps her greatest trick was the back-backward somersault. She stood with her back to the horse's head and did a complete somersault with a twist so that she landed facing forward. Though a terrific athlete and one of our brightest stars, she was so sweet and gentle that we all loved her.

Another charmer was Bird Millman, the first American girl to work on the tightwire with no pole or parasol for balance. Dressed in short fluffy skirts, with her long hair piled on top of her small head and a little balloon in her hand, she made a series of birdlike runs on the wire, chirped a couple of popular songs, and danced a hula while a chorus sang "Aloha." Con Colleano, of course, far exceeded her in daring and agility on the tightwire. This dashing if unpredictable fellow of Spanish-Irish-Australian descent wore toreador pants and a flowing white shirt as he danced a dazzling bolero, and wound up his act with a feet-to-feet forward somersault. He was the first man ever to accomplish this most difficult of all tightwire stunts.

Toward the end of this period, we acquired Mabel Stark and her tigers when Uncle John bought the Al G. Barnes Circus. Mabel was an Amazonian lady with masses of yellow-dyed ringlets on her head and a body covered with scars. And no wonder! For her specialty was wrestling with a full-grown Bengal tiger. Without whip or gun or fear in her heart, she worked sixteen of the great cats in the most commanding manner a lady ever had.

Though Mabel was so formidable, she could not have been without feminine wiles, for she had two ardent suitors whom she played off against each other to the delight of the entire circus. One of them was our manager, Fred Worral. Quarter-Pole Worral we called him, because he seemed always to be leaning against a quarter pole with his great paunch impressively decorated with an elk's-tooth watch charm and a skimpy little pipe sticking out from under his handle-bar mustache, the perfect, pompous picture of an old-time circus man.

Also, Andrew the giraffe man fell in love with Mabel. He must have been seventy-odd; but spring came into his life for the first time. As far as anyone knew, he had never before shown affection for anything but giraffes.

With extraordinary dexterity Mabel kept these suitors separate and unknown to each other, while each lavished gifts upon her and no doubt dreamed of sharing a rose-embowered cottage when Mabel should finally forsake her tigers for domestic bliss. It was an awful shock to both of them when they finally discovered the mutuality of their courtships. Poor Andrew was the worse affected, having waited so long for love. He went to Mabel and demanded his presents back. Hopeless rebellion! Eyes that could quell a Bengal tiger pierced and confounded him. Back he went to the gentle giraffes.

My favorite clown as a boy was Herman Joseph. Herman was Jewish and played the role to the hilt, exaggerating his already adequate nose. He worked in the main show, but his moment of limelight came in the Wild West after show which we still had in those days—twenty-five cents extra. Then he would dress himself up in a cowboy suit calculated

to end all cowboy suits, and clown throughout the show
with a constantly varied repertoire of gags and impromptu
wisecracks. For the finale Herman fired off an ancient blunderbuss that seemed to kick him halfway across the track.

Another clown—not a great one, but a great person—whom
I love dearly is Pat Valdo. He came to the Barnum show in
1902, seven years before I was born. He was a tall skinny
lad of twenty-one who, like my uncles, had seen one circus
in his home town—Binghamton, New York—and became
insanely inspired to become part of it. Pat worked up from
walk-ons to a good clown spot and married a circus girl. Together they developed a wonderful boomerang act which we
used for many years. Pat's executive ability was early noted
by my uncle John, who made him assistant equestrian director to Fred Bradna.

When he was over seventy years old my brother and I
retired him on a pension, but Pat refused to stay retired. He
is still a tall lanky lad with the sawdust oozing out of his ears;
and happy as a circus seal doing a great job as general
director of The Greatest Show. He is seventy-nine years old.

Bobby Clark was also with us when I was a boy. He was a
good clown who became a great comedian.

There were others almost as great, many others. Merle
Evans, the superb bandmaster who for thirty-seven years
produced the blare and cacophony, the sweet, soft strains, or
the roll of drums that accompanied each act; responding to a
couple of hundred cues twice every day and sending the
audiences with the brazen clangor of the loudest cornet in
show business. There were the Wallendas with their pyramid
of people riding a bicycle across a wire at the top of the tent;
Charlie Sigrest, a good acrobat, flier, tightwire man, and
equestrian, but spreading his talents too thin to be quite great;
Clyde Beatty was with us for a while. In the Wild West after
show we had Tom Mix, the good cowboy in the white hat

who in real life was just that, for he always played himself. We paid him $10,000 a week one season, and he lost it all when he started his own show. He was not quite smart enough for the black hats.

Another great character whom Uncle John brought to America in the twenties was Hugo Zacchini, who had himself fired out of a cannon. Of course, other people had done it before. I think the genesis of the act was in 1870, when some Italian invented a cannon that was supposed to shoot a soldier over the enemy lines. The idea was that he would float down on a parachute and wreak havoc in the rear. Lulu, a man dressed up as a girl, first did it in the circus in 1879. But Zacchini brought the act to dramatic perfection, with a huge cannon actuated by a spring—but lots of noise and smoke—which hurled him in a great arc the whole length of Madison Square Garden into a net. It is very dangerous, for if you do not fall into the net just right you can be badly hurt. To say nothing of the total damage if one misses the net entirely!

There were dozens more with us in the twenties, many of whom might have been greats today but who were overshadowed them by those who were even greater. It is impossible to speak of them all, though I knew and liked them all. But there was one, or rather two in one, whom I have saved—the best and dearest—for the last.

They were Lillian Leitzel and Alfredo Cadona, who in the circus firmament belong together like the Gemini. As in the case of all those inseparable pairs of lovers who walk forever side by side through history and myth, many fine writers have told their story. However, having known and loved Leitzel from the time I was five years old, and watched Alfredo at his apogee of greatness swooping as effortlessly as a barn swallow under the luminous peaks of the Big Top, perhaps I can add a fresh touch or two to their portraits.

Leitzel came first—she always came first, for she was the

greatest star of them all, personifying in her tiny lambent person the quintessential glamour of the circus. Like most of our other greats, she was a child of the tented arenas; reared, trained, and disciplined from babyhood for her profession. Unlike most of them, she was beautifully educated, knowing the literature and philosophy of five languages, and the language of music as well. Had she chosen, she could have been a fine concert pianist.

She came to America from her native Bohemia with a family trapeze-and-bicycle act, of which her mother was the star. From the age of nine she had been stealing the show from her mother, and when the family act went back to Europe, Leitzel elected to remain. She got her big break in a Hoboken honky-tonk and became a star of vaudeville before she joined the Ringling show in 1915.

At the time I met her, Leitzel was not only our brightest star but our smallest. She was only four feet ten inches tall, and her luxuriant golden hair covered her in glory. In all things but one she was exquisitely formed; with an incredibly narrow waist, lovely legs, and feet so small that she wore a child's size-1½ shoe. Exquisitely dainty and feminine, she had the shoulders of a Notre Dame tackle. This was due to the exigencies of her act.

It consisted of two parts. Wearing silk tights and a diaphanous short-short skirt, Leitzel would go up the web—as the dangling ropes for the aerialists are called—in a series of apparently effortless roll-overs until she reached a pair of roman rings high above the center ring. There was no net beneath them—Leitzel never used a net. For technique, grace, and style, her performance on the rings was unequaled. Where others labored, she floated; where others assumed grotesquely contorted positions, her body held the grace of a Grecian marble; where others wore the set smile of stress and fear, she laughed as joyously as a little girl playing on a swing.

Though Leitzel's artistry reached its height on the rings, it was the second part of her act which appealed to the Roman-holiday instincts of the crowd. When she had descended from the rings and taken a bow, she grasped another rope and was flown aloft to the top of the tent. Now everything in the whole great arena was stilled. Even the candy butchers were forbidden to hawk their sweets while Leitzel did her final turn.

As a single spot focused on her tiny glittering figure, she slipped her right wrist through a padded loop attached by a swivel to a hanging rope. Then she got up by momentum and hurled her entire body in a full circle over itself. This is called the full-arm plange, or "dislocate," for each time she did it her right shoulder was dislocated and was snapped back by its powerful muscles.

Over and over and over Leitzel went while the drums signaled each turn with a roll and crash and the audience chanted the count: "one—two—three—four . . . twenty-five—twenty-six . . . fifty-one—fifty-two . . . eighty-five—eighty-six. . . ." Often she did a hundred turns; her record count was two hundred and forty-nine. Incredible endurance! On a blazing August day up there in the peak of the tent, where the temperature was twenty or thirty degrees higher than at ground level, she would still complete the dizzy century of turns. As she spun around, her long hair gradually, artfully loosened from its pins and swung free, following the parabolas her body made like a golden comet's tail. . . .

Sensational as her performance was, it was not what Leitzel did, or even how she did it, that made her so great a star. It was her own self. She could walk out and simply stand there before ten thousand people, and win and own them before ever she made a move. They felt the incandescence of her personality back to the last row of the "blues."

Sometimes we wondered that she was not consumed by

the violence of her passions. Oh, she was a violent person! Without doubt, part of her flaming temperament was calculated showmanship. But where artifice ended and Leitzel took over, no one, not even Leitzel, knew. When she flew into one of her terrible rages everyone took cover. I think that even Uncle John was afraid of her. Cursing in all five languages, she often let fly with a right-arm slap that stunned the recipient. On the other hand, she could move in the most sophisticated society with perfect decorum; and talk at ease with kings.

She could be tender, too. There was no artifice in her love of children. There were many youngsters traveling with us in family troupes. They all called her Aunty Leitzel, and adored her. Whenever she went shopping she came back loaded with presents for them, and she was always giving them birthday parties with cake and all the trimmings.

There was no proper schooling for the performers' young families at that time, so every weekday Leitzel kept school in her luxurious dressing tent for the children of the circus. With infinite patience she taught them to read and write, and enjoy the beauty of music and poetry; and to understand noble thoughts. She also had a little trapeze rigged up in her tent, on which she showed the tots who wanted to emulate her the rudiments of her art.

It was because Leitzel first knew Johnny and me when we were young that she always loved us. In her blackest mood, when all else failed to move her, Johnny would go into her tent and whisper some secret magic words to her. She would start to laugh and quickly be on her way to the Big Top to charm the audience with her graciousness.

I remember one time when I was at Manlius she came to Syracuse with a little "winter circus" that Fred Bradna had put together. Some of my best friends at the Academy and I got leave to go over to see the matinee. As I entered the auditorium Bradna came up to me looking desperate. "That God-damned Leitzel is having a tantrum," he said. "She claims I hung her rigging wrong, and she won't go on. See if you can do anything with her, Buddy."

So I went to knock on her dressing-room door, and she screamed between lurid oaths that she wanted to be let alone.

"It's me, Buddy North," I yelled.

The door flew open and a radiant Leitzel jumped at me and hung around my neck. After the effervescence of her greeting subsided, she admired my uniform and I admired her lack of same, for she was nude to the waist. I asked her how things were going.

The lightning flashed around my head. "That triple-blanked son of a gun Fred Bradna hung my rigging wrong," she yelled.

"He's a dope," I said sympathetically. "But I've brought some friends over from Manlius just to see you, and we feel pretty bad that you aren't going on today."

"What God-damned fool told you I wasn't going on?" Leitzel demanded. Then she added sweetly, "Of course, I am. And you are going to introduce my act."

I was horrified, but I knew better than to refuse. So when the time came I stood on the stage and went through the spiel I'd heard Lew Graham give a hundred times to introduce Leitzel's act. Looking over my shoulder, I can see myself standing there very tall and lanky and young in my cadet uniform, with big frightened blue eyes and a small squeaky voice saying those grandiloquent phrases. The audience loved it. It was, in fact, superb showmanship, which Leitzel knew very well when she made me do it.

Leitzel was married three times, but only once that counted. The first time she was very young. She always claimed she could not remember her first husband's name. Certainly nobody else could. The second time she married Clyde Ingalls, our great side-show manager. On a certain tempestuous night she cut off one of his fingers with a butcher knife. Her third and true husband was Alfredo Cadona.

Again I say without fear of contradiction that Cadona was the greatest flier of all time. Though he was not the first to do a triple somersault from the flying trapeze to the hands of his catcher, who was his brother, Lalo Cadona, he did it better than anyone before or since. Arthur and Antoinette Concello both did the triple later, but they were never able to emulate Alfredo's apparently effortless style. Indeed, that word—style—was the mark of Cadona's greatness. Whether in the most difficult feats or a simple pirouette from the catcher back to the bar, his form was as classic as Nijinsky's in ballet. When he caught the bar he seemed merely to touch it weightlessly; and when he flew through the air it was as though he were moving in his natural element. Even if he missed and fell to the net, it was gracefully done.

Indeed, one of Alfredo's most hair-raising stunts was based on the time Lalo missed his catch and he fell into the net far off center, bounced high in the air, and came down through the spreader ropes at the side of the net. They broke his fall, but he hit ground quite hard. He got up and dusted himself off. Then he climbed up again to complete his famous triple amid a perfect tornado of applause.

Frequently after that, Alfredo would do this dangerous trick on purpose. Fred Bradna tells of how he got Cadona to do it one time when Uncle John was in the house. He says that in his agitation Uncle John swallowed his cigar.

Alfredo Cadona was of Mexican-German extraction. His father flew in a small one-ring circus in Mexico. He came to us first as a talented young flier, and promptly fell in love with Leitzel, as who did not? She had no time for him then, and he went away and married someone else. He came back to us about 1925 as a full-fledged star. By that time Leitzel was married to Clyde Ingalls, but no bonds of God or man could keep those two fated and fatal people apart. Cadona became a fixture in Leitzel's tent, which was furnished with oriental rugs and always adorned with fresh flowers provided by the management. There she taught him, as she taught the circus children, the pleasures of literature and the social graces.

Leitzel got a divorce and she and Alfredo were married in Chicago in 1928. I have a wonderful snapshot of them leaving the show grounds in an open landaulet plastered all over with Just-Married signs. Though Leitzel was well into her thirties that year, she looks like a high-school girl, and a small one at that; while Alfredo looks like the boy next door. They were so radiantly happy that their faces wore, not professional smiles, but broad grins.

Alfredo Cadona was nearly as great a star and almost as violently temperamental as his wife. No one could describe their marriage as serenely happy. It was gloriously impassioned. It lasted for three years.

In February 1931 Alfredo was flying at the Winter Garden in Berlin while Leitzel was performing at the Valencia Music Hall in Copenhagen. Frank McClosky, who later became general manager of our circus, was her head rigging man for this winter engagement.

On Friday the thirteenth—so obvious are the coincidences of real-life tragedy—Leitzel was doing the first part of her act on the roman rings. McClosky was standing beneath her anxiously watching every move. Something distracted his attention, and in that instant the swivel supporting one of the rings crystallized and snapped. Leitzel plunged headfirst twenty feet to the ground.

McClosky was beside her in a flash—too late a flash. In a moment or two she stood up shaking her golden head. The audience cheered wildly, and Leitzel said, "I'm all right. I can go on."

McClosky would not let her and took her to the hospital. Cadona canceled his performance in Berlin and rushed to her. On Saturday she seemed so well and gay that he let her persuade him to go back to Berlin. On Sunday, February 15, 1931, Leitzel died.

Leitzel's death saddened her admirers all over the world. It stunned us who had known and loved her so well. It destroyed Alfredo Cadona.

For many months he disappeared into some accursed solitude. Then he came back to fly again with the circus. Never had he been so brilliant. But now his brilliance had the raw edge of recklessness. Even the crowds watching him sensed that the flashing figure doing impossible feats was inviting death. As is his way, Death declined the invitation.

In his frantic effort to escape memory, Alfredo was married again, to Vera Bruce of the Australian equestrian family. He continued his reckless performances, with the inevitable result—not death, but a fall that tore his shoulder ligaments so that he could never fly again.

Now the descent from glory quickened. If he had saved any money, it quickly disappeared and he was forced to take unsuitable jobs—Vera's equestrian director in a one-ring show. That was too bitter to be borne. Then he was part proprietor of a gas station. One wonders if the casual customers were frightened by the bright gleam of hatred in his eyes; hatred or madness. . . .

No one could live with a man who could not live with himself. Vera sued for divorce. A conference was arranged at her lawyer's office.

Alfredo came there very calm and reasonable. He asked the lawyer if he might have a moment alone with his wife. At Vera's nod the attorney went out, closing the door.

On cue, at the click of the latch, Alfredo pulled a forty-five automatic from under his coat. As fast as his finger could pull and release the trigger he fired five shots into Vera Bruce's body—three of them unneeded. The sixth shot pierced his own brain. Thank God, at least he did not miss.

Alfredo Cadona was buried beside little Leitzel.

The dolorous story of Leitzel and Cadona emphasizes again my underlying theme of the violence and tragedy that stalk the back yard of the circus. This is the inevitable nature of an entertainment which endeavors to appeal to all the basic ideas of diversion—not only the enjoyment of beauty and glamour, courage and skill; but also the taste for the strange and exotic in the wild animals and primitive people, and titillation by the unnatural, such as the strange and often revolting deformities of the side shows. It is implicit above all in the circus' legacy from imperial Rome of a spectacle in which death, if no longer inevitable, yet plays a leading role, walking those high, thin wires in the peak of the Big Top and standing beside each Clyde Beatty and Mabel Stark every time they enter the arena cage.

Violence was made inevitable, also, by the heterogeneous collection of people and wild animals which made the back yard a little like a tented jungle. Consider the labor force which manned the great trains of the twenties. Apart from the wonderful and skillful people who were our permanent employees and the mainstays of the show, these thousand roustabouts and razorbacks came from the floating residue of labor. It was financially impossible to give so large a group permanent employment when the circus spent five months in Winter Quarters with no money coming in and nothing for them to do. Therefore, each spring we had to recruit a whole new army. They were mostly men who lacked either the capacity or the desire to hold permanent jobs. Rootless, reck-

less, and feckless, owing no loyalty to us—why should they?
—nor, in most cases, to families or communities, they were a
tough, anonymous lot—a sort of Foreign Legion of the Labor
Army. Throw a thousand such as these together in one
nomadic community and you have the makings of trouble
every day. It is wonderful that we had so little of it.

Sometimes the stench that rose from the crew's cars was
awe-inspiring. The performers were very clean even though
on the road they had to wash in pails of water. We had arrangements on the lot and in the dressing rooms to bring them
pails of hot water and you could get very good at taking a
bath out of a bucket.

But we could not possibly provide hot water for a thousand
roustabouts and razorbacks. Most of them managed to do
surprisingly well with cold water, but some became famous
for their polluted condition. I recall a character named Willy
Green, who boasted that he had not had a bath for forty
years. Willy came out of Bridgeport and was really a dis-
reputable character; but by the inevitability of his arrival
every spring and his blatant, almost impish uncleanliness, he
became a legendary and privileged figure.

I remember one night, when I was a boy, Willy approached
Uncle John on the lot. He looked like Red Skelton in his character of Freddy the Freeloader and smelled like a camel.
Uncle John was standing there with his hat and his cane,
his clothes beautifully pressed, and his shoes polished mirror
bright, looking, as he always did, as though he were just starting out for the Easter Parade.

"Hello, Jawn," said Willy. Nobody, not even Fred Bradna,
addressed John Ringling as anything but Mr. John.

"Hello, Willy," said Uncle John, who had known him for
thirty years. "How are you?"

Willy said, "Pretty good, but give me a light."

Uncle John puffed up the fire in his great double corona

and, bending over, held his cigar solicitously to Willy's cigarette while he puffed away. When he had the light, Willy said airily, "Thanks, Jawn." And strolled away like a circus king.

Another source of potential violence was the continuing tradition from the bad old days linking the circus and the underworld. Even the argot of the circus stemmed from it. Oddly enough, it did not come from contemporary criminal jargon, but straight from the umbrageous, fetid alleys of eighteenth-century London, from Polly Peachum's Newgate and the rogues who swung from Tyburn Tree.

When I first joined the circus I wrote my mother a show-off letter that was full of such words as dip (pickpocket), block (watch), shiv (knife), keyster (suitcase). She could not understand a word of it, but it would have been perfectly intelligible to Dick Turpin.

The price of comparative freedom from criminal camp followers was eternal vigilance. With all our efforts, and those of the Burns detectives as well, we could not keep it completely clean. Shell-game operators, confidence men, pickpockets, gamblers, and bootleggers all preyed on the circus. The parasites would attach themselves to the circus train like barnacles to the bottom of a ship in tropical waters. Every so often we would have the engineer stop in the middle of nowhere, preferably a desert, and delouse the train. We would go through it from end to end, digging the human rats out of baggage wagons and from under cages on the flats and heaving them ungently to the ground, where enthusiastic assistants would urge them on their way. Somehow they seemed to manage to rejoin us soon thereafter, but at least they had a nice long walk.

This was the sort of world in which Brother John and I served our apprenticeships to the circus. One thing we learned. Because it was a tough world, raw and savage, management had to be even tougher. To maintain the accurate timing of setup and teardown, the exact scheduling on which the whole great operation depended, required an iron discipline enforced by stern measures. But because these were very human sort of people and, in the case of the performers, very high-strung ones, it also required diplomacy and understanding.

The man who ran a circus train had to be harsh and utterly ruthless, wise and sympathetic; a general of the army, railroad executive, showman, and psychiatrist combined. He had to be a howling optimist, a compulsive gambler, and also capable of taking infinite pains to avoid disaster. Above all, he had to be dedicated to the circus.

CHAPTER XIV

THE HOUSE OF JOHN

There had never been anything but love and loyalty between the Ringling brothers until Alf T. died. But when Charles and John were left to divide their world between them, a ground mist of jealousy rose to cloud their relationship. This did not affect their management of the circus. There, as always, they acted in concert. But in their outside business ventures and their social life, the rivalry between them became more acute, even bitter. John Ringling went his own freewheeling way, and his wife Mable was very easygoing and still one of the most beautiful women in America; but Edith, though handsome, was gray-haired and matronly. She kept prodding Charles to outdo his rambunctious younger brother.

Whatever the cause, they carried this competition to ridiculous lengths. If Uncle John got a yacht, the *Zalophus*, Uncle Charles had to have an even bigger one, the *Symphonia*. Because John had formed the Bank of Sarasota, Charles founded the Ringling Trust and Savings Bank. Sarasota of that time needed two banks considerably less than a dog needs two tails; today, however, it boasts at least six, although the two Ringling banks are no more.

There is an amusing story in connection with the banks. Charley Kannally, Uncle John's circus secretary, worked in the winter in Uncle Charlie's bank. As the circus train started North one spring, Kannally came to see Uncle John in the Jomar. "I'm flat broke, Mr. John," he said. "Could you lend me fifty dollars until payday?"

"Mable, come here," Uncle John called. "I want you to witness a wonderful example of loyalty. Kannally, here, works at Charlie's bank but he still gives us his business."

One way in which Charles indicated his disapproval of his brother's offbeat hours was always to make business appointments with him at nine o'clock in the morning, knowing full well that he habitually breakfasted at three in the afternoon. John was invariably late for ordinary business conferences; in fact, his tardiness at one vital meeting helped to bring about his financial downfall. But his retort to Uncle Charlie was always to appear on the exact stroke of nine. I suspect he stayed up all night to make it.

The rivalry between the brothers reached its climax in the palaces—no lesser word describes them—that they built side by side facing the bay in Sarasota. Uncle Charles began his in 1924, immediately after hearing of Uncle John's grandiose plans for a Venetian *palazzo*. Charles Ringling's home was, and still is, an uncommonly beautiful house. Following the classically simple lines of eighteenth-century English architecture, it was built of Georgia marble tinged by the palest shade of pink. The spacious, beautifully proportioned rooms were filled with appropriate graceful furniture built by Sheraton and Hepplewhite in England nearly two hundred years ago. Because Charles Ringling loved music so much, he installed a magnificent organ, and the music room, with its carefully planned acoustics, was often filled by the voices of the great singers of the time, most of whom were his son Robert's friends.

Such a beautiful house, and $10,000,000 with which to maintain it, should have been enough to satisfy any man. It probably did content Uncle Charles, but not Aunt Edith. The trouble was that by 1924 Uncle John was reported to be one of the twenty richest men in the world. This, like so much else in our peculiar environment, was a wild exaggeration. Nevertheless, the oil wells were pouring out their wealth; the railroads were running to the limit of capacity; theaters, turned into movie houses, were packing them in; and in addition, the Florida boom was on, and John Ringling had bought those jungled islands across the bay from Sarasota— Bird Key, St. Armands, Coon, and Otter—and several miles of Longboat Key. He poured $700,000 into building the John Ringling Causeway with its drawbridge to connect his islands with the mainland, and began the business of laying them out in lots with streets and sewers, landscaping, and all the trimmings. In addition, with his friend Albert Keller of the Ritz-Carlton Hotel in New York, he began to build a luxury hotel on Longboat Key at an estimated cost of $2,000,000.

In 1925 Brother John brought him a firm offer of $10,000,-000 for his islands; which he turned down without blinking his heavy-lidded eyes. That year John Ringling was worth $100,000,000—on paper.

Then Uncle John built Ca' d'Zan—the name is Venetian patois for "House of John." At a time when the east coast of Florida was being dotted with extravagantly ornate castles from Spain whose fantastic design, evolving in the fecund brain of Addison Meizner, genuflected only slightly to the purported land of its origin, John Ringling out-Meiznered Meizner.

This must be said: Ca' d'Zan was not built to wipe Uncle Charlie's eye, or even to gratify Uncle John's and Aunt Mable's luxurious tastes. It was part of a long-range plan John Ringling had evolved to give the state of Florida a memorial to Mable and himself that would be at once as magnificent and much more useful than the Pyramids.

The plan also included a museum to house the superb old masters he was buying at an ever accelerating rate. A corps of art experts, headed by Julius Boehler, whom everybody called Lulu, combed the crumbling palaces of Europe for these pictures which Uncle John stored temporarily in a warehouse in Sarasota and with Manhattan Storage in New York.

Perhaps his most important purchase was the four huge Rubens cartoons for tapestries. These marvelously painted scenes from the Bible were bought from the then Duke of Westminster. When Uncle John went out to the Duke's estate to see them, he was horrified to find them stored in an outbuilding, rolled up like old rugs.

Though Lulu Boehler advised him, Uncle John liked to make the final deal himself, for he loved a horse trade like David Harum. He did not enjoy simple little business deals, but preferred intricate negotiations. The key to the moment when he was about to exert all his wizardry as a trader was when he would drape one arm over his victim's shoulder and say, "Now I want to be fair to you." Then look out!

My uncle had another trick of trading which he employed, whether consciously or not. He would never sit down; so, of course, his adversary could not either, with John Ringling standing imposingly or striding around the room puffing his long cigar. He would keep it up for hours, and I think the other fellow often yielded from sheer exhaustion.

In this way Uncle John acquired a great many pictures at bargain prices. For example, on a trip to Europe in 1927, he purchased a Frans Hals for about $100,000. On the very day it was unpacked in New York, Lord Duveen saw it and offered Uncle John $300,000. He was turned down. Hence it now hangs in Sarasota rather than in Washington, D.C., as Duveen was bidding for Andrew Mellon.

In addition to pictures, John Ringling was purchasing ancient sculpture, Renaissance columns and colonnades, heavily carved cinquecento furniture, tapestries; in fact, anything and everything that represented the ancient culture of Europe—particularly of Italy—which so many years ago had opened the eyes of a midwestern country boy to the beauty of great art.

John Ringling bought literally by the shipload. On one occasion at least, he chartered a freighter to bring his purchases directly from Genoa to Port Tampa. The lesser statuary he scattered among his keys to add a touch of ancient grace to his real-estate development. Arthur Vining Davis' roaring tractors dug them out of the renascent jungle thirty-five years later. The best pieces were reserved for the future John and Mable Ringling Museum of Art.

But though Ca' d'Zan was designed as a cultural monument, Uncle John and Aunt Mable proposed to have fun with it while they lived. It was built for them according to their specifications as to the smallest detail. Armed with sketches by Italian designers, they went to see New York architect Dwight James Baum and told him what they wanted—a Venetian-Gothic *palazzo* which would embody the best features of the Doge's Palace and the old Madison Square Garden, which Stanford White had designed after the Venetian manner. Mr. Baum is said to have turned pale.

In the end he succeeded in modifying their ideas somewhat, but Ca' d'Zan was still one of the most fantastic houses ever built anywhere. Two hundred feet long, the basic material of its exterior was rose-cream stucco, but you could see very little of that because of the elaborate decorative designs of glazed terra-cotta tiles baked in soft red, yellow, blue, green, or ivory tints. Columns faced with polished Mexican onyx supported the rounded-arch windows which exfoliated into clover-shaped Byzantine oriels.

Above the main body of the house rose a square tower, also embellished with colored tiles, which contained an open loggia. The landward side was ornamented by medallions with bas-relief figures. The central one, by the designer's whimsy, contained easily recognizable full-length sculptures of John and Mable Ringling costumed like Adam and Eve *before* the Fall. It happened that I was walking with Uncle John the day this medallion was unveiled. He looked up at it and for the only time in my remembrance blushed. "We've got to do something about that," he said. "Jesus, look at that!"

It was, in fact, plastered over, but later the state of Florida's great museum director, Chick Austin, would countenance no such prudery. Uncle John's fig leaf was removed.

The interior of Ca' d'Zan was, if anything, more gorgeous than its façade. You came into an immense three-story hall with a balcony running around three sides of it. Its pavement consisted of squares of black and white marble and its high, cambered ceiling, from which hung the biggest Venetian-glass chandelier I ever saw, was made of carved, pecky cypress framing a stained-glass skylight. Tall, small-paned windows of colored glass diffused the brilliant sunlight reflected from sky and water. The walls were hung with Renaissance tapestries. There was a great organ and perfectly enormous carved and gilded furniture. Aunt Mable worked for three years making exquisite needle-point upholstery for it.

On the right was the long ballroom divided halfway down by antique columns. It was much more gaily furnished and the lighthearted medallions in the ceiling were painted by a Hungarian artist, Willy Pogany. John and Mable again appeared in one of them; this time waltzing together in full evening dress. To the left, through the breakfast loggia, was the state dining room, paneled in dark walnut with crimson draperies. Its most startling feature was a wall-sized still life by the Flemish painter Frans Synders depicting the trophies of a hunt. Painted with meticulous realism was a heap of dead animals, including a deer, a swan, peacocks, rabbits, small birds, and a great boar sliced down the middle and running with gore. Weak-stomached guests faintly turned their eyes away. Uncle John suffered no qualms.

A catalogue of innumerable rooms grows exhausting, so let me but touch a few high spots—the barroom, with its long, polished bar bought complete with colored-glass panels from the famous Cicardi Winter Palace Restaurant in St. Louis; Uncle John's ballroom-sized bedroom, furnished in Empire for a change, with an anachronistic modern barber's chair, in which he was shaved every day; the master bathroom, walled with Siena marble, its tub cut from a solid block of the same, with gold-plated fixtures; Aunt Mable's suite, all curvilinear rococo Louis XV decor; Uncle John's office, a plain, businesslike room, but the telephone was repoussé silver; and, finally, the rumpus room, occupying most of the third floor, its groined ceiling frescoed by Pogany with a Venetian carnival scene featuring John and Mable in fancy dress surrounded by their exotic pets.

Ca' d'Zan stood right on the edge of the bay. A vast terrace of differently colored marbles in a streak-of-lightning pattern ended at the dock, to which the *Zalophus* was usually moored. Alongside her, hitched to a striped pole topped by a golden ball, lay an imported gondola. With its furnishings, not including the tapestries and works of art, Ca' d'Zan cost Uncle John $1,650,000.

If I have made fun of my dear uncle's house, it is not malicious but affectionate teasing. For I loved Ca' d'Zan. What roaring wonderful times we had there! What magnificent meals were cooked in its great kitchens! What superb wines we drank around that long refectory board! And what wonderful talk we heard from the brilliant guests, whose names were a Who's Who of the twenties! Flo Ziegfeld and vivacious Billie; Irvin Cobb, his brisket bulging with good food and jollity; S. Davies Warfield, whose niece Wallis almost made Queen of England; Tex Rickard; Al Smith; Frank Phillips, who started as a barber, married a banker's daughter, became a checker for the bank at the Coliseum in Chicago when the circus was there, and finally founded Phillips Petroleum; W. J. Burns, the top private eye; John McGraw of the Giants, who gave me a uniform and let me practice with them; Fred Albee, vaudeville king; Jimmy Walker; Will Rogers; dozens more, and all their lovely ladies. The echo of their long-stilled laughter may yet break the museum pall of that great house nights, when the tourists are tucked in their motels—at least, I like to think so.

And mistake me not! Ca' d'Zan was, with all its excesses, neither ugly nor vulgar. It was so riotously, exuberantly, gorgeously fantastic, so far out of the world of normality, that it surpassed the ordinary criteria of such things and emerged a thing of style and beauty by its magnificent indifference to all the so-called canons of good taste. It was, in fact, the epitome of its owner.

Take a look at him as I knew him at this his opulent peak, an intelligent, daring gambler whose luck was riding high and whose personality was as extravagant as Kublai Khan's. He stands better than six feet tall, heavy, as all the Ringlings were. But there was nothing paunchy about Uncle John in his superbly tailored clothes. You felt only massive power. He still had a moon-shaped face, but there was power in it, too, and in his round heavy-lidded eyes. Power? Arrogance? Perhaps—reinforced by a temper of torrential violence. But its blast was as short-lived as a thunderstorm. Ten minutes after he had laid you out, Uncle John was as warmly sunny as a summer day. This was not true of Uncle Charles. He was far more gentle and considerate, and his resentment was harder to arouse. But once ignited, it smoldered for years.

Even at his autocratic apogee Uncle John still loved fun. He was still and forever a wonderful clown. One of the delights of my youth was watching him have breakfast. Often my sister Salomé and I would go over to Ca' d'Zan in the afternoon just to see the show. Uncle John always put on a special performance for our benefit.

We would find him in the breakfast room surrounded by as strange a group of companions as ever Alice saw through her looking glass. On its perch was a gray African parrot named Jacob, with whom my uncle conversed in German. Both John and Jacob were very fond of the coffeecake my mother baked. My uncle would dunk some in his coffee and give it to his friend, who would say politely, "*Schmecks gut, Johann.*" Then the bird would whistle shrilly and call, "*Komme Tel! Komme Tel!*" and the big German police dog would arrive in a series of liquid leaps. Aunt Mable's white cockatoo, Laura, watched from another perch, while two lovely little African bullfinches perched nearby. The company was completed by six or seven delicately built little gray pinschers, who sat in a semicircle looking hopefully up at Uncle John.

Then the butler, Frank Tomlinson, entered carrying an enormous dish of fruit. Uncle John devastated it. I have seen him eat twelve king oranges and five grapefruits; or two pounds of Tokay grapes. Mangoes were the most fun. Nine was a fair average for him. He would wade into the soft pulpy fruit with juice running all over his face and hands and the special oilcloth bib he wore. Then Tomlinson would bring him a silver basin of water, and he would make a circus of his ablutions for our benefit, dunking his face, snorting, puffing, and blowing while he rolled those round clown eyes of his and made marvelous faces.

After the fruit he got down to the serious business of breakfast—a king-sized sirloin steak or a heaping dish of corned-beef hash with poached eggs all over it. Then the coffeecake and coffee.

When the show was over he disappeared to his room to dress. This process usually took about three and a half hours. I never knew what mysteries of toiletry he practiced that took so long; for he locked the door, and no one was allowed in, not even Aunt Mable; not even Tomlinson.

As I have indicated, Uncle John was very close with money in some ways, despite the splendor of his establishment. He would haggle over the price of a window screen or a small tradesman's bill. Yet when the Mexican onyx for Ca' d'Zan failed to arrive on time, he had it sent from California by railway express. The shipping bill was several thousand dollars.

And sometimes Uncle John made magnificent gestures. A brand-new two-tone Cadillac might drive up on Mother's birthday. He paid for my education at Manlius and Yale; and gave me a big allowance. In fact, he took great pride in my academic career, and sometimes forgetting our exact relationship, would introduce me as "my son who is at Yale."

I admit I loved him; never more than, when broken physically and financially, he leaned on me to be chauffeur and handyman and sometimes even cook in the great empty kitchen of Ca' d'Zan. So be warned that I am a prejudiced witness. For his very inconsistencies—his splendor and his meanness, his arrogance and kindness, his lashing temper and his bubbling humor, which he kept when all else was gone—made him the most fascinating man I have ever known.

You may imagine what chance gentle, conservative Charles Ringling had of rivaling Uncle John. Nor did the competition long continue. In the spring of 1926 Charles Ringling had a stroke. Aunt Edith would never admit the nature of his illness, but it was plainly evident. He came to Baraboo that summer with the writing of death on his face. Uncle John was there as well. The brothers conferred; and for the only time in the history of the family there was talk of selling the circus. Charles knew that he would ride the train no more, and John was deeply involved with his great affairs.

It was a momentary weakness. They agreed that economically it was the wise thing to do. But when it came to the point of decision neither brother could imagine the circus without a Ringling.

That fall Uncle Charlie came to Sarasota as usual. One day word came to Ca' d'Zan that he had had another stroke. Uncle John almost ran across the big lawns separating the two houses. When he arrived Aunt Edith said his brother was too ill to see him. So he waited alone all day in one of those splendid rooms. In the late afternoon he was told that he could go upstairs.

He found his brother lying unconscious, with our family

physician, Dr. Joseph Halton, sitting beside the bed. John had no need to question Dr. Joe; the enormous struggle each breath cost Charles was plainly too great a strain to be borne long. John sat down in a chair. He did not make a sound, but Dr. Joe saw that the tears were literally pouring down his cheeks.

So they sat silent and helpless. One would never know what Uncle John was thinking in his grief, though there may be a clue in what he said. Quite suddenly the horribly harsh sound of breathing stopped. Dr. Joe jumped up to feel his patient's pulse. John Ringling heaved himself to his feet with the difficulty of an old man. As he stood beside the doctor looking down at Charles, pawing at his eyes to clear his vision, he said somberly, "I'm the last one on the lot."

CHAPTER XV

BUST AND BOOM

On the death of his last brother, John Ringling considered himself the sole proprietor of Ringling Brothers–Barnum & Bailey Combined Shows. True, Aunt Edith had inherited a third share of it from her husband, and Cousin Richard also owned a third. But Richard had already been discounted in

Uncle John's mind and Edith Ringling was only a woman. The Ringlings traditionally paid no attention to women in business.

The fact was that he had been making circus policy for a long time. He could always dominate Charles in big decisions, though the latter had more to do with the actual management of the show.

One of the most important decisions that John Ringling had made, almost unilaterally, was to abandon the old Madison Square Garden and build a new one. He had been closely associated with Tex Rickard, that eminent promoter of lucrative sport, for a long time. Indeed, it was Uncle John who financed Rickard's promotion of the first "million-dollar gate," the Dempsey-Carpentier fight in 1921, and the building of Boyle's Thirty Acres, the arena in which it was held.

Whether Rickard came to Ringling, or vice versa, I do not know, but they both decided that New York needed a new amphitheater. The New Madison Square Corporation was formed with John Ringling as its largest stockholder and first chairman of its big-name board of directors. Of course, this was an enterprise that went far beyond the necessities of the circus for a five- or six-week stand in New York. Rickard regarded it mainly as a place for prize fights, and the promoters of other professional sports had their special interests at heart. But in John Ringling's mind it was built primarily for the circus. Ringling Brothers–Barnum & Bailey opened there in the spring of 1926.

It was not long before Uncle John got disputatious with his fellow directors and resigned as chairman. However, it is not true that he quarreled with Tex Rickard. In fact, when Tex got into trouble over his allegedly amorous attentions to a young lady who had not reached the age of consent, Uncle John raised $50,000 in a hurry and hired Max Steuer to defend him.

Nineteen twenty-six was in other ways a trying year for John Ringling. For it was then that the Florida boom burst with the second loudest financial bang of the century. It had been one of those seizures of mass madness which occasionally turn the public, and the smart guys, too, into packs of lemmings rushing to fiscal destruction. Though vast tracts of land were bought and sold at skyrocketing prices, very little property actually changed hands. So hectic was the pace that the trading was done in contracts to purchase with 10 per cent down. Nobody had time for formal deeds. As a result, when the bottom fell out, everybody owed everyone else and nobody owned anything. An exception was Uncle John, who still owned his islands.

However, he realized that you could not even give land in Florida away, so he cut his losses. Overnight the bulldozers stopped snorting, the trucks stood still, concrete solidified in the mixers, and, as silence settled on the keys, the jungle thrust its first tentative tendrils under roadways that led nowhere. Most melancholy spectacle of all was the rusting steelwork of the Sarasota Ritz-Carlton rising from the mangrove swamps like the skeleton of a gigantic dinosaur which had become obsolete before it had even evolved.

Though the Florida debacle put a considerable crimp in John Ringling's finances, it did not really shake them. His interests were too vast and too far-flung, and in those years, when the whole nation was exhibiting the preliminary symptoms of the speculative hysteria which had lured the Floridians to destruction, they were enormously profitable.

Though he stopped his grandiose plans for its development, Uncle John did not forsake Sarasota. He now regarded it as his home town, and he sought means to restore its fortunes.

He had been thinking up ways to publicize Sarasota for years. Back in 1923 he had conceived the idea of preparing the big Worcester house on Bird Key as a winter White House for his friend President Harding. It was a felicitous thought, for at that time Bird Key could only be reached by water and therefore would be easy to guard. And the spacious white mansion even had a circular veranda with Corinthian columns like the south portico of the real White House. The only trouble with the plan was that President Harding died in a miasma of government scandal that summer.

In the spring of 1927 Uncle John had an even better plan, which was to move the circus winter quarters from Bridgeport to Sarasota. He foresaw that it not only would be a great tourist attraction for his beloved little city but would reduce circus overhead. The great cost of heating those block-long brick animal barns in Bridgeport would be virtually eliminated, for only the most delicate animals would need artificial heat in Florida, and then only for a short time. In addition, he thought the circus people could live far more comfortably and cheaply in Florida. He was right, of course, but his abrupt decision caused considerable dismay at first.

Fred Bradna describes being called from Bridgeport to Ca' d'Zan in March 1927 and watching Mr. John absorb one of his huge afternoon breakfasts. Then my uncle told him of his decision to buy the old fairgrounds for winter quarters. According to Bradna, he said, "I can buy the land for twenty-nine cents on the dollar, now. I'm going to make Sarasota one of the sights of the South. Think of the tourists who would visit our winter quarters here and pay for it. Revenue in midwinter, that's the ticket!"

He ordered Bradna to break the news in Bridgeport, which the equestrian director was afraid to do. He knew that many of the permanent staff were born and bred Bridgeportians, and he thought they would take it hard. However, Fred was even more afraid of Uncle John, so he finally carried out his orders; and he was agreeably surprised that, after the first gasp of horror, most of the circus people sensibly began to look forward to wintering in the South. In fact, the only person who was really upset was "Good Luck" Lombard, who ran their favorite speak-easy. He just kept on moaning, "Say it isn't so!"

Uncle John gave a banquet for seventy prominent Floridians and imported big shots to announce his coup. On the menu were terrapin soup, to which his special terrapin pool at Ca' d'Zan contributed, and Sophie's (the Alsatian cook) chef-d'oeuvre, roast pheasant with wine kraut. The next day he went to the fairgrounds with Bradna and personally laid out the proposed winter quarters, staking out the barns, menagerie, workshops, roads, and railroad sidings, and an outdoor arena exactly the size of Madison Square Garden, in which the performers could practice and he could earn—while they learned—the dollars of gaping tourists.

However, according to Bradna, John Ringling's enthusiasm, for once, was generated less by the money than by what he was doing for Sarasota, which now commanded his loyalty second only to the circus itself.

For a few years more, life in Ca' d'Zan went on at full tilt. The house was filled with people all winter long, and often the kitchens produced dinner for a hundred guests. There were lawn parties to which all Sarasota was invited to eat and drink on the great terrace while Uncle John's favorite orchestra, which he had imported from Czechoslovakia, played on the deck of the *Zalophus*. On Sunday the band gave free public concerts on St. Armands Key.

Uncle John did not much care for sailing, and the yacht was more ornamental than useful to him. However, he often lent it to his friends. Indeed, his generosity led to the sad end of *Zalophus*, which might have been much sadder but for his quick thinking. He was in New York one spring, when he offered the boat to Mayor Jimmy Walker and his lovely lady of the theater, Betty Compton, for a Florida cruise. A well-known banker, who shall not here be named, and his sweetheart were also in the party.

The next thing Uncle John heard was a telephone call from his red-faced captain, Al Roan, who said, "I don't know how to tell you this, Mr. John, sir. But the fact is we hit an uncharted sand bar right in Sarasota Bay, and *Zalophus* sank."

"Jesus!" said Uncle John. "Anybody drowned?"

"No, sir. I got 'em off in the launch, but they act like they wish they had. They're scared wild of the publicity."

"Who knows about it?"

"Nobody yet. It was black night."

"Listen carefully, Al," Uncle John said. "You take those people to Tampa and put them aboard a train for New York or anywhere there's a train going. That boat won't sink until tomorrow morning!" Nor did she—according to the newspapers.

Maintaining the enormous flow of liquor at Ca' d'Zan in Prohibition days required some illegal ingenuity. Supplies of run-of-the-mill stuff were easy enough to get, but the fine wines and whiskies which my uncle loved were less easy to come by. Though he was a moderate drinker, or because of this, perhaps, he was very particular. His favorites were Peter Dawson's Old Curio scotch before dinner and either Pilsner or Beck's beer from Bremen afterward. A rumrunner's craft once felicitously foundered off Ca' d'Zan and my uncle, with his friend and neighbor Ralph Caples, profited thereby. They bought and salvaged the entire cargo.

To conserve his supply of Old Curio, which he had laid in years previously by direct purchase from his friend Sir Peter Dawson, he ordered Tomlinson to keep the dusty cobwebbed bottles and refill them with bootlegged White Horse. "I leave it to your discretion," he said to his butler, "which guests get the real thing and which won't know the difference."

Nevertheless, John Ringling was generous with liquor. His

standing order to Tomlinson was "Never ask a guest if he'll have another drink. Even if he's falling down drunk, just say, 'Will you have a drink, sir?'"

There was one time when Tomlinson got into trouble by following these instructions. It was during a visit by Jimmy Walker, who came to open a dog-racing track which my uncle had promoted. As the time drew near for the mayor of New York to go to the track to speak, Uncle John observed that he was incapable not only of speech but even of locomotion. A hurricane blew up around poor Tomlinson's head. "You ought to have better sense than to let him get like this," John Ringling thundered. "He's got to make a speech. Do something!"

Tomlinson told his wife Hedwig, "Make some strong coffee. Make it like licorice."

He fed cup after cup to the mayor, who drank it docilely— he was always courteous and amiable even when half-seas over. Tomlinson laced the last cup of coffee with brandy to complete His Honor's restoration. Those who heard him, say that Walker made one of the best speeches of his life.

Meanwhile the grand design of the museum was taking shape on the land just south of Ca' d'Zan. It must, of course, be Italian in feeling, and so Uncle John, with his architect, John H. Phillips of New York, planned it on the classic lines of an Italian villa. From the severely simple east façade, two long, low wings stretched westward toward the bay enclosing a formal garden filled with lovely ancient bronze and stone sculptures. The garden ended in a mirror pool, beyond which stood the heroic "David" of Michelangelo. It was one of three bronze replicas cast from the original marble on the four hundredth anniversary of Michelangelo's birth in 1874. Of the others one remains in Florence and the third is in the Vatican Museum in Rome. The museum itself was made of rose-pink stucco, and the rounded arches of the colonnades of the garden court were supported by nearly a hundred slender ancient marble columns brought from Italy. The flat balustraded roof was lined with the best statues in the collection. It was by any standard a thing of rare beauty, and it housed beauty incomparable.

By this time the John Ringling Collection consisted of over seven hundred pictures, not all of them good, but some of them great. In the museum the first room you entered was designed for the four great Rubens cartoons. They hang there now. As you come in, their sheer magnificence, the glory of color and design, literally stuns you, so that it takes a little time to compose yourself sufficiently to study them rationally.

Inevitably, the rest is something of an anticlimax, but a magnificent anticlimax. Uncle John loved, above all, the seventeenth-century Baroque, whose splendid exuberance was in harmony with his character. His taste was out of fashion then, so he was able to obtain great works of this period for a fraction of the price which the changing vogue makes them worth today. However, he did not let his personal preference unbalance the collection which he designed for the benefit of the people of Florida. Instead, he acquired masterpieces of all the great classic schools of painting, stopping, as though a curtain had fallen, at the beginning of modernism.

Since catalogues, even of the beautiful, are boring, I will drop only a few eminent names to show the range of the collection. In it are represented Fra Bartolommeo, Veronese, Tintoretto, Titian, Andrea del Sarto, Canaletto, Bassano, Sassoferrato, Piero di Cosimo, Lucas Cranach, Rembrandt, Frans Hals, Breughel, Cuyp, Jan Fyt, El Greco, Velázquez, Murillo, Goya, Jean Marc Nattier, Raeburn, Reynolds, Gainsborough, and Lawrence; and so on and so on, through pages and pages of great names whose mention stirs but a dim anticipation of the beauty they created.

In 1928, when work was only starting on the great project, though most of the pictures were already safely housed in warehouses in New York and Florida and in Ca' d'Zan, John Ringling publicly announced his gift to Florida. Mark you, he signed no deed of gift or any legal document. The whole great collection was still in his name and remained so on the day he died. But having given his word, he regarded himself merely as a trustee. So when the time came when the sale of just one of those masterpieces would have pulled him back from the verge of ruin, he refused to consider it. Thus, this uncle of mine, who began life as a barefoot boy on the banks of the Mississippi, made himself a millionaire, and loved to live the life of a Renaissance prince, ultimately risked all to leave intact the dream he had created.

Now the circus was having its golden autumnal age. Every year Uncle John brought back the cream of the European crop of new acts. He kept the best of the old ones and introduced such new faces as Con Colleano, the Wallendas, and Zacchini. I suspect that at this time it was not only The Greatest Show on Earth but the greatest show there ever had been on this planet.

Of course, such entertainment was dated. The world had moved—how it had moved! Because they have mellowed in retrospect, we forget what a violent contrast the twenties presented to the serene and secure years which had preceded World War I. This change was even more shattering than the difference between our era and the one which was blown to bits by the first atom bomb. For by now we have grown unhappily accustomed to mechanization, to ruthless war and genocide, to the disintegration of moral standards, and to a sense of total insecurity. But the adult population of those days had grown up believing that mankind had become civilized. They were utterly appalled by the sudden revelation of savagery erupting through its well-bred surface when for the first time the whole world went to war.

Despite the flush of materialistic triumphs, the great surge forward of mechanical and industrial techniques which were bringing tremendous advances in our standard of living during the postwar years, people were afraid. They were frightened by the very progress they had made and the changes it had brought about. Even while they gloried in their new freedoms from the necessity of long hours of drudgery and from the tyranny of puritanical conventions, they secretly longed for something permanent and unchanging. I think that is why the circus was so popular.

For it was almost the only thing in that era of flux which had not changed at all. In its essentials it followed the formula of the show which Mr. Barnum had put on rails in 1871— better, certainly, less crude and more artistic, but basically the same. Millions of people came to see it every year in a nostalgic return to remembered serenity. They brought their children to see the last remaining bit of the simple, happy America they had grown up in.

Uncle John was perfectly cognizant of this public reaction. In fact, it was why he worked so much harder for the circus than for all his other enterprises, though they were far greater in scope and far more lucrative. No matter how modern his personal life, how deeply he was involved in the hectic finance of the twenties, and how much he enjoyed the frenetic pace, he worked to keep the circus inviolate. Concerning it he was a starry-eyed romantic, for he felt that The Greatest Show on Earth was a precious part of the American heritage, which it was his responsibility to preserve.

CHAPTER XVI

THE MAN FROM "DREAMLAND"

John Ringling's troubled times began in 1929. Nothing unusual in that, except that in his case personal grief compounded them. For several years Aunt Mable had been keeping a secret. So well did she counterfeit that no one, except her doctor, certainly not Uncle John, knew that she was mortally ill of a complication of diabetes and Addison's disease. Early in 1929 strength of will could no longer overcome their ravages. That spring she took to her bed, and with her customary consideration for her husband, died very quickly in June 1929.

Uncle John was desolated. He was so much older than Mable and she was so vital and beautiful and gay that until the last few days he had never contemplated life without her. So little was he prepared that he, who hated black, had no proper clothes to wear. Tomlinson stripped the braid off his butler's trousers and lent them to his master to wear at the funeral.

I saw my uncle in New York soon after that. He was desperately grief-stricken, and completely convinced that "I will never be gay again." So sure was he of this that he presented me with his entire wardrobe of magnificent suits made for him by Bell. They hung like curtains on my lanky frame, but I was able to sell them very profitably to a secondhand-clothes dealer in New Haven. I am sure that part of the price was due to the labels sewn in the linings, which said, "Made expressly for John Ringling."

The violence of John Ringling's grief, like the storms of his rage, was bound to exhaust itself quickly. Nor could such a lusty man stop living. Within the year he was back at Bell's ordering a whole new outfit. In the summer of 1930 he fell in love, or thought he did, with an attractive widow named Mrs. Emily Haag Buck, whom he saw lose $32,000 one night in Monte Carlo. He was married to her by Mayor Frank Hague of Jersey City in December 1930.

Why they ever married is beyond all understanding; for two less compatible people have seldom promised to cleave only to each other. That my uncle was not easy to live with must be clear by now. Eccentric, egocentric, and arrogant, able to impose his will on outsiders by the power of his wealth, and accustomed to Aunt Mable's loving acquiescence in his home, John Ringling was unable to change even if he had wanted to.

Emily Buck was equally set in her ways. She was rich, attractive, and spoiled. She flitted around the house so much that Uncle John would roar at her, "For God's sake, Emily, light somewhere."

Quite early in their marriage Uncle John borrowed $50,000 from his new wife, pledging three of his fine pictures for the loan. This is not an exception to my statement that he would not part with his pictures. At the time he was not yet seriously embarrassed and thought it was merely a temporary accommodation.

Under such circumstances the marriage could hardly be expected to last. It did not. They were separated within two years and their divorce was within one week of becoming final when Uncle John died in 1936.

John Ringling's first step on the facile descent to insolvency was due to his faults and his virtues, to his pride and his ideals. In the spring of 1929 it was time to negotiate the usual circus contract with Madison Square Garden for the season of 1930. A date was set for a meeting with the officials of the Garden. Uncle John did not show up.

There is no explanation of why he did not keep this critical engagement, but it is no great mystery, either. He was quite accustomed to making engagements with important people and breaking them cavalierly. However, the directors of the Garden corporation were already irritated with him. When the meeting finally took place they told him that they would sign only on condition that the circus did not play Friday nights in order to permit the very profitable prize fights to take place. At the end of a violent scene Uncle John told them with anatomical exactitude precisely where they could put their contract, and announced that the circus would open at the 22nd Regiment Armory.

The Garden promptly made a contract with the American Circus Corporation, our only serious rivals, for April 1930. John Ringling was thunderstruck. He was so stricken and hurt that for a little while he was not even angry. Then, as he pondered what he thought of as blackhearted treachery, his rage generated in itself until it was all-consuming, destroying his business judgment.

There is considerable excuse for his intense emotion. For over fifty years either Barnum & Bailey or Ringling Brothers or the Combined Shows had opened in Madison Square Garden. In fact, both the old Garden and the new had been built for this very purpose. It was unthinkable to my uncle, and indeed to many other people, that a rival circus should play there.

In John Ringling's fiery brain there were only two possible alternatives—either to buy the Garden or the American Circus Corporation. The first he discarded because the other circus would still have a contract. He bought the American Circus Corporation from its owners, Jeremiah Mugivan, Albert Bowers, and Edward Ballard—all old circus friends of his —for about $2,000,000. He paid only a little cash down and gave his personal note for $1,700,000 to the Prudence Bond and Mortgage Company, which financed the deal. "I'm playing the Garden next year," said Uncle John.

Now, this transaction was not quite as foolish as it seemed; or to put it another way, it did not, at that time, seem as foolish as it was. The American Circus Corporation owned five good little circuses—Sells-Floto, Hagenbach-Wallace, John Robinson, Sparks, and Al G. Barnes. They had bought the last two in 1928. Their total assets included 150 railroad cars, 2000 animals, tents, baggage stock, and 4500 people. It was definitely a going concern.

John Ringling proposed to incorporate a new company and sell its shares to the stock-avid public, thus paying off the note. His Wall Street associates told him that they would have no trouble floating such an issue, backed as it was by very real assets and his own great name. That was the grave miscalculation.

Everyone who was in any way connected with finance re-
members the terrible days in October 1929, when the great
American dream of boundless prosperity burst on the floor of
the New York Stock Exchange in a bedlam of bellowing
brokers and chattering tickers, punctuated by occasional
pistol shots and the thuds of falling bodies. Everyone knows
that it was no local adjustment of the stock market, but a moment of truth, when the fact that they had been living beyond
their means began to dawn on the whole American people. It
was, in fact, the end of a historical era. It was also the end of
John Ringling's hope of selling an issue of circus stock.

Throughout the dismal years of the great depression, that
debt was a killing encumbrance to John Ringling. He succeeded in transferring it and the ownership of the American
Circus Corporation to Ringling Brothers, despite the justified
reluctance of Aunt Edith and Richard Ringling, but it was,
nevertheless, his obligation.

Of course, his other great interests went bad, too—almost
every business in America did. The circus, which had netted
$1,000,000 in 1929, was doing so badly that in 1931 it closed
down on September 14, the earliest date thus far in its long
history. But Uncle John would have been able to ride out the
storm had it not been for that piece of paper as heavy as a
granite boulder dragging him down into ever deeper water.

Another aspect of his character did not help. He had an
amazing faculty for ignoring bad news. It was as though his
mind were divided, like the hull of a ship, into thought-tight
compartments and he could close the doors on any fact he
did not want to face.

I remember once years later, after Uncle John had had his
stroke, in the darkest days at Ca' d'Zan, we were having dinner when the doorbell rang. Tomlinson had long since
departed along with most of the cash-consuming luxuries, so I

went to the door. It was a United States deputy marshal, and he wanted to see Mr. Ringling.

Knowing well that this meant another action for debt—there were over a hundred suits pending—I went back and told Uncle John.

"For God's sake, tell him I'm not here," he said.

"I'm afraid he knows you are."

"How does he know?"

"You haven't gone out."

"Buddy, don't argue with me," Uncle John said sharply. "Tell the man I'm not in."

But I was young and inexperienced and had let the marshal follow me far enough to see and hear Uncle John. So I had to brave my uncle's ire and tell him that the man was in and refused to leave.

"Very well," said Uncle John. "Tell him to wait."

Then, just as though nothing had happened, we went on with dinner, which, incidentally, was the result of a combined operation of his trained nurse, myself, and Uncle John. As we lingered over coffee he was never more charming, telling wonderfully amusing stories of the old days. You would have thought that he had not a care in the world, and the fact is he did not, while the meal lasted. Then I helped him into the great hall, where we found the marshal looking a little lonely amid its splendors. Uncle John put him at ease with the charming affability of an English duke greeting his favorite bailiff, was served with the papers, and undoubtedly forgot all about them.

This strange ability to ignore trouble was probably an asset to John Ringling in the good days. It saved him from unnecessary worry, which has reduced other men in positions of great stress to ulcer-ridden misanthropes. But it was almost fatal in such a time of crisis. So little did Uncle John concern himself about his crumbling fortunes that in 1931, when they were tottering toward the final disaster, he went to Europe as usual and attended a sale at Christie's in London, where he bought more paintings for his beloved museum.

That year my cousin Richard Ringling died. He had gone through five or six million dollars and his estate was a tangled mess whose principal asset was his one-third interest in the Combined Shows. To help his widow, Aubrey Barlow Ringling, in her distress, Uncle John squeezed some money for her out of the hard-pressed circus.

John Ringling's personal crash came in 1932. In the spring of that year he suffered a clot in an artery in his leg which threatened blood poisoning and amputation. His superb constitution and ability not to worry pulled him through, but he was told he must have a period of rest free from the pressure of affairs and the importunities of creditors. For his hideaway he chose the Half Moon Hotel in Coney Island, which along with Dreamland Amusement Park was owned by his great and good friend Sam Gumpertz, with whom he had been associated in several business ventures and who sometimes accompanied him to Europe. There he would be peaceful and safe—so he thought.

Samuel W. Gumpertz was an ambitious man who had started his career as an acrobat at the age of nine. He had been, in turn, a candy butcher, usher, actor, singer, press agent, and, in an off moment, a cowboy, before he became a producer of kinetoscopes, as the earliest moving pictures were called. He was on the road with a flicker called *The Coronation of the Czar* in 1897 when the fantastically extravagant Bradley Martin fancy-dress ball hit all the newspapers. Gumpertz changed the name of his picture to *The Bradley Martin Ball* and raised the price from a nickel to fifteen cents. That put him on the road to fortune as a successful theatrical producer, showman, and real-estate operator. What Uncle

John did not know was that Sam's ambitions included owning The Greatest Show on Earth.

While John Ringling was recuperating at the Half Moon Hotel, two things were happening. An interest payment on the circus note, which had been reduced to $1,017,000, was defaulted; and Sam Gumpertz organized two groups of businessmen, who, under the corporate titles of Allied Owners and New York Investors, bought the note from the Prudence Company.

Gumpertz also gained the confidence of Edith and Aubrey Ringling. This was easy enough in the case of Aunt Edith, who had disliked her brother-in-law for years and who had been further incensed by his cavalier treatment of her rights in the circus. Aubrey was, I believe, fond of Uncle John, but her share of the circus was the only support of herself and her children. Gumpertz succeeded in convincing her that John Ringling had lost his grip and was bringing the show to ruin.

Now only one thing more remained before they snapped the trap on the unsuspecting invalid. This was to get a complete list of John Ringling's vast and scattered assets. This they did, down to the very last laundry, through one of his most trusted employees.

In July 1932 John Ringling was summoned to a meeting of the circus creditors and his relative-partners. When he limped into that luxurious office he was utterly dumfounded and confused to find who were his enemies. He looked dumbly from Edith to Aubrey, his close Wall Street friend William Greve, who represented Allied Owners, and to Sam Gumpertz. Though he may have been autocratic and foolish in his dealings with Aunt Edith, he believed he had guarded her interests. To Aubrey he had shown great kindness. To find them arrayed against him was a fearful shock because of his strong feeling of family solidarity.

He was almost as shaken by the implacable attitude of

Gumpertz, who up to that moment had been so solicitous for his health, so warm in his professions of friendship.

It was Gumpertz who delivered the carefully thought-out ultimatum. Because one installment of interest on the note had not been paid, Allied Owners claimed they were in a position to throw Ringling Brothers–Barnum & Bailey into bankruptcy and to take it over. They would refrain from doing so only on the following conditions:

1. The circus would be turned into a stock company to be chartered in Delaware.

2. The creditor groups would receive 10 per cent of the stock as a bonus for their work in forming the corporation. The remainder of the stock would be divided one third to each of the partners—Edith, Aubrey, and John Ringling.

3. The note for $1,017,000 would be assumed by the new corporation; but to secure it John Ringling would pledge all of his personal assets, a full, itemized list of which was appended. The banking group would hold them as collateral until the note was paid off.

Probably for the first time since he had started his own business at the age of twelve, John Ringling felt unable to cope with a situation. He was in a state of shock, beaten down and bewildered by the sudden onslaught of misfortune, and undone by the disloyalty of his friends and kin. In fact, he did not even have a lawyer to consult, for the circus attorney, John M. Kelly, was advising the opposition. Had Uncle John had a good lawyer of his own, he would have been advised that it was legally impossible to throw the circus into bankruptcy without a long-drawn-out lawsuit. As it was, John Ringling did not know where to turn.

Even a year or two previously he would have fought back with flashing power that would have left his enemies holding their severed financial heads. But Uncle John had been enfeebled by his illness. Now he broke under the strain.

The terrible dilemma, to his mind, was that the ultimatum posed a conflict of loyalties between the things dearest to his heart: the circus and his magnificent gift to the state of Florida—his pictures. For Allied Owners demanded that these be pledged as collateral as well. Even in those depression days Uncle John could have sold a few masterpieces and cleared himself—but this was unthinkable to him. So, too, was the idea of hocking them to the creditors. Most unthinkable of all was permitting the circus to be thrown into bankruptcy and losing it forever.

In the end he surrendered almost unconditionally. The one concession he demanded, and got, was that another corporation be formed called the Rembrandt Corporation, to which he deeded his art collection. He then put up the stock of his corporation as part of the collateral his creditors demanded. All his other assets were also pledged.

Ringling Brothers–Barnum & Bailey Combined Shows, Incorporated, was duly formed in Wilmington, Delaware. Then came the dramatic moment of the first stockholders' meeting, at which John Ringling received the ultimate blow. After the preliminaries had been completed, it was proposed and seconded that John Ringling be elected titular president of the new corporation—for the sake of his name—at the token salary of $5000 a year—his drawing account had always been $50,000. Sam Gumpertz was to be general manager in complete charge of running the circus—he had no experience in circus management. Edith and Aubrey Ringling and John M. Kelly were to be vice-presidents.

Almost incredulous of his hearing, John Ringling voted his 30 per cent of the stock against the proposition. Edith voted her 30 per cent for it; and, of course, Gumpertz's group voted their 10 per cent of the stock in favor. Thus the balloting stood 40 per cent for, 30 per cent against. At this moment, Aubrey, who seemed terribly unhappy about the situation, said, "Now there have been enough votes cast. It's all settled, so I don't have to vote at all."

Uncle John focused his bulldog eyes on her. He would spare neither her nor himself. "You will vote, Aubrey," he said. "I must know where you stand."

Aubrey voted, and the balloting now stood 70 per cent for the opposition slate, 30 per cent against. Thus the last of the brothers lost control of their circus.

There remains a tragic anticlimax. That autumn John Ringling began negotiating a contract with the Christiani family, who had the greatest equestrian act left in the world. One afternoon, as he was sitting in his little office, he suffered a paralytic stroke. He managed to stagger part way to the door in an attempt to get home, and collapsed.

Crumpled in the pocket of the suit he was wearing we found a telegram informing him that he must cease his negotiations with the Christianis—they afterward came to the show—and, furthermore, if in the future he tried to take any part in the operation of the circus, "we will hold a stockholders' meeting and turn you out." It was signed "Sam Gumpertz."

CHAPTER XVII

THE LAST PARADE

In one sense, Uncle John made an amazing recovery from his illness, due to that tremendous vitality of his. After five or six weeks rest his speech cleared and he partly recovered the use of his paralyzed right side. In another sense, he never recovered. His power of instantaneous, imperious decision was gone. He was frightened and suspicious of everyone. Nor can I blame him.

These were the years when my brother John and I came to know him well and love him; for there was no one left to look after him but us and our mother. At this time Johnny was working for the fine old Wall Street firm of Parish and Company, but he devoted the best part of his energies to what can only be described as a desperate struggle to help Uncle John regain control of his fortune and the circus. After I graduated from Yale, I was with my uncle almost constantly.

Remembering an incident in the early spring of my junior year, I realize how much I owe him. We were coming down in the elevator from his apartment when he said to me casually, "Buddy, do you really care about going back to Yale next year?"

Astonished, I said, "Of course I do, Uncle John. It's my senior year, the best one of all."

He just said, "O.K., Buddy."

So I went back with the same allowances and unrestricted charge accounts at the co-op I had always had. When I learned how hard-pressed he then was for ready cash, I realized what an effort it had been for him to give me that final uninhibited year. If he had told me of his circumstances I would probably have said, "No, Uncle John, I'll go with the circus." The casual way he put it to me showed an unsuspected sensitivity in his character.

From the time he desperately signed his assets over to the banking groups, John Ringling's position was increasingly precarious. The fact is that the last four years of his life were a period of financial cliff hanging. Though he still had a great fortune, he also had large fixed charges, such as the taxes on his properties in Florida, the rent of his apartment at the Marguery in New York—636 Fifth Avenue was torn down to make room for Rockefeller Center—and many other unavoidable obligations. According to his agreement with the bankers, a large percentage of his income was automatically diverted to paying off the note. They could have allowed him to keep a little more to live on without imperiling their interests; but they would not. With all his capital assets frozen in their hands, he had no room to maneuver.

It is not only fraternal affection which makes me state that my brother John was remarkably resourceful and steadfast in his handling of Uncle John's affairs. He had absorbed a business know-how during his Wall Street experience and with his real-estate agency in Florida and his service with the red wagon of the circus; but his financial ingenuity was his own. He displayed it a hundred times in those years, particularly in the worst crisis of all—the attempt to throw Uncle John into bankruptcy in 1934.

When the Florida boom broke in 1926, Owen Burns, a friend and business associate of my uncle's, had almost completed a beautiful hotel in Sarasota. It was advantageously situated on the bay close to the business district. He went into bankruptcy, and the Prudence Company—mother of all our misfortunes—took it over. John Ringling bought it from them; paying no cash, just giving his personal note for $55,000. It was a bargain even for those depressed prices, as everyone knows who has stayed at the John Ringling Hotel. Of course, the hotel was part of the collateral held by Allied Owners. It was frozen.

In 1934 the note came due, and payment was demanded on the threat of bankruptcy proceedings against my uncle. Two other small debtors joined in what, I believe, was a concerted effort to finish him off financially. We had to get the $55,000, and we had hardly enough cash to eat on. But Brother John discovered some hidden assets.

One was a disbanded branch of one of the short-line railroads that the creditors had not thought worth taking. John sold the old rails for $20,000. He sold some bonds of our mother's with her consent and threw that money into the pot. Then he succeeded in borrowing $25,000 from a money-lender in New York for six months at the incredible rate of interest of 25 per cent. When he heard about it, Uncle John screamed, "For God's sake, Johnny, are you trying to break me?"

We needed $10,000 more. I knew that in a special closet in the New York apartment Uncle John had 400 cases of bourbon whisky distilled in 1893, which he had bought from Ed Ballard just before Prohibition went into effect. However, even though the Eighteenth Amendment had been repealed, we needed a wholesale liquor license, costing $4000, to sell it. As John says, "We did not have four cents"; nor could we borrow a nickel more. And we had to procure the money in two days.

In this emergency John went to a friend who was in the liquor business. This man agreed to buy the whisky, paying $40 a case for 300 cases—he sold the last few bottles for $50 apiece. Uncle John agreed to the sale by telephone and we had $12,000.

So John got the money and Uncle John was saved. It was like those old-fashioned melodramas with the prodigal son galloping up just in time to pay off the mortgage. In the last confused months of his life Uncle John told people in Sarasota that Johnny had stolen the whisky.

Life was very strange during the years I spent at Ca' d'Zan with Uncle John, serving him as business agent, chauffeur, handyman, and sometimes cook. The only employees were his trained nurse, Miss Saunders, and faithful Al Roan, the yacht captain in happier days, who did his best to keep the grounds and gardens from going back to the jungle.

Yet we lived in a setting of magnificence. The huge house was so well built that there were few signs of decay even though nothing was spent on upkeep. The substantial furnishings got very little wear and tear; and the superb paintings still hung on the walls to light the rooms with beauty.

Since Uncle John could not make up his mind to part with any of his personal possessions, he still had two Pierce-Arrows and five Rolls-Royces, some in New York, but most of them at Ca' d'Zan. One of the Rollses had been built especially for the Czarina of Russia in 1914. It got as far as Berlin when World War I broke out. Uncle John bought it there in 1919. We used only two of the cars, a Pierce-Arrow and Uncle John's favorite 1924 Rolls-Royce touring car.

With all this I was terribly pressed to find cash to buy our groceries—our credit with the local merchants was nil. Out on the rejungled keys were piles of hardware from the old Waldorf Astoria and vast supplies of plumbing—bathtubs, toilets, and other fixtures—intended for the Sarasota Ritz-Carlton. We survived by selling these piecemeal for the new buildings that were beginning to spring up in Sarasota. I became a very good salesman of sewer pipe.

Another source of revenue was big piles of Spanish tiles on the grounds of Ca' d'Zan. While the house was being built Uncle John had gone to Barcelona, where a lot of old buildings were being torn down. He had bought the softly weathered tiles from the roofs and sent two shiploads of them direct to Port Tampa. That was more than was needed for Ca' d'Zan and the museum. We ate off the proceeds from the rest.

A thing that troubled me greatly was the deterioration of the paintings in that sea-damp climate. Varnish was cracking and paint peeling off. Though the museum was open and some money came in through the turnstiles, it was not enough to keep the place staffed, let alone keeping it up. So I bought or borrowed books from the library and studied a quarterly technical paper from Harvard University, giving myself a how-to-do-it course in art restoration. Then I went through the museum, the house, and the storage vaults carefully cleaning the paintings that seemed most in need of it, stripping and revarnishing those whose varnish had cracked, patching weakened canvases, and gluing back peeling patches of paint.

It makes my curly hair stand straight up to think back on messing with works of art that are the heritage of all mankind. But it was better to have a dub get some good mucilage and stick the paint back on than to lose it altogether. Uncle John was very pleased with me.

The extraordinary thing about our penury was that it was all unnecessary. In spite of the crippling restrictions placed on John Ringling's resources, Brother John worked out several deals that would have relieved us; only to lose them through Uncle John's fatal suspicion and indecision. One time Johnny came to him with a firm offer from one of the big oil companies of $200,000 cash and 25 per cent of the gross to be allowed to sink a well on one of his unencumbered oil properties. Uncle John said furiously, "Those crooks are trying to steal my oil."

The offer was good for sixty days. Just after it expired Uncle John decided to accept it. He was too late.

One would think that, subject to such frustrations, the life of a young man in a great empty, fading mansion with an elderly invalid who was facing ruin would be distinctly grim. The contrary was true. It had for me a curious kind of charm. Of course, I had many young friends in Sarasota, with whom I occasionally went out, but in the main I was tied pretty closely to the house. It was Uncle John himself who made it bearable.

This, again, came from that thought-compartmented mind of his which could lock out not only monetary difficulties but also the evident signs of failing health. He was as gay a companion as though the sap of youth were boiling through his veins and the money were rolling in. He even threw off a near-fatal heart attack he had in 1934 without losing his nerve, or his verve.

In the evening we would dine in the loggia, looking through tall windows at silvered waters with a quarter moon sinking over Longboat Key. The china we ate from was delicate spode; the glasses were Venetian crystal; the wines were light and dry; and the food, however hardly come by, was delicious. My uncle was a perfectionist at table and I reckon that I inherited some of his taste. My mother, as I have said, was a master of Alsatian cookery. There was nothing my uncle liked better than to have dinner at our house, when she would cook for him all those dishes he had loved from the time they were children together.

At Ca' d'Zan I would push him into the cavernous kitchen in his wheel chair and he would sit there directing operations while Miss Saunders and I prepared the food. With this and that I became quite an accomplished chef.

But the best part of the meal came when we lighted our cigars and sipped our coffee and liqueurs while Uncle John bubbled with the fun of living, clowning outrageously for our benefit. One night, when his divorce proceedings from Emily were in full swing, the telephone rang. It was long distance calling "Mrs. John Ringling." Uncle John screwed his face up in a wonderfully woebegone expression and said, "Tell them that Annie doesn't live here anymore."

During these sessions he told hilarious tales of the old times and made witty comments on current affairs. These were the early days of the New Deal, when Franklin Roosevelt's liberal leadership offered plenty of opportunity for amusingly acrid comments by an old die-hard who believed that the income tax was unconstitutional; and did not pay a cent of it for the last ten years of his life.

However reactionary his political views, there were many nuggets of real wisdom and insight gleaming through my uncle's conversation. I remember him saying of my brother, "The trouble with Johnny is that every time he gets fifty cents he thinks he's a millionaire." This, of course, was perfectly true, but on the other hand, it was Johnny's ineradicable optimism that eventually made him a millionaire.

A bit of prudent advice from Uncle John on business tactics was "Never go after a Masai warrior with a buggy whip."

On another occasion he said, "Don't put your faith in receiving gold coins from the little bluebirds—they are definitely more prone to drop an entirely different sort of commodity."

One of my uncle's great pleasures and mine was to have me wheel him through the museum, stopping before his favorite pictures while he reveled in their radiance and made illuminating critical comments. Guercino's rendition of Joseph's spurning of Potiphar's opulently proportioned wife invariably provoked my uncle to remark, "What a chump!" Never one to defer his judgment to the experts, he always made me stop in front of a certain painting. Unfailingly he remarked, "They say it's not, but I am convinced it's an early Titian." And years later it was authenticated as such by no less an authority than Dr. Wilhelm Suida.

Certainly his judgment had frequently been vindicated, as once when he was walking past a small art shop in New York and a picture in the window caught his eye. There was something about the painting of the head that rang a bell in his brain. He bought it for $200. When the overpainting was scraped off, it turned out to be a Tintoretto, which was valued by the appraisers of his estate at $50,000.

And how he would have chuckled at having overruled Boehler and bought the Duke of Westminster's Rubens for $150,000 if he could have known that in 1959 the Duke's

"Adoration of the Magi" by the great Flemish master was sold at auction in London for $770,000.

Perhaps the finest times we had together were our long automobiles rides. Uncle John, who seldom forgot anything, might say to me, "There is a wonderful royal poinciana tree south of Fort Myers that must be in bloom now. I'd like to see it once again."

So we would drive a hundred miles or so to see a tree. And well worth it!

This brings me to what was almost our last drive together. It was just before the cloud of suspicion was aroused in his failing mind that broke the close bonds between him and my brother and me. I shall write of that in a later chapter, but not here. For Brother John expressed our feelings about it when he said, "Nothing that Uncle John did or said in the last six months of his life makes any difference. What counts is the years before."

The ride came about when Uncle John looked up from the local paper and said, "The Cole Brothers Circus is going to parade in Pensacola next Thursday. I'd like to see it."

It was fifteen years since either of us had seen a circus parade. When we combined the shows, "The Big One" proved too monstrous to parade. The last time we did it, in 1919, the three-mile-long line of tableau wagons, cages, band wagons, elephants, horses, clowns, and steam calliopes snarled up traffic for hours. In one parade, only the spectacular driving of Jake Posey at the reins of the forty-horse hitch of the band wagon averted a massacre when the brakes failed on the seven-ton vehicle with its iron-shod wheels. The horses began to run down Beacon Hill in Boston like a cavalry charge toward the crowd massed at the end. No one, not even Posey himself, knew how he managed to turn that torrent of horse-flesh safely around the corner at the bottom of the hill.

On the appointed day I drove Uncle John in the open

Rolls to Pensacola. There was a small hotel with a second-story balcony overlooking the main street, and I arranged a comfortable chair on it for my uncle. While we waited he sat absolutely silent staring down at the gathering crowd— the small boys running about and roughhousing, parents and just people buying pennants and whips and those familiar whirly birds from the vendors, little girls in frilly dresses staring big-eyed up the cleared roadway, and the inevitable mongrel pups dashing madly back and forth. I was silent, too, with a rising sense of excitement mixed with something like dread of nostalgia too bitter to be borne.

The thump of a drum and a wind-borne blast of music brought a complete hush. Just like the kids, I was straining my eyes up the street. I saw the eight horses with nodding plumes of the band wagon round the corner. Then the full blast of sound hit us, the gay, raucous blare of brass playing circus music. It got louder and louder and behind the tootling musicians I could see red-and-gold howdahs rolling and pitching on the stately gray backs of the elephants.

As the procession passed beneath us my professional eyes automatically noted certain deficiencies—gold paint flaking from gaudy tableau wagons, spangles missing from worn costumes, the decrepit condition of a tired Bengal tiger. And these things did not matter at all. I was almost choking with excitement, my eyes riveted on the spectacle. Then I thought to look at Uncle John.

He was sitting absolutely motionless in his chair and tears were streaming like miniature cascades from his eyes. That he could not see that terribly gay scene below him was evident; but having been so close to him, I shared his inward vision. At no other time would I presume to hypothesize what went on in my uncle's mind; but that afternoon I *knew*.

As though our brains were meshed together in telepathic television, I saw with him the Ringling band led by white-

whiskered Yankee Robinson come down Broadway in Baraboo—Al and Alf T., Charles blowing mightily on his trombone,
and Otto lambasting the big bass drum. And capering along
with a French horn wound around his shoulder, a gangling
young musician-clown . . .

I saw the heavy work teams and the farmer boys guiding
our spring wagons with their pathetic homemade decorations.
Then, in an Einsteinian relativity of time, the procession
lengthened. There went the ferocious, man-eating hyena, the
dusty brown bear, and the glowering bald eagle; elk, lions,
monkeys, a deer; Aunt Louise wrapped in a boa constrictor;
and, very proudly, Babylon and Fannie, those first ponderous
pachyderms.

Time accelerated and vision overlapped. Now came a
multi-team hitch of horses that filled the whole thoroughfare
from curb to curb, pulling a crimson-and-gold band wagon
as long as a railroad car with thirty musicians playing for
dear life. A herd of forty elephants in gorgeous trappings
with gorgeous girls on their backs went past; a white horse
curvetting all alone carried young Ella Bradna, while further
back rode a schoolgirl named May Wirth. Smiling from a
splendid carriage was little Leitzel. Another stream of horses
drew the Bell Wagon, its carillon chiming sweetly after the
noise of the band. Clowns cavorted along, led by old Herman;
cage after cage of sleek, pacing jungle beasts were followed
by the open dens with tamer creatures—Louise the hippo,
and Katy, bowing her long reticulate neck. More and ever
more magnificent tableau wagons, iron wheels rumbling on
cobblestones; riding on them, glimpsed for only an instant
but with brilliant clarity, familiar faces—young radiant
faces . . .

Then, blasting us with its cacophony until the buildings
seemed to rock, came the biggest steam calliope of them all.

Time stopped. The real calliope was passing out of sight

followed by a swarming mass of children young and old. Uncle John pushed himself out of his chair with enormous difficulty, and clung to my shoulder. "Time to go home, Buddy," he said.

On December 2, 1936, John Ringling died. He had $311 in the bank. His estate was officially appraised at $23,500,000.

Part IV
JOHN RINGLING NORTH

CHAPTER XVIII

WE NORTHS AGAIN

In following the fortunes and misfortunes of Uncle John, the personal affairs of my brother and me have been left behind. What we were doing while the main narrative proceeded to its almost Aeschylean conclusion is important only in its bearing on what we, and more particularly John, did later, and to show the impact of the circus on our private lives.

As to Brother John, then. He had curly dark hair and piercing hazel eyes under heavy brows. His powerful stocky body radiated vitality. He looked more than a little like Uncle John, with a dash of the Black Irish to him.

In his youth he was a genuine romantic. In fact, despite his hard-boiled exterior, he still is one; otherwise he would have taken the easy, sensible way out and no show would now have the right to call itself The Greatest on Earth.

As a young man, John fell in and out of love with the same apparent ease that Cadona flew through the air. There was the time he loved a lass in the circus. The lass was May Wirth, who gave him lessons in bareback riding when he was twelve. Unfortunately he sprained his ankle, and there ended a promising equestrian career.

In a more adult state, but before his position became so powerful as to make him follow Uncle John's precept that trifling with performers was unsporting, he loved another circus girl and nearly broke his neck. He was riding the train on a long night haul. The cars were not connected like ordinary Pullmans, and if you desired to visit someone in another part of the train, you waited until it stopped and then ran like a son of a gun alongside until you reached the fair one's car. Johnny had paid his call and it was time to retire to the staff car, where he bunked. The train stopped in a deserted countryside and John got off and started running through the darkness alongside the rails. Suddenly solid ground vanished. He caught the end of a tie as he dropped, and found himself hanging under the train on a trestle over a gorge. The only lesson this taught him was to wait until the train reached a station.

When John turned twenty-one he was in love with a girl named Anne. Her claim to fame is that he composed the first of his many lovely songs to her. Oddly enough, it was called "Anne."

As he passed the magic milestone that made him officially a man John went to Baraboo to collect a legacy of $20,000, which Uncle Al had left him. His plan was to return to New York and marry Anne. Instead, he met Jane Connelly of Connellsville, Pennsylvania; Jane was visiting her aunt, who was married to our family physician, Dr. Dan Kelly of Baraboo. They were married without giving it too great thought in 1924. Since in those days Yale students were not permitted to marry, John left college at the beginning of his junior year.

Jane was a very nice girl—in fact, all the women we have ever married were. Blame our matrimonial failures on ourselves if you like, for they were not the ladies' fault. Or blame them on the circus. It was probably half and half. This, though, I will repeat: to be happily married to a circus man, a girl must be part gypsy. Whether hereditarily or merely figuratively, all the great circus people who lived and loved and raised fine families with the show had more than a drop of Romany blood in their veins.

John and Jane had a lovely long honeymoon. It lasted six months. He went through the $20,000 in that time. Then he had that lucrative year as a real-estate salesman in the Florida boom, during which he came to New York and sold Texas Guinan a lot for $5000—Hello, sucker!

However, each summer he went off on the circus train for six to eight months. Once Jane went with him, but she could not stand a life to which she was so unaccustomed and in which she could take no active part. So, in sum total, they spent about four months a year together. It was not enough. They were divorced in 1927.

Now, it is not to be supposed that after his divorce John led a celibate existence. Far, very far, from it. Life with the circus is hardly conducive to that. (Later, when he was in Wall Street, he was more noted for his taste in beauty than his acumen in finance.) Thus, in an astonishing manner he eventually reversed the life cycle of the Lepidoptera. From an emperor moth fluttering in the spotlights of a hundred night clubs, responsibility turned him into a sort of financial caterpillar, whose voracious appetite for, and uncanny ability to acquire, the lovely green leaves printed by the United States Mint earned him the respect and credit of the banking community. However, his mutability included the ability to change himself back again each night, when the sun set and the baby spots came out over Broadway. He remains a nocturnal creature.

Our sister Salomé was twice wedded by this time. She was a lively but amiable girl raised in the Ringling tradition of female obedience. As she often says, "The only time I disobeyed my mother was when I got married while she was out shopping."

Sally's first husband was Lieutenant Roy Biggs Stratton, U.S.N., whose bulky build earned him the nickname of Beef. He sailed into Sarasota Bay on a destroyer and promptly fell in love with my sister. When he sailed on to Port Tampa she motored up there with Mother to lunch with him and, quite literally, married him while Mother was in Tampa shopping.

The marriage had little chance of perpetuity. Beef was away in his ship for months at a time. When he was home on leave the young couple lived with Mother, who despite her many virtues was intensely possessive of her family. She made poor Beef feel like an intruder. Soon after their daughter, Salomé, Jr., was born, they were divorced.

Sally's second marriage was forever. Randolph L. (Duck) Wadsworth was—and is—a tall, rangy gentleman from Fort Thomas, Kentucky, who was several years older than she. He came to Sarasota in 1930. Despite his conventional upbringing, Duck fitted into the ebullient North family like the last piece of a picture puzzle. Even Mother loved him. Uncle

John, who had recently married Emily, offered to have the wedding at Ca' d'Zan on Christmas night 1930.

There was a slight difficulty about the ceremony. The Episcopal minister refused to marry them because of Sally's divorce. The Methodist minister stood on his dignity because his colleague had first refusal. Finally, a young Presbyterian, who had just been called to the church of that faith in Sarasota, agreed to perform the ceremony.

Duck and Sally talked the arrangements over with him. Wadsworth, a stout Episcopalian, said that he would not feel truly married with the plain Presbyterian service. The amiable young minister had no objection to using the Episcopal form. Then Duck asked, "What are you going to wear?"

"Since it is in the evening, I thought I would wear my tux."

Broad-minded though he was, Wadsworth turned a trifle pale at the thought of being married by a minister in a "tux." "A friend of mine was married by a Presbyterian minister who wore his doctor's robes," he suggested tactfully.

The poor young fellow blushed. "I have not taken my doctorate yet," he admitted, "so I have no robes." Then, seeing Wadsworth's consternated expression, he added, "I'll try to arrange something."

He hurried off to call on our wonderful Catholic priest, Father Elslander, who quickly agreed to provide suitable habiliments.

So Salomé was married amid the splendor of Ca' d'Zan with the Episcopal service said by a Presbyterian minister wearing the full canonicals of a Catholic priest. It was a wonderfully happy occasion. Most of the living Ringlings were present, and for once they were all speaking to each other. The trisectarian nature of the ceremony was a good omen, for thirty years later Duck and Sally are as much in love as any two people I know.

For the record, I was first married on New Year's Day 1933. No doubt luckily for my young bride, her parents interfered before the marriage could be consummated, and it was annulled.

After the break with Uncle John in 1936, I went to work for the Chronicle Publishing Company in Marion, Indiana, under my friend David Lindsay. There I met Ada Mae Thornburgh, a lovely petite blonde. We were married in the autumn of 1936. Ada Mae and I were very happy together until the circus recalled me to her exacting service.

CHAPTER XIX

THE FIRST FIGHT FOR THE CIRCUS

In his time John Ringling made many wills, but I have definite knowledge of only the last two and a half. In the first of these he left the art Museum and Ca' d'Zan to the state of Florida and the residuary estate to his only sister, my mother. About 1934 Brother John suggested that since, if all the residuary

estate were left to Mother, the new high inheritance taxes
would take most of it, he leave only half of it to Mother and
the rest in trust to Florida to maintain the museum and add
to the collection. This he did, naming my mother and John
co-executors of the will, and Randolph Wadsworth, John, and
myself trustees for the state of Florida.

Now came our unhappy falling out with Uncle John. My
brother had proposed that he use a new law firm. Uncle John
gaily said, "Who is this new mouthpiece you're bringing me?"
and agreed.

However, a little later, when the new lawyers demanded
that he post security for their ultimate fee, Uncle John flew
into one of his towering rages and blamed John bitterly for
"this horrible mistake." He evidently felt that I shared John's
guilt by association, for while he was still fuming, Uncle John
had Eugene Garey of Garey and Garey draw a codicil to his
will specifically cutting John and me off—though we had
never been legatees—and reducing Mother's legacy to $5000
a year for life. However, nothing was said about new
executors.

Later still, Uncle John was sued by the first firm for a large
fee. My brother testified on his uncle's behalf, and he won.
After that Uncle John told a mutual friend of ours that he had
torn up the codicil.

However, none of us ever saw my uncle alive again. It is
my belief that during those last months we were deliberately
kept apart. He was tired and sick and a prey to suspicions,
which may well have been fanned by the jealous people who
surrounded him. Whether this be true or not, I agree with
my brother that whatever he did then should not affect our
feelings for him.

That was the situation when Uncle John died. It was typical
of his shifting suspicions that after the funeral that infernal

codicil turned up in the office of still another lawyer, whom he had secretly employed.

I shall never forget the day we were summoned to this gentleman's office to hear it read. It may have been my imagination, but he seemed to take an evil glee in our discomfiture.

Naturally we were grieved by it. I do not expect to be believed when I say that this feeling was more because it showed our loss of Uncle John's affection than because of the money; but this statement will seem more plausible if I add that at this time we did not think there would be any money left after the bequest to Florida.

However, we had our moment of triumph. John handed a copy of the will, of which the document we had just heard was a codicil, to the lawyer, who had never seen it, and asked him to read it. When he came to provisions naming John and Mother co-executors, and myself a trustee, he looked absolutely thunderstruck. The codicil had no effect on that. So we Norths were struck out of inheriting what seemed unlikely to be worth anything, but given the whole responsibility for the administration of the estate, together with the large executor's fee.

What a welter of imbroglios resulted! There were at least a hundred lawsuits pending against my uncle when he died. Soon a whole new crop arose. Emily sued for her widow's third—she had previously waived her dower rights. Nine Ringlings, headed by Robert, sued to have John and Mother ousted as executors on the grounds that the codicil indicated John Ringling's intention to cut them out of the will and left the disposition of Mother's original bequest unclear. Lots of other people got into the act, and on top of it all the United States Government put forward a claim for $13,500,000 for estate taxes and unpaid income taxes.

John Ringling North, aged thirty-three, with the reputation

of a playboy and a contested claim to be executor of the
estate, was the only hope of averting utter chaos, and
incidentally, of saving the circus. It looked as though he did
not have a chance.

I very much doubt if John himself knows how he got
through the next year. Looking back, it seems to me that in
three hundred and sixty-five days there were at least a thousand crises, which works out at about three a day. Of course,
twenty-four hours sometimes passed without any new emergency, but on really busy days we had at least ten. John met
them by a combination of bluff bravado, ruthless determination, and some of the fanciest financial footwork since the
Mississippi Bubble.

In his maneuvers John had extremely able assistance from
Leonard G. Bisco of Newman and Bisco. He was attorney for
the Manufacturers Trust Company, which held a personal
loan from John Ringling for $200,000 made back in the lush
days. John had met Bisco when he was helping Uncle John
stave off bankruptcy and he had proved very helpful. John
asked Bisco to handle an appeal case in New York. When
he won, John appointed him general counsel for the estate.
Meanwhile I had given up my job in Indiana and come East
to act as John's assistant. Because the worse things got, the
less Uncle John wished to know about them, his books and
records in Florida were in a state of confusion that would
have baffled Univac. John engaged James A. Haley, a Sarasota
accountant, for the herculean task of ordering this chaos.
Haley did an excellent job, but added another complication
to this tangled tale.

In dealing with the multiple lawsuits we adopted the tactics
by which the foxy old Roman General Fabius wore Hannibal's armies down—delay after delay, and never, if possible,
coming to grips with the enemy. In this way we exhausted

many of the litigants until they were willing to settle on easy terms.

But where offensive action was possible, John moved with a daring that would have been foolhardy had our case not been so desperate. One of his strategic coups was not to fight the codicil, but to probate it uncontested. This put the state of Florida on our side—a powerful ally. Since practically the entire estate was a charitable bequest, we claimed that this knocked out the federal government's right to estate taxes. Naturally, Florida backed us ardently. Eventually John was able to settle with the government for $850,000. As Leonard Bisco put it, "That thirteen million was only a telephone number. There was no real basis for it."

When we came to look into the affairs of the circus we were appalled. With a $2,500,000 gross in 1929, Uncle John had cleared nearly $1,000,000. The total net for five years under Gumpertz's management was only $300,000 on a gross of over $20,000,000 from the Ringling show and all its subsidiaries. Furthermore, in order to get even this meager return, everything had been allowed to run down. Wagons and cars were shabby and unpainted; the quality of the performance had deteriorated because penny-pinching salaries failed to attract first-class new acts; even the big cats and other animals looked mangy. All this was reflected in loss of patronage. By 1937 the circus was losing money like a broken hydrant gushing water. As has often been the case since ancient Rome, people said the circus was done for. They would be proved right unless something were done fast.

Saving it and gaining control of it by hook or crook became my brother's main motivation, as it still is. Whether by hereditary or environmental influence, he was dedicated to this purpose almost to the point of fanaticism. As will be seen, he recklessly sacrificed far more lucrative assets, throwing oil wells, lands, and other solid cargo overboard to lighten the leaky ship. No rules bound him. Had he seen such tactics in the prize ring, the Marquis of Queensbury would have fainted.

On November 6, 1937, the circus note to Allied Owners and New York investors would become due. It had been somewhat reduced, but still amounted to approximately $850,000. The banking groups were as anxious as ever to take control of the Combined Shows. Not only would they give us no time, but they stood on every technicality in an endeavor to grab it. Although by now John Ringling's estate had been appraised at $23,500,000, there was virtually no cash in the till. Almost all the assets were still frozen as collateral for the note; and the federal government was still suing for that thirteen million. November 6 rushed upon us with the inevitability of an avalanche.

Late in October not even hope was left. It was then that John went to pay a call on his friend Harvey Gibson of the Manufacturers Trust Company. He was quickly shown into Mr. Gibson's walnut-paneled office. He walked across the deep pile rug with his bouncy, confident stride and greeted the banker with his open-faced Irish charm working at full throttle.

When they were seated, Mr. Gibson asked, "Well, Johnny, what can I do for you?"

"Lend me a million dollars," said John.

Without the quiver of an eyelid Mr. Gibson said, "Just give me the facts, Johnny."

John gave him the facts and figures with a command of convincing detail that must have impressed the banker. John's proposition was that the Manufacturers Trust should lend the Ringling estate $950,000 to pay off the circus note and take care of some other minor matters. This would not only reclaim the circus but get all the collateral out of hock and enable the executors to dispose of the assets, which were at least twenty-three times the value of the loan.

This in brief was the plus side of John's case. Against him, besides his youth and raffish reputation, were all those lawsuits and the federal government's gigantic claim.

"What makes you think that the circus can still make money?" Mr. Gibson asked.

"If I run it, it will," John said confidently.

"Are you going to run it?" the banker asked.

"If I can't get my relatives to agree to that, the deal's off," John said.

"I believe you," said Mr. Gibson.

He sent for Bisco and asked him whether, in view of the litigation, "we will come out all right."

Bisco, bless his black heart, said, "Yes."

Then Gibson said, "Yes," provided Edith and Aubrey Ringling agreed.

If that was John's greatest piece of salesmanship, his greatest stroke of diplomacy followed. His aunt and his cousin were inclined to think of him as an ally of Uncle John's against them, which was the truth. To make an agreement placing him in charge of the circus for five years or until the note was paid off was abhorrent to them. In fact, it sounded crazy. John told them that it was the only chance of the Ringlings keeping control of the great institution which they had founded.

Whatever may have been our differences before or since, Aunt Edith and Cousin Aubrey had strong family feelings. Though Ringlings by marriage only, they were completely imbued with our tremendous loyalty to The Greatest Show on Earth. Among ourselves we might fight like alley cats; but for our circus we stood together against the world. John's evident emotion and total sincerity overcame their prejudice. With slightly wry faces they swallowed the pill, bit the bullet; and signed on the dotted line.

On the other hand, the banking groups fought to the end. Even after the loan was repaid, their representative refused to resign from Ringling Brothers–Barnum & Bailey's board of directors. Their 10 per cent of the stock was entitled to special voting privileges by the fatal agreement Uncle John had made with them. We finally signed a contract with them for the circus to purchase their 10 per cent (100 shares) holding of its stock for $137,000, paying $52,000 down and giving them its note for $85,000. They were to hold the stock as collateral, but since it was no longer in their name they could not vote it.

A little later the bankers got their comeuppance. The circus was in such bad financial shape that it could not meet the second payment on the note. John consulted Bisco, who advised, "Let them keep the stock. The voting trust was broken by its sale, so it won't do them any good."

Later still, New York Investors went into bankruptcy. Bisco bought their 18 shares of Ringling stock for $3000. At the same time he secured a ninety-day option to purchase the 82 shares held by Allied Owners for $25,000. Thus, the cost of the whole 100 shares was $28,000. "I bought them in my own name," Bisco says, "but I wanted them for Johnny."

At a meeting with Edith, Aubrey, and Robert Ringling, Bisco persuaded them to let John have 70 shares while they divided the remaining 30. This insignificant 7 per cent of the stock was the small beginning of John Ringling North's holdings in Ringling Brothers–Barnum & Bailey's Combined Shows.

After we first got rid of the bankers, the circus stock was held as follows:

Edith Conway Ringling	300 shares (30%)
Aubrey Ringling	300 shares (30%)
Estate of John Ringling (voted by John Ringling North, Executor)	300 shares (30%)
Treasury stock (not voted)	100 shares (10%)

According to our voting trust agreement, Aubrey and Edith, though holding 60 per cent of the stock, were entitled to only three directors on the board. John was entitled to name three directors. The seventh director, with the deciding vote, was William P. Dunn, Jr., of the Manufacturers Trust Company. The new board elected John Ringling North president of the circus. I was elected vice-president and assistant to the president.

Thus, in a few hectic weeks John achieved his first great ambition—absolute control of the management of the circus. And as yet he owned not a share of stock in it, since his purchase of 7 per cent came later. Putting him in charge was a splendid gamble on the part of our relatives and the Manufacturers Trust Company. It was a tremendous challenge to him. His task was to pull a disintegrating, has-been institution out of its doldrums and make it once again The Greatest Show on Earth. Johnny never doubted for a moment that he could do it.

CHAPTER XX

THE NEW CIRCUS

In taking command of the circus my brother and I did not rush blindly into a situation and improvise a solution. In the middle of all the legal sound and fury we had been doing some very hard thinking. In the course of it we had developed a philosophy of circus showmanship to fit the new age in which we were living. We were very harshly criticized for modernizing the show. The hard-shells and nostalgics said that we had ruined it. We were even criticized for making it less odoriferous. Well, people may think they want bad smells, but I am willing to bet odds on that, if we were to put those awful stinks back just as they used to be, these same people would yell the house down through closely held noses.

As we saw it, the mood of the American people was vastly different in the thirties from what it was in the rip-roaring twenties. Then they had felt themselves hurtling forward into a future of irresistible progress. So they looked fondly over their shoulders at a seemingly serene past. Progress had been stopped dead by the depression; and the zest had gone out of living. The mood now was one of *Weltschmerz*, world-woe. The past was thoroughly discredited by the hardships of the present. In their stagnation, people looked, not too hopefully, to the future. They sought a "new deal," a Brave New World.

Another thing. The generation that had been raised on the tinsel glitter of the old-fashioned circus, and had taken their children to see it in an effort to recapture the past, had moved on. The young parents who now brought their children to the circus had been raised on more sophisticated entertainment, and their children were more sophisticated than they. Automobiles and movies, to which color and sound had just been added, had done that. People expected more entertainment, more value, for their money. You just could not offer them the tired old stuff and expect to get away with it.

What John and I tried to do was to cater to this new sophistication while keeping the best of the old circus. We wanted to give our audiences beauty and style; well-designed, harmonious costumes; artistic lighting; the big, handsome production numbers they had become accustomed to; and a unity of theme instead of a hodgepodge of unrelated acts.

At the same time we had no intention of losing the magnificently exciting atmosphere of wild animals, elephants, aerialists, equestrians, and clowns that made the circus a unique
form of entertainment. Above all, we thought it needed an
infusion of Barnumesque showmanship tuned to the age of
radio.

Our aim, then, was something added but nothing lost.
Inevitably we fell short of perfection. Something was lost; but
a great deal was gained. I am sure that we were right, and
that had we not done as we did, Ringling Brothers–Barnum &
Bailey Combined Shows would have ended, not with a bang,
but, in the pessimistic words of the poet, "with a whimper."

The first year we ran the show, 1938, we had so short a
time that we could not make too many changes. What we
could do was to give it unity and glamour. To design it we
engaged Charles Le Maire, who had mounted *The Ziegfeld
Follies* and *George White's Scandals*. He was rightfully
billed in the program as "the noted master of color tone and
exquisite fabrics."

Until that time the performers in the different acts had
brought their own costumes. John changed that by supplying
them with costumes especially designed for harmonious
effects in all the three rings and four stages. He also introduced what, I believe, was an original contribution to circus
entertainment. The aerial ballet, a production number with
sixty beautifully costumed girls performing acrobatics high
above the arena on the webs. *

And we did add showmanship. In this connection John
pulled off two coups that were worthy of the old master himself. The first was to hire Frank Buck at a salary of $1000 a
week, along with a private car—how the stockholders howled
over that. But Buck was worth the money. He was at the

* Canvas-covered ropes suspended from swivels.

height of his reputation as the apotheosis of the white hunter and about the last of the truly glamourous adventurer types, in the tradition of Livingstone, Stanley, and Paul du Chaillu, to come out of darkest Africa.

I shall never forget the day he reported at Winter Quarters in Sarasota. So great was his prestige that the performers were in a dither and even the blasé waiters in the cookhouse were excited. The head chef sent all the way to Tampa for a steak fit to serve so robust a character.

When Frank came into the cookhouse with us, everybody was standing up or jumping on benches to get a better look. The chef bustled out in his tall white hat and asked very deferentially, "How would you like your steak, Mr. Buck? Very rare, I suppose."

Frank looked up at him and said apologetically, "My stomach's a little upset today. May I have some milk toast?"

I almost wept for our chef; all the childlike tragedy of disillusionment was written on his face.

We built the show that year around Frank Buck. John dreamed up and Charles Le Maire designed an opening spec called "Nepal." To quote the florid circusese of the program, "It portrays in fantasy, splendor, and exotic opulence the royal welcome to 'Bring 'Em Back Alive' Frank Buck by the Maharajah of Nepal and his native court."

Frank, in his famous pith helmet, was to arrive riding on a hunting elephant in a basket howdah, accompanied by a wildly picturesque train of native hunters and beaters, dancing girls garlanded with hibiscus and wild orchids, and an odd assortment of jungle animals, including Lotus, the hippopotamus and Edith the giraffe. The Maharajah was no slouch when it came to oriental splendor. He awaited Frank on his magnificently caparisoned state elephant, surrounded by maharanis, glittering native princesses, guards, and a troop of dancing girls in diaphanous saris. Supposedly he had managed, too, to borrow a troop of Bengal Lancers from the British Government.

The Indian-jungle theme was carried throughout most of the show. Even Merle Evans' band wore Bengal Lancer uniforms. A special feature was Terrell Jacobs in the center arena with twelve particularly vicious black panthers—supplied by Frank Buck, of course. No one had ever dared to handle so large a group of those beasts before. Terrell was a rough-and-ready character who had lost one eye to a lion. His was the old-fashioned, brutal, whip-and-pistol technique that I hate; but he was very, very brave.

The only big non-oriental feature was the second production number, a beautiful pageant based on Disney's *Snow White and the Seven Dwarfs*. The latter, of course, were played by our famous group of little people.

When the time came to start North in 1938, we felt we had a show that justified its resounding title. In order to build up the traditional aspects of it, John had engaged the two greatest equestrian acts in the world, the Christianis and the Loyal-Repenski troupe. He was warned that these two equestrian families had feuded for generations like the Hatfields and the McCoys, but this did not deter him.

I was very fond of the Christianis, who now have a circus of their own. They were a great big family—it took half a railroad car to transport them. There were Poppa and Mamma Christiani, six sons, and five daughters, all in the act. Cosetta, the second sister, was a wonderful girl and a great acrobat. Just to give you an idea of how nice a circus girl could be to have around, I will tell you about one night when I took Cosetta out to dinner at Max's in New York after the show. A drunk came into the crowded room and stumbled over my long legs. Instead of apologizing, he belligerently offered to knock my block off.

I thought I'd have to do something about it, but before I could make a move, Cosetta was up like a flash. She grabbed the drunk by the collar, lined him up, and let him have a right to the jaw that knocked him over two tables. "Nothing to worry about, Buddy," she said as she sat down.

The Christianis did some tremendously spectacular bareback riding. The climax of their act came when five of the brothers ran at a galloping horse, leaped in unison, and landed standing on the animal's back. A variation of this was all five boys making the same amazing jump and landing astride the rosin-back.

In addition to the equestrian acts, we had the Flying Concellos, who, as I have said, were the only man-and-wife aerialist team who could *both* do the triple somersault from the swinging bar to the hands of the catcher. Antoinette Concello was a lovely person, pretty and graceful. Her husband, Arthur, though below medium height, was an enormously strong, wiry, tough-talking fellow with a brilliant mind and surprising executive ability. He owned a school for aerialists in Bloomington, Illinois, where he trained youngsters and put other aerial acts together. When he stopped flying in 1942, John made him general manager of the circus. He is still general manager of the Combined Shows.

The Wallendas were with us still, and we had added William Heyer, the master of manège, who also had a wonderful troupe of liberty horses, and Ralph Clark, who jumped two horses Roman standing style over a flaming automobile.

Begging and borrowing the money to do the job, we completely refurbished the physical aspects of the show. Everything was repainted and regilded until it blazed with glorious glitter. Like everything else, the old Jomar had been allowed to go to seed. John had it redecorated for us.

Whenever the papers want to make a story out of John's Medicean splendors they play up his magnificent private car.

Actually, as a place to live eight months of the year, combined with an office from which to run a multimillion-dollar business, it was barely adequate. There was a sitting room at the rear with a couple of easy chairs, two settees, a glass-topped coffee table, and a small icebox-bar. Then came a single room followed by Uncle John's double stateroom connecting by a bath with Aunt Mable's single. Beyond that was a small dining room with a wall table that seated five people comfortably or seven jammed together. A small serving pantry, kitchen, and the chef's and valet's quarters completed the picture.

All the crimson draperies, glass beads, lace curtains, and fretwork, which had delighted Uncle John, were ripped out when the ceilings were lowered for air conditioning. We put in severely functional furniture and plain pine cabinets and lockers. The color scheme was pale green and cream. Such was the austere scene of those alleged Lucullan revels. We jazzed it up later by hanging over the dining room a charming fantasy of a bobbed-haired Lady Godiva dismounting after her ride assisted by two flamboyant Negro mammies and a blindfolded stableboy, which Charles Baskerville painted for John in honor of a delightfully disgraceful incident at the World's Fair of 1939.

As in Baraboo long ago, the departure of the circus train was a great event in Sarasota. For the first two stands, in Madison Square Garden and the Boston Garden, we used only two sections—the other two, carrying the Big Top and forty-one other tents, the tent crews, transport wagons, and three hundred work horses, would join us when we went under canvas in Brooklyn. The first train had the flats with the tableau wagons, floats, props, and the roaring, howling, grunting, braying, hissing, screeching menagerie. Fifty elephants were jammed side by side in three large cars. The precious ring stock rode in luxurious box stalls. The giraffes were snugged down in odd-shaped well-padded boxes that were underslung in the rear to give them enough room. Seals and hippopotamuses traveled in their comfortable tanks.

The second train carried the extra-long sleeping cars for the performers and staff and, of course, the Jomar.

It seemed that all the people of Sarasota and the hinterland were there to say good-by. They lined the tracks from Winter Quarters to far out on the main line. Mother came down to see her two sons off. With the wind whipping his priestly robes, Father Elslander, assisted by two acolytes swinging censers, blessed the trains in sonorous Latin and sprinkled them with holy water.

The first section moved off in a tremendous hubbub of shouting people and yowling animals. Then our big engine huffed and puffed and the long line of cars painted in glistening silver and "Ringling red" began to move. John and I swung ourselves aboard the Jomar and Mother called, "Be careful in the yards!"

We slid along between the cheering crowds, with every performer leaning out of windows or crowded on platforms exchanging good-bys and wisecracks with their friends. John and I, on the rear platform, were more excited than any of them.

When we had left the station behind and were rattling through the pinewoods, we retired to the bar for a much needed drink. As we toasted each other and The Greatest Show on Earth, we were wildly elated, without a thought that we were heading for trouble at forty-five miles an hour.

One of the things that saved us was Gargantua, "The Most Terrifying Creature the World Has Ever Seen."

CHAPTER XXI

"THE MOST TERRIFYING CREATURE THE WORLD HAS EVER SEEN"

Probably the most publicized animal ever shown was Jumbo, the huge African elephant that put Barnum in business and

ABOVE: Arthur Concello (left)—a
great aerialist. RIGHT: Arthur
Concello today as executive director.

Brother John and I "never trust the cats." (*Acme Newspictures Inc.*)

Gargantua, "the most terrifying creature the world has ever seen," John and I found in a quiet little lady's back-yard shed in Brooklyn.

John's ex-wife, Germaine Aussey, was a French movie star, and a fine horse-woman.

The great days in the Big Top (opening spec). *(Knickerbocker Pictures)*
The six-pole Big Tops and satellite tents. *(Chester Photo Service)*

Loading the menagerie at Winter Quarters. *(Steinmetz)*

Alfred Court, greatest of all wild-animal trainers, trusted the cats.

Pinita del Oro, at home on the trapeze.

The great Christianis practicing at Winter Quarters.

The Hartford fire. "The horrors of war paled by comparison." *(United Press International Photo)*

Coffee cups—the most famous slack-wire act.

Emmett Kelly contemplates the glory that was Ringling. *(Steinmetz)*

"That year . . . we traveled 17,117 miles and showed in twenty-seven states."
(*Steinmetz*)

a new word in the English language. In the annals of show-manship, Gargantua runs Jumbo a close second. His han-dling of the great gorilla showed that Brother John had the magic touch and the calculated recklessness that a successful circus man must have.

Back in November 1937, when we were still at the Ritz Ho-tel in New York anxiously awaiting the issue of the intricate negotiations over the future of Ringling Brothers, the tele-phone rang one evening. A lady on the other end introduced herself as Mrs. Lintz. She said she had a full-grown gorilla. Would John be interested in buying it for the circus? John said, "I certainly would. When can I see it?"

At this point the lady became somewhat evasive, but finally invited us to come to tea at her home in Brooklyn.

John, who did not yet have control of the circus and only a hazardous prospect of getting it, said excitedly, "Buddy, we've got to have that gorilla!"

In a taxicab—John's chauffeur-driven Cadillac was still in the equivocal future—we drove to Brooklyn, winding through dismal streets of rubber-plant-decorated houses, down into a tenement district, and up again to a once elegant, water-front street. We mounted the brownstone stoop of a mansion of faded grandeur straight out of Charles Addams' macabre cartoons. A small middle-aged lady let us in, and we sat down on rosewood and horsehair chairs to drink tea with her. We drank gallons of tea and chatted inconsequentially and looked at the magnificent view of the lighted towers of Manhattan until we both began to suspect that we were the victims of an old lady's fantasy.

Finally, John said abruptly, "Now we would like to see the gorilla."

Mrs. Lintz fluttered nervously. "Oh, yes, yes. You must see the gorilla. We'll go out now."

She led the way through her big old house, down worn

stairs to the basement kitchen and across a yard to a shed
that had once stabled the owner's horses. Inside, one naked
electric bulb hung from the rafters lighting dust and cobwebs,
and a man was sitting on a wooden chair. He was introduced
as the gorilla's keeper, Richard Kroner.

"Dear little Buddy lives in there," said Mrs. Lintz.

This was shock number one to me; dear little Buddy
indeed! So my namesake lived in there. I saw a big rectangular wooden box standing on end. It looked something like an
oversized coffin. The peculiar thing about it was that it was
braced on three sides by heavy timbers set against the walls
and one coming down from the ceiling. We learned later that
it was lined with steel.

"Before you see Buddy, I want to tell you his story," Mrs.
Lintz said.

She told the tale which all the world now knows, about a
baby gorilla being brought from Africa on a ship and some
disgruntled member of the crew throwing acid in the poor
little thing's face, burning it horribly. "I bought him from the
captain," Mrs. Lintz said. "He thought the gorilla's value was
ruined and sold him cheap." (Ruined? Heavenly day! That
acid was worth a million to us.)

It seemed that Mrs. Lintz's late husband was a plastic sur-
geon. He had tried to do some repair work on Buddy without
too much success. "But he was the sweetest little thing," Mrs.
Lintz continued. "We all loved him. He used to come into
the parlor and have tea with me every afternoon."

"Well, let's see him," said John.

The front of the box had a slatted sliding door. Kroner
raised it, revealing iron bars, and behind the bars glowered
the most fearful face I have ever looked upon. A tremendous
hairy head, great dripping fangs, and the horrible sinister leer
of the acid-twisted mouth. In that dim light, cribbed in his
box, he looked even bigger than life. Gigantic!

While we looked in horror, Mrs. Lintz kept talking about how dear and lovable Buddy was, and moving closer to the box. Suddenly the whole building shook as the creature hurled himself against the bars in a slavering, raging effort to get at her. With a shriek in the excruciating key of terror, our hostess ran for her life. We saw her no more that day.

John was absolutely determined to have that gorilla. He was eight years old, and very few gorillas had then survived that long in captivity. Uncle John had imported two which lived only about six months. John figured that if Buddy had lasted eight years he was well acclimated.

Mrs. Lintz was equally determined to sell him. According to Kroner, there had been some carelessness a while back, before they had built up the cage so strongly, and the gorilla had gotten out. Mrs. Lintz woke up in the middle of the night to find lovable little Buddy in her bedroom. It was enough.

So John and I bought him for $10,000. We signed the contract with Mrs. Lintz even before we got control of the circus, but John said, "We just can't afford to miss having the most terrifying creature the world has ever seen."

"All right," I agreed, "but one thing I insist: we're not going to have a vice-president of the circus and a gorilla both named Buddy."

"It isn't a good name for a gorilla anyhow," John remarked. "What do you suggest?"

Still full of my classical education from Yale, I had perhaps my brightest flash of inspiration. "Let's call him Gargantua," I said.

Then came the question of getting Gargantua the Great to Florida. We did not want any premature publicity that fall. Rather let him burst on the world in his full ferocity when the circus went out in the spring. So John called up our uncle's old friend Bill Eagan, stationmaster for the Pennsylvania Railroad. I heard only his end of the conversation: "Look, Bill, I want to arrange to take a gorilla down to Sarasota with me on the *Orange Blossom Special* on December second."

There was a long harangue and voluble explanations from Eagan. Then I heard John say, "Gorilla, Bill? Who's talking about gorillas? You must be hearing things. This is a delicate little monkey. The reason I want him to go with us is that he'll die of loneliness in a freight car."

They talked a lot more and Eagan evidently agreed. When John hung up he said, "Eagan says that ever since one of Dr. Ditmars' boa constrictors got loose in a Pullman they've made a rule against carrying dangerous animals in the baggage cars of passenger trains. We've got to work this carefully, Buddy."

We all got down to the station early. The only newspaperman there was our friend Gladwyn Hill, then of the Associated Press and now Los Angeles bureau chief, who had promised to hold the story until we were ready. Presently Gargantua's huge box arrived, accompanied by Kroner. It was carefully placed upright in the baggage car. At this point Frank Eagan arrived to see how we were doing. He eyed the box balefully. "A small monkey?" he asked.

"He needs room to exercise," John said.

Gargantua exercised, and the box shivered and rocked.

"I think he's feeling chilly," Kroner said. A small diamond-shaped hole had been cut in the front of the box. Kroner stuffed a corner of a full-sized blanket in it. It was whipped through like a handkerchief.

"Small monkey?" said Eagan.

I was looking hypnotically at the top of the box, where great big nails had been driven in and bent over to hold the shutter down. Those nails were slowly, incredibly, straightening out.

Then I looked down and saw eight black fingers as big as cigars under the shutter. Wham! It flew up in the air, crashing against the roof of the car. Gargantua and Bill Eagan were eye to eye.

At that blessed moment whistles blew, the engine bell clanged, and the *Orange Blossom Special* began to move. Bill Eagan jumped for the platform and stood there shaking his fist at Johnny's impudent Irish grin.

When we got Gargantua to Sarasota we had a wonderful time with him. There have been many discussions among anthropologists as to which is the smarter animal, the gorilla or the chimpanzee. I vote for the gorilla. Gargantua was without doubt a thinking character. His mind was about equal to that of a maliciously capricious moron, and, like a child, he loved to play games. Catch was one of his favorites. We always used a softball. We would throw it into his cage and he would catch it and toss it back underhand. Then all of a sudden he would change from toss to throw and wham it at your head like a big-league pitcher. You would not want to play that game with croquet balls.

Another game he liked was tug of war. You threw the end of a rope into his cage. He took it and you both pulled. Sometimes he politely let you win, but he could always win if he wanted to. Four or five men might get on the other end, and Gargantua would take the rope in his hand and wind it back under his arm for leverage and jerk them all right off their feet. Then he would throw the end of the rope out to you because he wanted to play some more. But each time he threw it, he would give you a shorter length, trying to lure you nearer. Then that son of a gun would try to jerk you close enough so he could grab you and bite you. He was a wonderful animal.

The moment we released the news about him, Gargantua

became an international celebrity. Arthur Brisbane wrote a syndicated column about whether he could beat heavyweight champion Gene Tunney. Gene, who was a friend of ours, went along with the gag and gave an interview saying that he could take Gargantua in nothing flat. But he did not try it.

A number of scientific people came to Sarasota just to see the gorilla, Dr. Yerkes the great anthropologist from Yale among them. Another visitor was Bernard Baruch's brother, Dr. Sailong Baruch. Dr. Baruch was a distinguished-looking man who wore a handsome beard. When we took him to see Gargantua it was a tossup as to whether the doctor or the gorilla was more interested by the other. Gargantua, who had never seen a bearded man before, was absolutely fascinated. He walked all over his cage studying this phenomenon from different angles. Suddenly he made up his mind that he didn't like it, and picked up all the loose things in his cage and hurled them at the doctor.

One of the great stories about Gargantua—he made the cover of *Life,* with a double spread inside—came when he bit my brother. John was playing with him and got a little too close. Gargantua grabbed him in his tremendous grip and began biting his arm. John bellowed for help and Dick Kroner hurried up and beat the gorilla over the head with a pole until he let go.

Did John rush to a hopital with his mangled arm? Yes, but not until he had stopped at the advertising car to give the news to a palpitating world. Our famous old press agent, Roland Butler, released a dispatch stating that John had received "the most massive antitetanus shot ever given to a human being."

John was not too badly bitten, but Roland's round-the-world headlines were so bloodcurdling that my brother's current fiancée, a lovely German girl named Carlotta Gertz, called him in the middle of the night from Berlin. When the

connection was made she sobbed, "Are you dead, Johnny?"
He answered, "I'm not dead. I'm talking to you."

But she kept on repeating, "Are you dead, Johnny? Are you dead?"

Gargantua thrived in Florida, but as the time came to take him on the road John became more and more worried. Living normally in germfree jungles, gorillas are terribly susceptible to human respiratory diseases. We were afraid that Gargantua would literally catch his death of cold from the circus crowds. As to so many of us, inspiration came to John in the still hours; unlike most of us, he did not wait until morning to act. Reaching out of bed for the telephone, he called his friend Lemuel Bulware of the Carrier Corporation in Syracuse, New York. "My God, what are you calling me for at this hour?" Lem asked angrily.

"Cool off," John said. "You'll be delighted when you hear this. I want you to build an air-conditioned cage for Gargantua. Good tie-up, great publicity for us both."

That was a time when air conditioning was just getting started. Bulware saw the possibilities right away. "It's four A.M., John," he said, "but I'll start working on it right now."

Bill Yeske, who had built our wagons for forty years, built the magnificent cage wagon in which Gargantua was exhibited. Carrier did not just air-condition it; they made tests of climatic conditions in the Congo and fitted up the cage with thermostatic controls and humidifiers that reproduced them exactly. The phrase "jungle-conditioned cage" won them the advertisers' award for 1938.

Gargantua lived as happily as his nature permitted in that cage for twelve years. Once he got pneumonia in New York, when the air conditioner could not cope with the concentration of germs in Madison Square Garden. John called in the greatest diagnostician and the best man for pneumonia in America. There they were, in the basement of the Garden at five o'clock in the morning, fighting for a gorilla's life. They had a battery of oxygen flasks connected to the air ducts of the air conditioner, feeding him pure oxygen.

Gargantua was a good patient. The poor fellow was almost gone, and he was like a sick child. The doctors had no fear of his great strength. He seemed to know he was sick and that they were trying to help him. We were all happy when his old ferocity returned.

After that, Gargantua remained in good health until the close of his life. In his prime he weighed five hundred and fifty pounds and was five feet seven and one half inches tall. His enormously powerful arms had a total span of over nine feet. He ate everything we did except meat, but he did get boiled liver and cod-liver oil for vitamins.

In 1941 John heard of a lady gorilla in Cuba who was for sale. Her name was M'Toto, which means "Little One" in Swahili. John went to Havana to call on M'Toto, who was living in a pretty little house of her own on the grounds of her opulent owner, Mrs. Stephen Hoyt. The reason Toto was for sale was that one day, when she was having tea in the garden with Mrs. Hoyt, she playfully broke both the lady's wrists. It was an accident, for Toto had a sweet disposition.

John bought Toto. This was the beginning of the wonderful idea of the marriage of Gargantua and Toto. We planned a lovely wedding on Washington's Birthday 1941, with a cake flown down from Schrafft's in New York. Mrs. Hoyt, in flowing chiffon and a picture hat, was matron of honor, and lots of reporters were invited. The ceremony took place in a bower of flowers under a canvas canopy at Winter Quarters.

The strains of *Lohengrin's* Processional hailed the approach of Toto's chaste white cage, bearing a placard, "Mrs. Gargantua the Great." Toto's trainer, José Thomas, was riding in the cage with her. A snorting tractor backed it into position end to end with Gargantua's monster cage. The great ape was pacing the floor in an amiable humor. When the backboard of Toto's cage was removed, Gargantua stopped dead in his tracks. An expression of dawning amazement grew on his terrible countenance. As he moved forward to grasp the bars he was plainly thunderstruck.

Toto had her back to him. She must have felt that someone was following her, for she glanced over her shoulder. One look and she lurched forward and flung her arms around the trainer's neck. This evidently made her feel secure, for she turned and bellowed at her husband.

At that, they both went into tantrums. From a docile, pampered pet, Toto became a raging jungle beast. Gargantua exceeded his previous high of ferocity. Roaring and yelling, he pelted his wife with half-eaten vegetables and shook the cage in his raging efforts to tear out the bars. The congregation was hysterical between laughter and terror.

I regret to say that the marriage was never consummated. When the bridal couple got a little used to each other we connected their cages, with only bars between, in the hope that propinquity would foster love. Toto showed signs of interest. She made coy advances, like throwing an overripe melon at her husband. But Gargantua spurned her. George Jean Nathan always claimed he was a fairy.

Each cage had two compartments so that you could shut the gorilla in one end and clean out the other. When we got to the Garden that year, Mrs. Hoyt came to call on Toto. To get into the unoccupied end of her cage, she had to pass Gargantua's. Incautiously she turned her back on him. He grabbed for her and just got her dress. A loud rip and there was Mrs. Hoyt in nothing but her bra and panties screaming bloody murder.

Anthropologists say that a gorilla's normal life span is the same as that of primitive man—forty-five or fifty years. However, Gargantua began to age visibly when he was twenty-one. His coat turned the color of a silver fox and he became progressively more feeble throughout 1949. Our last stand of the season was Miami and that night Gargantua died. Even his passing was publicity-timed, for our press agents wrote that he had waited until the last night of the season to die like the good trouper that he was.

I had promised Dr. Yerkes to send Gargantua's body to Johns Hopkins for autopsy. We sadly packed him in a piano case full of dry ice and flew him to Baltimore. After they were through with him, his skeleton went to New Haven, where it now stands in company with some of our most famous animals. Harvard wanted him, but Gargantua was a Yale man.

CHAPTER XXII

LABOR PAINS

We brought the circus into New York in March 1938, allowing one week for rehearsals. This seems like a short time to put an entire show together, but James A. Bailey used to allow only three days. It can be done if everybody knows his business. The performers are all old pros. They don't have to think about the entire circus, just the five, seven, or twelve minutes they are allotted out of the total running time.

Fitting them together and planning a balanced performance was up to John and Fred Bradna, our great equestrian director, and their assistants. You have your specs and production numbers, your wild-animal acts, acrobatic numbers, clowns, aerialists, equestrians, trained elephants, and so forth, and you always plan so that either the clowns or a little aerial act is going on while the crew is tearing down after an act that requires heavy props, such as the arenas for the trained cats.

Normally, planning for next year's show begins the day after you open in the Garden; but, of course, in 1938 we did not have that much time. However, Bradna and Valdo had been programing the shows for so long that they did not find it too difficult. The big production numbers had been routined, rehearsed, and timed in Sarasota. Acts had been arriving from Europe for a month, but some of them did not reach New York until a few days before we opened. Then it was just a matter of dropping them into the slots that had been held open for them. Merle Evans, our veteran bandmaster, had to learn over two hundred music cues.

The night of the dress rehearsal ran the unholy time of four hours, but this was largely due to Terrell Jacobs' trouble with his panthers. You cannot cut an animal act short. They must be forced to go through their entire routine every time; otherwise, they will quit at that spot and have to be withdrawn for a week or so of retraining. So one balky cat can hold up the whole circus. That night Jacobs' act lasted an hour instead of its allotted twelve minutes. Otherwise, things ran very smoothly. Superstitious show people said this was a bad omen. They were right.

To go back briefly. In May 1937 Sam Gumpertz had signed a five-year contract with the American Federation of

Actors, an A. F. of L.-affiliated union that represented the working crews and handlers, doubling their minimum wage. A slightly smaller scale prevailed while in Winter Quarters, and traditionally this continued during the New York and Boston engagements until we actually went under canvas.

A few hours before opening night a union delegation headed by Ralph Whitehead came to John and demanded full scale immediately. John knew they were pointing a pistol at his head. The famous Ringling rage boiled up. He told them to go to hell. Shortly before the performance every man jack walked out, except the staff, the performers, and the freaks.

It looked like total disaster. The Garden was our biggest stand. Everything hinged on it, from the publicity which spread throughout the country to the profits which carried us over many a rough spot on the road. We had stretched our credit to the breaking point to refurbish the show. If we disappointed the large opening-night audience, it would deal us a blow from which we might never recover.

We all knew that if we lost the circus again it was gone for good. In the back yard, down in the cavernous basements of the Garden, the performers were milling around, a leaderless, panicky mob, asking, "What happens now? What shall we do?"

Pat Valdo, our personnel director, shouted the answer: "Mr. Johnny says we show!"

That was a frantic night. The house, though not packed, was well dressed. To dress a house is to distribute the tickets so that most sections are peopled and there are no glaring expanses of empty seats. Rumors were running through the crowd that made them irritable and uneasy. Then the lights went down. Merle Evans gave us a blare and ruffle of drums. Under a single spot John stood at the microphone. He told the crowd what had happened and announced that we would try to go on anyhow. He ended with the sentence that has become a tradition of all the opening nights we have played since: "I welcome you to The Greatest Show on Earth."

The audience answered with a full-throated roar vastly different in power and emotion from the usual polite applause. Then the floodlights came on, the band played furiously, and the show began.

The spec was terribly different from the way we had pictured it. There were no grooms for the horses, no bull men to bring up the elephants, not even a small donkey. Led by an unelephanted Maharajah of Nepal, the royal court—maharanis, princesses, and all—trudged into the arena fairly staggering under their heavy gold-encrusted costumes. Sixty Bengal Lancers shuffled along in cavalry boots and spurs. The final irony was the appearance of the Great White Hunter, Frank Buck, in riding breeches, sport shirt, and sola topee, limping along carrying his pet cheetah in his arms. But at sight of him our loyal audience shouted the roof down.

Loyalty was, in fact, the leitmotiv of that night. Not loyalty to us, for we had not been with the show long enough to deserve it, but loyalty of the audience to the sporting spirit of the performers, and, in turn, their loyalty to their art. Beyond that, the loyalty of all concerned to the circus itself.

We gave a pretty ragged performance—a hodgepodge to end all the hodgepodges, which John had planned so carefully to avoid. The first problem was getting Terrell Jacobs' big iron cage up. John, Artie Concello, Pat Valdo, Clyde Ingalls, myself, and a lot more good people I don't remember, and a midget named Harry Earle, pulled and hauled ineptly. When we finally got it set, the audience applauded wildly.

When it came time to strike the cage, our artist friend Charlie Baskerville vaulted over the arena railing and ran to help. He was followed by hundreds of other men in ringside seats. At times the arena was so full of society razorbacks,

and reporters taking their pictures, that we had to beg them
to return to their seats.

Amateur bull men helped lead the performing elephants on;
very dangerous it was, too. The feuding Loyal-Repenskis
acted as hostlers for the Christianis, and the Christianis, in
turn, performed this menial service for their arch enemies. It
usually took a six-horse team to haul Gargantua's huge cage.
A great crowd of performers and civilians pushed it around
the arena. It was pretty hard to see Gargantua, but the
audience went wild.

How long the show ran that night I don't exactly know,
because nobody checked. But it was dawn by the time John
and I, with our faces blackened and our evening clothes in
tatters, got back to the Ritz. We never wanted another night
like that. But the strikers had really done us a favor. The
publicity was magnificent.

After two more makeshift performances to packed houses,
the union settled for a small compromise. After that, there
was only one more untoward incident of the run. This was
caused by a tigress named Lady, a magnificent animal who
had been raised on the bottle. She was as gentle as a kitten
and had never been known to unsheath her claws. When she
first came to Sarasota, John and I used to walk her around
Winter Quarters on a leash.

So in the great Nepal spec we had her keeper parade her
around the hippodrome. He had the leash and a little cane
to push her away if she got too playful. She seemed to enjoy
walking along among the other animals, a group which
included old Edith the giraffe, Lotus the hippo, and a troupe
of tiny Sicilian donkeys.

Then one night, as she waited among the crowd of people
and animals to go on, the strange jungle madness seized her.
Without the slightest warning she sprang at a poor little don-

key and bit his whole rear end off with one massive crunch. Then in long, sinuous bounds she started up the tunnel passage headed for the crowded foyer of the Garden. People were paralyzed around the bloody corpse of the donkey. Mayhem and the dreadful self-slaughter of a panic-stricken mob loomed if she reached the foyer.

In the corridor was a brave little midget named Paul Runkel, dressed for the role of Dopey in the "Seven Dwarfs." As the great beast loped toward him he stepped out and hit her squarely on the nose with his little rubber hammer. The sudden shock startled her back into her own sweet self. Her keeper snapped the leash on and led her docilely back to her cage.

We thought we had troubles in the Garden; but it was not until we went on the road that things really got tough. The first blow fell on a cold, rainy night as we began to load the show after the final performance in Brooklyn. With the Big Top about half down and everything sodden and flapping in the wet wind, work suddenly ceased. Ralph Whitehead and Judge Padway of Milwaukee, who was the A. F. of L. counsel, were both out there in the rain. John and I met them and we adjourned to a saloon near the lot to talk things over. They said that we owed the union some money that had not been paid. It amounted to $3500, so these two said, and the circus would not move until it was paid.

We were to open in Washington the next day. To miss even two performances there would cost us at least $25,000, and our operating expenses that year were about $17,000 a day. John threw up his hands, and I went back through the rain to the red wagon and got $3500. I offered the cash to Judge Padway, who refused to touch it. But another member of the union took it, and everybody went back to work. We got off the lot at 7:30 A.M. and opened in Washington that night.

Oddly enough, the union found that there had been a similar error in our accounts with the union the night we pulled out of Washington. These tactics were typical of the union in those days. They did it to let you know that the ax was over your head.

Right here I want to state that both John and I are not anti-union. Our own father was a member of the Brotherhood of Locomotive Engineers and we were brought up in sympathy with organized labor and an understanding of what it had done, not only for working men but for everyone in the United States. Our feelings in this respect is shown by our friendship with many labor leaders, especially that grand old gentleman Matthew Woll, and by the fact that in the year of our greatest battles with the union we had the circus take part in the Labor Day parade in Wichita, Kansas, where we were playing.

However, when labor got tough with the circus we got tougher. It was the only way to save it. For the circus is terribly vulnerable to mischance. Bad weather can come at any time; wrecks and disasters are an ever present possibility; if, in addition, there is the constant threat of a strike, you are in an impossible position.

A railroad show like ours must keep its schedule or perish. Even a few hours' delay can upset the carefully planned timetable of the railroad; a day's delay is extremely costly; and an idle week could spell financial disaster. Not only that, but there is the public to be considered. If we failed to show, it seriously damaged our carefully nurtured popularity—thousands of people, who had planned to make a fete of circus day, disappointed and disgruntled.

We considered it extremely reprehensible of unscrupulous labor leaders to take advantage of this vulnerability. So we fought them as viciously as they fought us; just as we fought every other threat to our circus.

The next blow came when all our teamsters struck in Toledo, suddenly refusing to drive the wagons from the lot to the runs. We were expecting trouble and had prepared an unpleasant surprise for them. John had a battery of tractors ready to take over. Again the strikers had done us a favor by forcing mechanization upon us. The circus was operating exactly as it had fifty years before, just as though the internal-combustion engine had never been invented. The wagons were still unloaded from the flats by hand and hauled to the lot by horses; and the Big Top was still raised by elephant power. Eighteen tractors replaced three hundred horses with all the problems of transportation, feeding, and handling that they involved.

Naturally this raised a howl. "People love the horses," our conservative managers said. "They'll miss them."

"We still have lots of horses for the equestrian acts," John pointed out. "If people want to see horses we'll pitch the horse top near the Big Top and open it to the public."

It became a very popular attraction.

We sent all the horses to our farm in Peru, Indiana, to be sold. When John and I reached the lot next evening, Jim Pepper, a wonderful old character who drove the gilly wagon, was waiting for us. He was literally in tears.

"What's the matter, Jim?" I asked.

"Mr. Johnny sold Bill."

"What's this? Who's Bill?" John asked.

"You know Bill," Jim almost sobbed. "He's pulled my gilly wagon for ten years. He's not a horse, he's a friend."

We could not break the old boy's heart, so we had Bill sent back from Indiana. As long as Jim lived, he hitched Bill to the gilly wagon every night and drove it around the lot picking up the tent stakes. When Jim died we retired Bill to Winter Quarters. That was the last horse-drawn gilly wagon.

The final showdown with the union came in Scranton, Pennsylvania. From the time we had gone on the road we had been losing money and our reserves were getting thin. In Syracuse, John announced that if the show was to go on, everybody, including the president, must take a 25 per cent cut in salary. My pay as vice-president was reduced from $100 to $75 a week. All the performers cheerfully agreed, but the workers stood on their contract. John offered to show them our books, but they just laughed at him and said, "We've got a contract covering a minimum wage, and you'll pay it or else!"

Boarding each man cost about $45 a month, which brought their pay to a point much higher than the prevailing average wage for unskilled labor. In fact, even after a 25 per cent cut it was still above average.

In a ground swell of grumbling we moved from Syracuse to Scranton. We set up and gave the matinee. Then the working crew struck. We could go on in the Garden without them; under canvas we could not do it safely. Ringling Brothers–Barnum & Bailey Combined Shows ended its season that day, June 26, 1938.

John and I and my roommate from Yale, Charlie Bedcaux, whose father was the famous efficiency expert, were virtually barricaded in the Casey Hotel in Scranton. We were in considerable danger. That was an era of labor violence; of sit-down strikes and pitched battles between specially trained labor goons and professional strikebreakers hired by employers. Feeling was often bitter. It was very bitter in Scranton.

For five days we were besieged in the Casey Hotel, with the circus stalled on the lot. We could not move it out, and the left-wing mayor of Scranton was disinclined to help us or offer much protection. The union leaders thought that if they held us there we would have to go on under the contract

Gumpertz had signed with them. We knew that to do so was financial suicide.

I remember one conference with Ralph Whitehead, who was an old Shakespearean actor given to dramatic speeches. John told him that all we wanted to do was to close up and move back to Winter Quarters in Sarasota.

"You can't mean that you would close the circus in mid-season!" Whitehead said incredulously.

"We have no choice," John answered.

Whitehead struck his chest and, voice at full diapason, said, "John, would that the ground would open up and swallow me before this dreadful thing should come to pass!"

Very quietly John said, "You know, Ralph, I wish to God it would, too."

After five days we managed to round up enough men to move us out. Even then the union would not allow us to go. They said we had to pay strike costs of about $12,000 or face a full-scale fight. It was an obvious injustice, but we had to yield. However, we made the most of it. I alerted the press and photographers. When Mr. Whitehead came for the pay-off they were all there. John ostentatiously took the money in cash out of his pocket and ceremoniously handed it to him while flash bulbs started popping. The pictures were run in papers all over the country under captions such as "Whitehead Getting His Pound of Flesh."

We still had an ace in the hole. When Ringling Brothers was incorporated in 1932, the American Circus Company was incorporated as a separate subsidiary company under the name of Circus Cities Zoological Gardens Corporation. While we were playing the East we had that corporation running the Sells-Floto–Al G. Barnes Combined Shows out West. This circus had no union contract. John went to all our best acts and asked the performers if they would sign at reduced salaries with Sells-Floto. They did. Frank Buck took a cut from $1000 to $250 a week.

Then I took The Big One back to Winter Quarters. We got in on a Friday. The following Monday afternoon I left Sarasota with twenty-five railroad cars loaded with motorized equipment, the Big Top, and most of the feature acts—Gargantua, of course, Frank Buck, the Christianis, Heyer's dressage display and liberty horses, Terrell Jacobs' animals, the Flying Concellos, and Ralph Clark's Jump over the Flaming Automobile. We joined Sells-Floto at Redfield, South Dakota. We had closed in Scranton on June 26; we opened at Redfield on July 7. It was fast work. While I was readying the show and effecting the transfer and amalgamation, John had not been idle. He had devised entirely new billing and publicity, which proved a miracle of improvisation—the newspaper ads and bills stated in small print: "The Al G. Barnes–Sells-Floto Circus PRESENTS [in larger type] RINGLING BROTHERS AND BARNUM AND BAILEY'S STUPENDOUS NEW FEATURES [the biggest type].

The new combination was quite a show—in fact, The Greatest left on Earth. Sells-Floto already had some splendid displays, including Mabel Stark, billed as "The Queen of the Jungle presenting a Notable Congress of the Earth's Most Ferocious Performing Lions and Tigers." Another feature was a charming girl named Dolly Jacobs with a lion that rode on horseback. Since the show was designed for a more provincial audience than The Big One, it had the traditional "Thrilling Roman Chariot Races."

We began to make money again.

Of course, the A.F.A. still dogged us. They picketed every performance; and their pickets even rode our trains and sneaked meals in the cookhouse. But it was a losing struggle. People in general were tired of labor strife; even the pickets seemed lackadaisical.

In Omaha, John and I came on the lot about noon to see how things were going. One bedraggled union picket was stalking up and down in front of the midway. John stopped to chat with him. "How are you enjoying your work?" he asked.

With a sour grin the man said, "Not very much."

"How would you like to stop doing this and work for the circus?" John asked.

The picket threw down his sign and said, "I sure would!"

We gave him a note and sent him over to the boss canvasman. I suppose that could be called tampering with a union employee.

John had deliberately dated the show into Houston, Texas, to coincide with the American Federation of Labor convention there. We did good business with the delegates. Matthew Woll asked John for some seats, and we gave him the best we had. Then our friend Tom Hogg, son of a former governor of Texas and one of those Texan conservatives who are so far right they make the Morgan partners look like Commies, came to town. When he asked for seats we warned him that Woll would be in the audience. He let loose a blast of profanity— it seemed that there had been trouble out on his oil rigs and a striker had taken a pot shot at him, which put him in the hospital for a while. However, he said he'd be "thus and so" if he'd let any "this and that" labor leader keep him away from the circus.

We had to give him seats near Woll's party. Tom was snorting fire when he saw them. In the middle of the show he said loudly to his chauffeur, "Go back to the hotel and get my six-guns. I don't feel easy without 'em in such low company."

The chauffeur brought the guns. Hogg checked them carefully and stuffed them in his belt. He sat there for a few moments more glaring at Woll, and then stalked out, saying, "I can't stand the smell of skunks."

Luckily Woll was amused.

Much to our surprise, we snatched a nice profit from apparent disaster. The show made back all our losses and closed the season of 1938 with more than enough to see us through the winter. It was the final appearance of the Sells-Floto–Al G. Barnes Circus.

In 1939 nobody knew whether The Greatest Show would disappear from earth forever or not. We had learned that it was impossible to operate it under the Gumpertz contract. John invited the union leaders to confer with us. The meeting was set up in the New York offices of our friend Matthew Woll, who, we hoped, would exercise a moderating influence on his colleagues.

The conference began very pleasantly. We were all glad to see each other again. It was "How've you been, John?" And "Great, thanks, Ralph," with Matt Woll beaming benevolently. We talked informally all afternoon, and, we thought, constructively. A late dinner was sent in—paid for by the circus, naturally—and we were the happiest people you ever saw. After dinner we sat down at Woll's long walnut conference table to hammer out an agreement.

It was at this point that Whitehead said they would accept the same contract they'd had before. John looked as thunderstruck as poor old Gargantua when he first saw Toto. "What have we been talking about all day?" he gasped. "You know I'm not going to stick my neck in the same noose that strangled us last year. I thought we were trying to work out something that would give us a break and still be fair to you."

The union people grinned at such naïvete. "You have a contract with us," Whitehead pointed out. "It's got three years more to run and we've never recognized that it can be changed. You have to go on with it."

We tossed it back and forth for a few minutes without the slightest change. There was no more give to them than to casehardened steel. Then my brother made one of the shortest addresses in the history of labor relations. He stood up, short and stocky and electric, facing the union bigwigs across the table. "Well, gentlemen," he began, "I have listened to everything. Now I have only two words to add to it." They don't need repeating. Then: "Come on, Buddy, let's go!"

Matt Woll and Judge Padway caught us at the elevators. Each took one of us soothingly by the arm. "Come back, Johnny . . . Buddy. We can still work something out."

We went back. An hour later we had a contract we could live with.

CHAPTER XXIII

LADY GODIVA GOES TO THE WORLD'S FAIR

Even before we knew that the circus would show in 1939, John was going full speed ahead with his plans for modernizing it. Perhaps his greatest innovation was the design for a new Big Top. The old six-pole tent had not been designed; it "just growed." In the beginning there was a round top. Long ago, when the five brothers needed more space, they put in a center section with the half-round tops at each end. As the show grew and the crowds increased, more center sections were added and the tent stretched out and out, becoming impractically long and narrow—510 feet long by 210 feet wide. It was almost impossible for people at the ends of the arena to see what was going on in the center ring. But so unchangeable are circus traditions that this inefficient monster remained in use for fifty years.

Remember that the Big Top was not just an inanimate mobile structure in which to seat an audience, but a living thing of vital canvas, rope and wood that was brought to life each day by our wonderful old boss canvasman, Captain Bill Curtis, and his men. The fact that it had this kind of life of its own was an essential ingredient of the circus; we had to change it without destroying its vital essence.

John's new Big Top was shaped like an oval stadium, with four center poles instead of six. It was his idea, but the detail and construction was by our boss sailmaker, Leif Osmondson. The new design enabled us to increase the diameter of the center ring to fifty feet, the biggest we had ever used. These improvements naturally brought criticism upon us, but what really roiled the traditionalists was the question of color.

The harmonious lighting effects which Le Maire had worked out were beautiful in the Garden and at night performances under canvas. But they were obliterated at matinees by sun blazing through the white canvas. John said, "Let's make the canvas blue."

The Big Top was, to quote the *Circus Magazine* for 1939, "reborn in shades of blue—dark blue at the peaks, paling, down its slopes, to tints of lighter blue. The center poles were gold and the scores of quarter poles were silver. The vast oval of boxes and grandstand were painted a new shade of 'Ringling red,' and the draperies at the ends of the grandstand and the rail draperies along the entire circumference of the

hippodrome track were deep blue with giant gold tassels. . . .
Golden stars glittered in the center of the ring carpets, on
drapes and on the poles. . . ." It was a child's-eye view of
heaven.

Another problem of the matinees on the road was heat.
Once people had been willing to swelter in the hundred-
degree temperatures built up by a Kansas sun beating on a
couple of acres of canvas; not so the modern American. On
hot days we played to half-empty houses, and this affected
the evening show as well, for there were fewer people circu-
lating through town talking of the wonders of The Greatest
Show. Air conditioning was the answer, but everyone said,
"You can't air-condition a tent."

Well, that is the truth; for a tent leaks hot air through many
orifices. But if you cannot attain perfection, you can improve
conditions. We bought eight motor-driven units operating on
the blower system from the Buffalo Forge Corporation. It took
three extra flatcars to transport them and an additional crew
of fifty men to run them; but they performed a near miracle.
Matinee crowds increased and our ushers reported people
saying that they came to get out of the heat as much as to see
the show.

Many less obvious but quite as important operating
improvements were made. Diesel generators supplanted our
outmoded gasoline plants, increasing our electrical output at
decreased costs. Huge-wheeled tractors replaced the pull-up
teams at the runs. Caterpillar-mounted booms loaded and unloaded the canvas and the Big Top rigging. Somewhere
around this time John had an idea for a mechanical stake
puller, which our boss wagon builder, Bill Yeske, realized for
him along with improvements on the mechanical stake
drivers already in use. Later still came a machine for guying
out the tent ropes, an operation which had been performed
by large gangs of men. As soon as we saw it demonstrated

John and I decided to use it; but as we walked away, despite
our enthusiasm for modernization, we both were sad that
never again would we hear the resonant chant of "Heebie!
Heebie! Hobie! Hold! Golong!" which was the euphoni-
ous rendition of "Heave it! Heave it! Heavy! Hold! Go on!"

Meanwhile we were not neglecting the show itself. Just as
he had given the performance a theme and over-all unity,
John now took the music in hand. Heretofore the band had
played totally unrelated bits and snatches of music. There
was lots of noise and lots of brass, but the tunes did not tie
up with anything except the individual acts with their
required drum rolls, gallops, and so forth. John decided to
program each year's circus music as an entity, and he hired
one of Broadway's best arrangers to give unity to the arrangements.

My brother was well equipped to organize the musical programs. He had a considerable share of the Ringling's musical
talent. He had loved and studied music for years—classical,
modern, and jazz. In addition to playing a hot saxophone,
he had studied composition. For years now he has composed
the music for the production numbers of the circus himself,
working in collaboration with such top lyric writers as Irving
Caesar, Ray Goetz, and in recent times with Tony Valona.
Though John is not a great musician, he has produced some
lovely melodies for the circus; among them "Lovely Launana
Lady," a hit tune of the De Mille's movie *The Greatest Show
on Earth.*

However, John did not rely on his own talents to provide
original music for the circus. When he dreamed up the idea
of an elephant ballet for the 1942 show, he had the effrontery
to ask Igor Stravinsky to write the music for it. To the surprise
of everybody but John, Stravinsky accepted, and produced
a classic composition. Thus encouraged, John engaged

George Balanchine as choreographer, and his lovely wife of that time, Vera Zorina, danced in the center ring on opening night. That was the year the show was staged by Norman Bel Geddes, directed by John Murray Anderson, and costumed by Miles White.

I suppose everybody loves circus music, gay and noisy and brassy though it be. John helped to make it good as well as noisy. Writing of the music in one of our shows, Lauritz Melchior said, "I could not leave Madison Square Garden while the circus band was playing 'Thunder and Blazes,' not even for *Tannhäuser*. Of course, I had a little something to worry about. I was supposed to be singing *Tannhäuser*."

In 1939 we decided not to send out the Sells-Floto–Al G. Barnes Circus, and its best acts, including Mabel Stark and the riding lion, were incorporated into The Big One. As a variation, we also had a Bengal tiger riding on the back of his deadly enemy, an elephant.

Gargantua was a greater star than ever. In the autumn of 1939 John took him to London. He was booked to sail on the new *Queen Mary*, but when it came time to load him, the hatches proved too small to pass his cage. So he went ignominiously by freighter. He was the star attraction of the Bertram Mills Circus at the Olympia several weeks.

A new revival of elegance was in sight that last spring before World War II. People were getting tired of the "Age of the Common Man"—especially the common man himself, who began making money and, as was right and proper, aspiring to the niceties of life. Like our uncles before us, we anticipated this trend. One of the productions for 1939 was called "Blue Grass Beauties." It reproduced the atmosphere of Louisville, Kentucky, on Derby Day.

It was, in fact, a glorified manège number. Where formerly such an act had one man or woman riding a dressage horse in each ring, John turned it into a big production, for which he used special lilting music. We hired several of the best gaited-horse riders in America. We brought thoroughbreds and saddle horses up from Kentucky. Some of the former were trained as liberty horses. I also acquired coaches which had belonged to August Belmont and Mrs. Vanderbilt, Sr. We filled them with our prettiest girls dressed in the flowing-skirted, picture-hatted fashion of the nineties. As they drove around the hippodrome behind the high-steppers, whose silver-mounted harness jingled softly, they were a lovely sight. Old August Ringling would have approved.

The opening spec that year, which set the theme of the show, was "The World Comes to the World's Fair." To quote the program again: "Europe, South America, South Africa, Canada and the United States march in almost indescribable splendor, followed by glittering sections from the Orient in the traditional glory of chromatic costumes and jewelled turbans, all supposedly bringing precious gifts to the World's Fair. They come mounted on gold and silver draped elephants, ahorse or on camels, in palanquins or afoot. . . ."

It was, in truth, almost that good.

The World's Fair management was so delighted by the idea that they put me on the art committee and asked John to stage a wild West show. He said bluntly, "The wild West idea couldn't be worse; but I'll do an international horse show that will knock your eyes out."

Grover Whalen agreed that it was a splendid idea and signed John to stage it. Immediately John's imagination began to flourish and exfoliate. Through Karl Bickel, former president of United Press, he contacted an Arab sheik for a contingent of desert horsemen on Arabian steeds. From all over the world he brought almost every kind of horse used by man. Everything had to be as real as the Arabians. There were a band of Cherokee Indians, Mexican cowboys, real

bullfighters—to cape, but not kill, bulls—and Argentine
Gauchos, who were experts in bringing steers to their knees
with the bolas. We induced our friends Jack and Charlie of
New York's 21 Club to set up a frontier bar—a real one,
from the film *Dodge City*. As the final fantastic Ringling
touch, John envisaged a Lady Godiva chorus riding white
horses clad in nothing but long golden wigs. It was a magnificent conception—evidently too magnificent for the limited
imaginations of officialdom. Suddenly everything went
wrong.

Let the lamentable tale be told in John's own terse words:
"They had promised me $12,000 a week for expenses. In a
wave of economy they cut me down to $4000. The Fair
management demanded that Jack and Charlie give the Fair
25 per cent of their gross. Since they had planned to invest
$250,000 of their own money, they naturally refused and
pulled out. The S.P.C.A. said that even though the bulls
would not be touched it was cruel to cape them. They said
the Gauchos could not use the bolas. So the bullfighters and
Gauchos were out.

"On opening night everything was lousy. We had absolutely nothing. Not even a publicity agent. I let a Brahma
bull loose in the Fair the day before. We got some publicity
all right!

"The final blow came a few hours before we went on. The
ukase came down from on high, 'no nudity.' There went my
Lady Godivas. I thought of Charlie Baskerville and all my
other friends waiting expectantly in the grandstand. To see a
shambles!

"We finally lined up for the Coventry pageant. The Indians
were all drunk. The cowboys were sober, but very cross.
Mayor La Guardia and Grover Whalen were out in front in
cowboy getups mounted on ancient cow ponies. The little

mayor was almost lost under his Stetson hat. Whalen was even funnier. Whoever saw a cowboy with a toothbrush mustache? John Krimsky wore the pink coat and topper of an M.F.H.

"Immediately behind Mayor La Guardia and Whalen rode Anne Wilson, a perfectly beautiful Model in a blond wig. When the order 'no nudity' came she had been draped in an Indian blanket. I took a handkerchief and tied it around her head. Then I plucked a feather out of an Indian's headdress and stuck it in the handkerchief. 'What are you wearing under that blanket, Anne?' I asked.

" 'Just a bra,' she answered.

" 'Give it to me.'

"She was a nice obedient girl who did exactly as she was told.

" 'Now listen carefully, Anne,' I said. 'Not right away, but when you get out there, well out, throw away the blanket. Then throw away the feather. Then the handkerchief. Get it?'

"Anne laughingly said, 'Yes.'

"The band played. Mayor La Guardia rode out ahead, with Whalen a little behind. Polite applause. As they got to the center of the arena there was a wild burst of cheering. The two of them waved their cowboy hats and grinned with delight. Came a second frenzy of cheers and yells like to burst your ears. Then a third, almost hysterical salvo of shouts as Anne threw the handkerchief away. Even those two applause-conscious politicians could not believe it was all for them. They looked over their shoulders and saw Anne riding in glorious nudity. . . ."

Grover Whalen called John on the carpet the next morning. "Are you familiar with clause five of your contract?" he asked. (Clause five said that if John's management should prove unsatisfactory he could be dismissed at the discretion of the officials.)

"Yes," John said. "May I ask if you have examined clause six?"

"No," said the Fair's president, "but I intend to fire you anyway."

"Yes, sir," John said. "About clause six. It says that if I am dismissed you have to pay me $1500 a week for fifteen weeks."

John rode the train with me in 1939, nursing the show through most of the summer. When he was with us, I devoted myself mainly to personnel problems and publicity. This was appropriate, since I had begun getting publicity for the circus at the age of two, when I fell out of a second-story window in Baraboo. It did not hurt me, but papers all over the country gave it a big play with a circus tie-in.

That year we took the circus all around the perimeter of the United States. After looping through Pennsylvania, New York, and the New England states, we went west along the northern border with a foray into Canada. Then down the West Coast to the Mexican border and along that to El Paso and the great Texas cities, looping back to Corpus Christi and Alabama. Then up to Atlanta, down the Florida east coast to Miami, and across the state for our final stand in Tampa. We traveled 17,117 miles and showed in twenty-seven states.

This, our first full season, was a splendid tour. The crowds who came to see the show proved to us that the public would support a modern circus. Money flowed into the red wagon.

Incidentally, of the hundreds of red wagons with the circus, only one was *the* red wagon. To this fiery caravan came tradesmen with their bills, staff performers and workingmen alike for the money due them, press agents with expense accounts, and politicians with outstretched hands. Within its armored walls reposed each night the day's take.

Like everything else with the circus, the red wagon was personalized, taking its being from its current incumbent. In my early days this was dear, crusty old Mr. Hutch. Fred de Wolfe was its custodian in 1939, and the ink was black. Despite our unusually large expenditures for the new Big Top, air conditioning, and mechanization, we closed the season with a net profit of over $400,000 on a total gross income of $2,635,000.

As we gaily traversed the wide plowlands, plains, and forests of the western states, playing the pleasant, appreciative little towns and the thriving big cities, we could almost kid ourselves that, except for superficial things like automobiles, this was the same secure, happy, prosperous world our uncles had known before the Age of Terror dawned. But there was a ring around the moon.

Over in Europe the towering thunderheads of war were piling up black-purple warnings. Then they burst, sending the lightning of diving Stukas spewing death on the hot Polish plains, which are so like our own Midwest. The world was at war again.

The moment he realized war was imminent, John decided to go to Europe to get what new acts he could before the supply was cut off as it had been in Uncle John's time. The danger of submarines did not deter him, but it caused the cancellation of every ship he booked on. Flying plays havoc with his stomach, but there was nothing else for it. Arming himself with Pepto-Bismol he took off in one of the new Pan American Clippers.

In spite of the difficulties and dangers of wartime conditions, John's trip was very fruitful. He signed up a number of excellent acts. He also discovered Max Weldy and brought him to America as our costume designer. He has been in charge of The Big One's wardrobe department ever since.

The most important feature which John brought back was Alfred Court and his assistant, Damoo Dhotre of India, with a genuinely terrific wild-animal act. It consisted of three rings of mixed wild animals: lions, tigers, mountain lions, and black leopards; a Kodiak bear, Himalayan bears, polar bears, great Danes, and a wonderful white snow leopard—all mixed up together.

To my mind Alfred Court is the greatest wild-animal trainer the world has ever seen. I realize that statement sounds like circus-style talk, but it is the truth. He is none of your whip-and-pistol bully boys, pretending to stand in deadly danger while cowing the cats by sheer brutality and the alleged power of the human eye. Instead, he makes it all seem as easy and polite as an Arthur Murray class in ballroom dancing.

Court, a slender, gentle man with a fine aquiline face, trained all these animals himself, though, of course, he had assistants. It is not usually a pretty sight to see the big cats trained. If they are full-grown they are quite capable of killing their trainer, so he takes precautions. When he starts off they are all chained to their pedestals, and ropes are put around their necks to choke them down and make them obey. All sorts of other brutalities are used to force them to respect the trainer and learn their tricks. They work from fear.

But Alfred did not use such methods. He did start off with the animals collared and chained to their pedestals, but he began by making friends with them. He went into the training ring with a leather pouch full of beef cut into small morsels. He would put a piece of beef on the end of a sharp stick and offer it to the animal, whatever it was. Then he would talk to it, coming closer until he was alongside. The next thing you knew he was stroking it. Of course, it took several days to gain an animal's confidence.

Then he took it off its leash and taught it its first lesson, which was to know its own pedestal, to which it must always return after its act.

As I have repeatedly said, a wild animal is always potentially savage. Association with man is contrary to his nature, so danger is ever present. But Court, through his patience and system of reward for effort, got his animals to respect him without fear. Of course, when it came to teaching them the more involved tricks he had to use a whip.

In fact, he had the greatest whip hand I have ever seen— very strong with absolute accuracy. If an animal got out of line, he would flick that animal in the most sensitive place you can hit either a male or female. He hit, but only because the animal had made a mistake, and had to know, at that very second, that it had done wrong. However, any animal which performed properly got his reward immediately.

Because of his methods, Court's animals always looked wonderful. They were glossy and full of spirit and seemed to treat him with real affection, especially the leopards. He introduced the trick of letting a full-grown Bengal tiger leap over him while he stood holding a small baton in his upraised hands for the animal to gauge his spring by.

I am not going to bore you with a catalogue of all the wonderful people my brother brought home on that last trip to Europe. They were sufficient to keep the show going throughout the sad years when the ring of Nazi steel closed around Europe. Of course, he had great difficulty getting them all out and onto ships. With nearly every noncombatant who had the price of an ocean passage trying to get out of there, it presented quite a problem—for example, Alfred Court and his animals came on four different ships. The way John solved it was by ingenuity, charm, arrogance, bullying, and *pourboires*.

However, I will speak of the most exotic, brilliant, and difficult of all the people he brought back. She did not come for the circus or for money, but for love. Her name was Germaine Aussey.

CHAPTER XXIV

BIRD KEY

When John and I took over the circus we began to spend
our winters with Mother in Sarasota. Back in 1932 Uncle
John had suggested that she move from the small bungalow
she was occupying to the big Worcester house in Bird Key. It
was a wonderful place to live.

Bird Key was an island in the middle of Sarasota Bay only five minutes from the center of town via Uncle John's causeway. In a place where even millionaires lived in one another's back yards, the big white house stood alone, except for a gardener's cottage, in a grove of coconut palms on its twenty-two-acre island. We were careful not to spoil its natural beauty with manicured lawns and artificial planting. Except for the formal gardens near the house everything was left so wild and shaggy that the island lived up to its name. Birds of all sorts nested there. As you drove up the long drive between two rows of Australian pines a white heron might take off on laboring wings before the car, or a crane zoom over you trailing his long legs. Along its banks were flocks of wild ducks, and pelicans surveyed the harbor from the dock. The only nonindigenous characters were John's peacocks strolling on the terrace.

The house was ideal for our way of life. It had big high-ceilinged rooms that were fine for entertaining and equally good for the lively games we liked to play when we were alone. I had a fine billiard table in one of them to practice my favorite indoor sport.

Upstairs there was plenty of room for us and our guests. Ada Mae and I had a bedroom, study, and bath. Our small son, John Ringling North II, slept nearby with his nurse. Brother John added a spacious bedroom-study-dressing-room suite over the kitchen. Its walls were paneled in pecky cypress, and a terrifying picture of Gargantua hung over the fireplace, on which he could look fondly when he woke every afternoon. Mother slept in a downstairs bedroom, and the rest of the house was available for guests, of whom there were almost as many as birds.

It was to this house that John brought his bride in 1940.

Her name was Germaine Aussey. She was very beautiful in an exotic European way, aquiline features, large greenish-blue eyes, and masses of auburn hair. Her figure was quite as enticing as Marilyn Monroe's and far more graceful. She was a French movie star.

John met her in a Paris black-out on Christmas Eve 1939. For the second, and probably the last time, in his life he fell truly in love. My brother has had many beautiful fiancées whom he always managed to elude just before the nuptial knot was tied. But his engagement to Germaine was for real.

In fact, John was so much in love that he even betrayed his instinct for showmanship. When Germaine arrived in America with him the circus publicity people were entranced. They dreamed up a wonderful fantasy for the marriage of the president of The Greatest Show on Earth and the "gorgeous, glamourous, glittering French movie star."

They pictured the wedding as taking place in the center ring under a battery of spotlights while Merle Evans' brasses gave everything they had, and the wedding party entered on white horses between two rows of elephants holding American flags in their upraised trunks.

John vetoed the whole idea as undignified and unworthy of true love. He and Germaine were married very quietly in Philadelphia on May 11, 1940. Soon thereafter he sent Mother a telegram that he was bringing his bride to Bird Key. The poor girl did not know what she was getting into.

Since I was off with the circus, I cannot give an eyewitness account of Germaine's entrance into the family, although I understand it was quite dramatic, like all her entrances. However, I did participate in her first winter there. It was the maddest we ever had.

John had the house all done over, for Germaine, the columned porches gleaming with fresh white paint, everything shining and polished. The household consisted of Mother, myself, Ada Mae, young John, and his nurse; Duck and Sally Wadsworth, Sally, Jr., Ducky, Jr., and their nurse; Charles, the French chef from the Jomar; René, the Italian butler; two helpers for Charles; and Brother John, Germaine, and her personal maid. It was as explosive a mixture as anything Nobel ever cooked up in his dynamite days.

Add to it our guests and the brilliant temperamental people who were working on next year's show and who often dropped in at dinnertime to talk things over. I am not sure if they were ever all there at once, but at one time or another in 1940 and 1941 we had John Murray Anderson, putting on the production numbers; Peter Arno, designing the circus program and magazine; Max Weldy on wardrobe; Balanchine for ballet; Stravinsky, writing music for the elephant ballet; Norman Bel Geddes for engineering; Miles White for costumes; Jimmy Strook of Brooks Costume Company; and Charlie Baskerville, Heywood Broun, and Monte Woolley, just for fun. We seldom sat down less than eighteen or twenty for dinner.

Mother loved the exciting theatrical whirl, which brought back memories of the days in Baraboo with her tremendous brothers arguing over next year's show. She went to a great deal of trouble to provide marvelous meals for us. Trouble is not the right word; it was a pleasure to her, for she was a *cordon bleu* in everything but name. She would hang around the kitchen giving directions, finally ordering everyone out and cooking the meal herself. One night Charles could take it no longer and chased her out of the kitchen with a carving knife.

Meanwhile, René conceived an irresistible passion for my sister's children's governess, who reciprocated, adding to the confusion belowstairs.

Confusion above was even further compounded. While Mother gaily cooked and played bridge all day and poker all night, poor Germaine could not stand the pace. As she once confided to a columnist, "I didn't marry one man, I married a whole family."

Indeed, her European upbringing and the acclaim she had known in France completely unfitted her for a life where she was just one member of a big family of robust extroverts and their friends. We would sit around in the great hall of Bird Key in casual clothes having cocktails before our nine o'clock dinner. Down the staircase would sweep Germaine in a Paris couturier's dream of high fashion with egrets in her hair. This endeared her not at all to my forthright wife and sister.

Another difficulty was that it literally made Germaine sick to stay up late. She had been a hard-working actress, used to getting on the set at 8 A.M. and going to bed at a reasonable hour. We hardly ever went to bed until four or five in the morning. Germaine, hating cards and parlor games, would go upstairs around midnight to be kept awake all night by roars of merriment from below, while she burned with jealousy that Johnny should be enjoying himself without her.

Not that Germaine was a bad sport. She rode the circus train for three seasons with John, posing prettily for publicity pictures with lions and elephants and on our beautiful dressage horses—she rode very well—and helping to entertain his swarm of friends all over the country. But circus life was wrong for her. As she said, "Traveling seven months of the year, even though it was in John's private car, did not fit well with our private lives. It was fun in the big towns, but in the small provinces I had nothing to do except sit alone in the Jomar."

Even when they stayed together at the Ritz in New York, it was hardly any better. They were out every night at El Morocco or the Stork, with breakfast at Reuben's. When she remonstrated with her husband, he said, "Why can't I stay out late? Uncle John always did."

To expect a private life married to the head of a circus is wishful thinking.

Inevitably the marriage did not last. With the sad little comment that "it is not always fun to be married to a genius," Germaine announced their separation in 1943, the year our dear relatives got the circus away from us.

However, she was loyal to John in the face of scandal-mongers who said that she was leaving him because he was a playboy who had let the circus slip through his fingers. In answer to this nonsense she wrote a dignified letter to the press, in which she said:

Dear Sirs:

Your article of November 16 [1943] . . . is thoroughly false to say the least. . . . I want to point out that I knew exactly when Mr. John Ringling North asked me to marry him . . . what his standing was with the "wealthy" circus as well as with the "fabulous estate" of his uncle. May I say at this point that the circus was not wealthy to everybody's knowledge. On the contrary, Mr. North is the one who took it over when it was bankrupt and put it back on its own feet out of the ditch. . . . But you see, sirs, I have married Mr. North for love and not for the glamor of the circus. . . . I like this country, and the prospect of living in it with the man I loved appealed to me.

I have always admired my husband's business ability and your calling him a playboy will not change them, nor will it lessen the strength and quality of the friendship of countless important people who are our friends throughout the United States. The Ringling personnel have always been extremely nice to me during the three seasons I lived with the circus on the road. . . . I know that the great majority of them regretted John Ringling North's withdrawal from the management post. . . .

I beg to remain
Yours very truly,
GERMAINE A. NORTH
(Mrs. John Ringling North)

Though John's nocturnal habits and her incompatibility with our admittedly difficult family contributed to the breakup of his marriage with Germaine, it was primarily the fault of the circus. Had it not forced an abnormal way of life upon them, they would have had a home of their own where they might well have lived happily ever after.

I am delighted to say that Germaine is happily remarried, and living the much less exotic life of a Long Island matron. Every spring, when the circus comes to New York, John sends his Cadillac to bring her and her children to the Garden, where they sit in his center box to enjoy the show Germaine still loves.

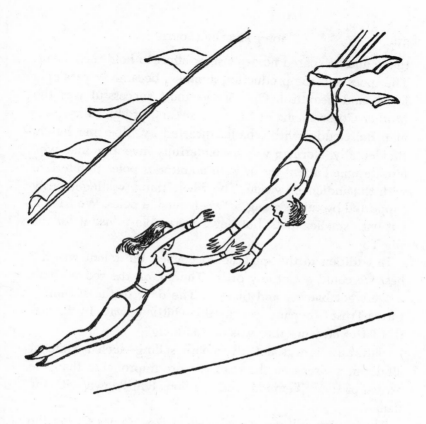

CHAPTER XXV

HELL ON WHEELS

In those last prewar years, the circus did extremely well financially. With the shadow of war hanging over them the American people once again turned to their old-time favorite form of entertainment. Whatever some critics might say about John's "razzle-dazzle" innovations, the public loved them; and he spared no expense or effort to hold their favor. The specs and the production numbers became increasingly lavish and beautiful. One of the most successful was the Mother Goose theme of the 1941 season, produced by Norman Bel Geddes with a ballet directed by Albertina Rasch. Incidentally, Norman was a wonderfully inventive man who also designed a tent for us with no interior poles to interfere with the audience's vision. The whole thing was ingeniously supported by cables slung between outside poles. We tried it out with smaller tents, but never were able to use it for the Big Top.

In addition to the splendid spectacles, the talent was the best we could get at any price. The ink on the red wagon's ledgers got blacker and blacker. The debt to the Manufacturers Trust Company was rapidly whittled away. In the end this latter circumstance was our undoing.

Naturally, it was not all smooth sailing—such a state of affairs in a circus on the road is more improbable than the arrival of the millennium and our lions lying down with the llamas.

There were still occasional flash strikes. James C. Petrillo and his musicians' union pulled one on us in 1940. When the strike was announced, John sent for Merle Evans, who had been with the circus all these years in a position of trust, and asked if out of loyalty he would not come out alone and play his famous cornet. Merle expressed his sympathy but said, "What can I do?" When the fateful hour came there was no band and no Merle either.

But we had not been asleep at the switch. We had made arrangements for recording all our music. We played the rest of the season to canned music. It saved the circus about $50,000.

The next year we made an agreement with Petrillo, and the band came back with Merle as musical director. But John never forgave Merle for what the bandmaster felt was loyalty to his colleagues but what my brother considered treason to the circus.

On the whole, our labor relations were excellent. What troubled us most was the manpower shortage as America became ever more deeply engaged in building her defenses against the slow, irresistible approach of war. After the draft started and we were more and more shorthanded, I did a great deal of physical work myself, more to set an example to the men than because one man's efforts at stake setting, for instance, would make much difference.

This stood me in good stead in 1942, when between the matinee and the evening show the bull men threatened to strike. John was in New York planning next year's show and I had the train. So I thought I should do what I could to reverse the situation. I asked the bosses to have all the workingmen called together in the menagerie top. They had seen their vice-president working side by side with them, so it was not like someone shooting off his mouth who did not know anything about their problems. Five or six hundred men gathered inside the tent. I climbed on one of the big piles of baled hay stacked up for the stock. I have never been good at public addresses, but this was an emergency.

As I started to speak the professional agitators who were stirring the men up began to heckle me. I was feeling lost and rattled when an unexpected ally turned up. He was the huge Negro boss of the horse tops, who had been with us for many years. His name was Blue, because he was so black that he looked blue.

Seeing my distress, Blue stood up. He loomed gigantic among the smaller men and he had a great iron stake in his hand. He waved it gently and spoke in a soft voice. "You all had better shut up and listen to Mr. Buddy!" he said.

They shut up. I made no promises except that if they would

move the show that night and set it up at the next town, I
would meet with their representatives in the morning and
try to work out their grievances. I think they knew I wished
them well and that I appreciated the loyalty they had shown
under increasingly difficult conditions. They roared acceptance of my offer. The next day I sat down with them and
negotiated a moderate wage increase. That was the last labor
trouble we had that year.

Being shorthanded, we tried harder than ever to maintain
safety practices. But in anything like the circus, with its constant movement, the trains, and the ordered confusion on the
lot—trucks moving in and out, tractors towing wagons and
cages around in daylight and darkness—accidents were almost
inevitable. Because it was well ordered and well organized
they were kept to a minimum, but they did occur.

For example, there were forty quarter poles, each weighing
over six hundred pounds, to be set up and taken down every
day. One night a lowering rope broke and a big quarter pole
fell on poor old Cigarette Bill, a character who had been with
the circus for many years, whom we all liked and respected.
Les Thomas, our seat boss, was also once nearly killed by a
falling quarter pole.

Whenever it was possible to save a life we spared no expense. In Oklahoma one of our young fellows, named Pat
Graham, was an innocent bystander in a barroom shooting.
He was hit by a bullet that went right through his chest. He
was taken to a local hospital and I was notified. I grabbed
a circus car and rushed there only to be told by the doctor
in residence that it was only a question of time. There was
nothing to be done because Pat had an internal hemorrhage.

"Have you given him blood transfusions?" I asked.

"No, we haven't," the doctor said.

"Why the hell not?"

"It would be a waste of blood," he answered. "We can't stop the internal bleeding."

I had just read an article in *Time* magazine about a new drug that caused quick coagulation of blood. I asked if they had any, and the doctor said yes but he did not think it would work in this case.

"You must try everything," I said.

"Well, who's going to pay for it?" the doctor asked.

I realized then that I was up against the old prejudice and distrust of circus people. Evidently even yet they were regarded as not quite human. In a rage I pledged the credit of Ringling Brothers, and my chauffeur and I volunteered our blood for the transfusion. Graham's life was saved.

Sudden windstorms were always a menace to our acres of canvas. Once at Chattanooga we were tearing down in near-tornado winds. We dropped the Big Top, and the men rushed from the sides along the lines of lacing undoing them so the canvas would be rolled up. This night two canvas hands were on the center section, which was two hundred feet long and sixty feet wide. As they started unlacing it the wind tore underneath, ballooning the great tent and hurling the men high in the air. Down they came, and up again as though tossed in a gigantic blanket while canvas thundered and cracked with loud reports and the gale howled through the rigging like an old square-rigger taken aback.

The Big Top gang just stood there laughing hilariously at those doll-like figures flying into the air to be caught on the billowing canvas and tossed up again. But I knew it was not funny. If the wind suddenly dropped, the poor boys might fall sixty or seventy feet to the ground. Shouting for the men to join me, I laid hold of a side rope. With dozens of hands hauling on the ropes, we brought the section down and landed our men unhurt.

That same night a cloudburst hit us, and the lot was

flooded. The wagons were mired to their axles, but we had to get moving. If one tractor failed to budge them we teamed up two or three or four. In the old days I have seen sixty horses hitched to one wagon and the teamsters cracking their bull whips to get them heaving in unison. Ordinary vehicles would pull apart under such a strain, but Bill Yeske built our wagons to take it.

I was never in a serious train wreck, though I well know how terrible that could be. Sometimes, however, when the train made an emergency stop the wagons on the flats would break loose from their chocks and roll off. Our men—and the "trailers" sneaking rides on the train—might be sleeping under them in spite of our warnings. Three of them were killed in one such stop in South Carolina.

Nor could we always prevent accidents among the performers. The thrill of watching men and women defy death is a traditional titillation for a circus audience, and there are plenty of performers willing to gratify this appetite. In fact, these professional daredevils resent safety precautions. Recently, when New York State law forced us to put a safety net under Harold Alzana while he performed his perilous feats on a wire stretched sixty feet high in the roof of the Garden, he was furious. "You're spoiling my act," he complained bitterly.

The menagerie was always liable to accidents. Sometimes it was sudden jungle madness, as when, in 1940, one of Alfred Court's "friendly" cats attacked him, and in the roaring, spitting rhubarb that ensued in the big cage, his beautiful snow leopard was accidently killed. That same year eleven seals got loaded by mistake in a different section from their trainer. Without anyone to keep them wetted down, they all died of dehydration. A little later four polar bears suffocated because the attendant forgot to open the ventilators of their car in very hot weather.

These were minor disasters. But because of their helplessness, a painful accident to one of our animals affected me more profoundly, perhaps, than the injury of a human being who knew and willingly accepted the risks of our business. In this connection, the most sickening sight I ever beheld in peacetime occurred on August 4, 1942.

We almost decided not to send the show out that year. Pearl Harbor and the entry of the United States into the war made the circus seem pretty frivolous. In addition, we did not see how we could recruit the necessary workers and we were well aware that an undermanned show was dangerous.

In this situation we sounded out opinion in Washington as to the wisdom of continuing. It was almost unanimously in favor of it as a morale builder in a time of sorrow and public uncertainty. As a result of these discussions we issued a statement:

"The Management of Ringling Brothers–Barnum & Bailey Circus thinks it timely and fitting to state its policy and hopes for the future at this critical period in our national history. Through letters from many individuals, wide editorial comment . . . and direct expressions from the country's Army, Navy, and political leaders, it has been made clear that the public wants The Greatest Show on Earth to carry on during wartime. . . . President Roosevelt personally has expressed his appreciation of the fact that the Show is Going On. . . ."

We then described the co-operation of draft boards and the Selective Service System in Washington in deferring key personnel; and the War Production Board's grants of priorities for necessary materials. We ended by expressing "our hope that our circus will continue just as our American Way of Life certainly will!–John and Henry Ringling North."

As key personnel, I was, of course, deferred; but I did not feel that I was quite that essential, so I enlisted in the Navy in the spring of 1942. However, the authorities did not see fit to call me for active duty until January 1943.

We put on one of our greatest shows that year. It was staged by John Murray Anderson and designed by Norman Bel Geddes. We had the elephant ballet with Stravinsky music and Balanchine choreography. Even the programs were special, enlivened by Peter Arno's witty cartoons.

From the point of view of attendance it was a banner year. Just as had been foreseen, the public flocked to the circus to find brief forgetfulness from grinding work and the terrible anxiety for their menfolk going overseas. From the point of view of operating a railroad show it was hell on wheels.

There was never enough of anything. Every question of supply was a crisis; every move we made, which, of course, happened almost every day, was bedeviled by lack of manpower and shortage of equipment on the hard-pressed railroads. And every performance was a critical risk.

My troubles began early. The first of them was over George Smith, our general manager. George was an old circus hand and a dear friend who knew all the intricate technicalities of moving the circus army. But infirmities gradually overcame him, and he kept getting worse. Finally it reached a point where he could no longer handle the show.

We were on our way from Sarasota to New York with the great, long trains and had just reached the Jersey terminal, where we had to transfer the coaches and equipment to railroad ferries to get across the Hudson. It became evident to me that George was in no condition to handle that complicated operation and get the show set up in the Garden. So I sent for Arthur Concello and asked him if he thought he could take over.

Arthur, who is a confident fellow, said, "I am sure I can."

"All right," I said, "you've got the job."

That is how the great aerialist became general manager of

Ringling Brothers—Barnum & Bailey Combined Shows. Today he is executive director and a member of the board. It may seem strange to give a flier a position of such great executive responsibility, but Arthur is an extraordinary man. Even when he was still very young, he was ambitious to become part of the management of the circus. He was interested in everything about it. He stayed on the lot late and got there early in the morning, studying all the various operations. He realized even then that the life of a flier cannot last long; for even if he escapes serious injury there is no escaping the slowdown of age.

From 1938 on, John and I had watched the progress of this dynamic Concello, and when the moment came I gave him the post for which he had been fitting himself all those years. He performed wonderfully well in it. Later he threw his considerable fortune into the pot to help refinance the circus in one of our periodical fiscal crises.

One of the things we feared most in 1942 was fire. Although fireproof canvas had been invented, the government needed an absolute priority of it. The Big Top was a compromise flame-resistant canvas that leaked. The other tents were the old-fashioned kind, waterproofed with a solution of paraffin and benzene. Baked in the blazing prairie sun they were terribly inflammable. We countered the danger by choosing lots with an ample water supply and surrounding the Big Top with our own fire-fighting equipment, fully manned with engines running. Nevertheless, our fears were tragically justified.

On the soft and sunny morning of August 4, 1942, our tents were pitched on a lakeside lot in Cleveland, Ohio, for a five-day stand. At eleven-thirty that morning the menagerie top suddenly flashed into fire. We never knew how it happened. One moment it was standing there normally in the sunshine, and the next it was a roaring inferno of flames hundreds of feet high. Three minutes later there was nothing left but charred, tottering poles, smoking bits of canvas, still-burning cages, and a wild confusion of frantic, tortured animals.

Men rushed into the ruins through the smoke and the horrible stench of burning flesh to get the animals out. Walter McClain, boss of the bull men, shouted an order to his elephants. They pulled up their stakes and paraded out trunk to tail. But what a fearful sight they were! In some cases their flesh was peeling off in long sheets and their thin, floppy ears were seared completely off.

The camels would not move at all, but lay there looking calmly at us as they died. We snaked some of them out with tractors and saved their lives. Badly burned zebras were running wild all over the place. Giraffes galloped about frantic with fear. Dear old Edith jumped the fence and ran away down the avenue. We found her four hours later quite unhurt.

Many of the caged animals were cooked by the burning straw of their bedding. Our wonderful veterinary, Dr. J. Y. Henderson, borrowed a pistol from a policeman and ran through the ruins shooting those suffering creatures whose cases were hopeless. The most terrible thing was that they suffered and died in utter silence with their eyes full of pain and wonder.

To treat the animals who had a chance for life, Doc Henderson filled spray guns with a healing preparation called Foille and set men to spraying every creature in sight. He put ladders against the sides of the elephants and had the bull men with big paint brushes slathering Foille all over them. In that way many were saved.

The matinee was canceled that day because everybody was taking care of the animals. But we gave the evening performance to a packed house. It may appear heartless, but it was in the cherished tradition of the circus.

When we came to count our losses the toll was terrible. Sixty-five animals died of burns—4 elephants, 12 zebras, 2 giraffes, 13 camels, an ostrich, 4 lions, 3 tigers, 4 Pinzgavens, 3 pumas, 16 monkeys, 2 black bucks, and a sacred cow from India.

Not one human being was injured. All John and I could think of was "Thank God it wasn't the Big Top!"

CHAPTER XXVI

THE HARTFORD FIRE

In spite of our difficulties the 1942 season was the best we
have ever had. The circus netted over $900,000 before taxes.
This was a good thing and a bad thing; good, because it re-
established the circus as a going institution and vindicated
John's management; bad, because our dear relatives felt they
no longer needed John.

At the end of the season John and I decided that no matter how profitable it might be we were not going to take the show out again in wartime—I would be in the Navy in any event. We had run it with as few as 350 workers and we needed 800 to do it right. This resulted in inefficiency, the stress and strain of overwork, and, most important of all, danger to the public. The fire in the menagerie top was a terrible portent. In all its fifty-nine seasons our circus had never killed a single customer. We would not risk breaking that wonderful record.

We knew we would have a difficult time convincing Edith and Aubrey Ringling, who still held 63 per cent of the stock between them, that it was necessary to close the circus for the duration of the war. You may recall that under the agreement of 1937 John was to have control of the show for five years or until the note to the Manufacturers Trust Company was paid off. The five years was almost up, and the note had been liquidated, partly with $450,000 in bonds which the federal government had released to the John Ringling Estate and partly from the earnings of the circus. For the first time in many years, Ringling Brothers paid dividends in 1941 and 1942.

Late in 1941, anticipating the end of the trust agreement, Aunt Edith and Cousin Aubrey had gotten together and signed a mutal contract to vote their majority stock together. In the event that they could not agree on how to vote it, their lawyer, Karl D. Loos, was to decide between them. This was known as The Ladies' Agreement. Its purpose was to kick John and me out of the management of Ringling Brothers.

We were perfectly aware of this mobilization of strength against us. John made the first move in the summer of 1942. He wrote to Aunt Edith and Cousin Aubrey asking if they would sell him enough of their circus stock to give him 51 per cent. They refused, as he expected.

The showdown meeting of the board of directors was called for January 1943. At that time it consisted of, on our side:

John Ringling North, president, Henry Ringling North, vice-president, and George Woods.

On the ladies' side were Robert Ringling, Sr., vice-president, Edith C. Ringling, vice-president, and Aubrey B. Ringling, vice-president.

Holding the balance of power was William P. Dunn, Jr., secretary and treasurer.

John had prepared for the meeting very carefully. In his speech to the board he described the difficulties and dangers of the past year's operation, dwelling heavily on the fire hazard. He then offered two carefully thought-out alternatives. The first was to offer to run the circus for the United States Government for the duration of the war as a nonprofit national institution, playing wherever it was sent, especially for the benefit of servicemen. He had reason to believe that President Roosevelt would accept the offer. If the circus came under government sponsorship it would receive much higher priorities, enabling it to get fireproof canvas and operate safely.

John's second alternative was to keep the circus in Winter Quarters on a caretaker basis for the duration. He pointed out that the new excess-profits tax made it impossible for the circus to make any real money. Moreover, as the result of the carry-back and carry-over provisions of the tax law, Ringling Brothers could keep a much larger percentage of recent earnings and possible future earnings. The circus could therefore remain in Winter Quarters for two and a half years without suffering any serious loss. The $1,000,000 which it had in the bank would be ample to see it through. At this point he rested his case.

There ensued a sneering silence. Then the ladies voiced

disgust with John's ideas and his management. Robert naturally went along with his mother.

Aunt Edith was especially implacable. Stout, grim-faced, with her hat riding high on her white hair, she was a commanding personality. In many ways she was a very lovable lady; but in other ways not so lovable. I believe she disliked John because his character resembled Uncle John's, whom she could not abide. She resented my brother's unspoken attitude that "I've saved the circus and it's mine." Finally, she had a burning ambition to make her son Robert president of the circus.

There was always a lot of jealousy in the distaff side of the Ringling family. If the brothers had not had their strong German love of family to bind them together, and if they had ever listened to their various wives, I am sure they would never have stayed together in harmony all those years. This is one of the reasons why I believe that it was no wish of Robert's that got him into the circus business, but his mother's ambition.

Aubrey Ringling, thin-faced and tense, peering rather nervously at the other directors through her rimless spectacles, was in a different position. In addition, Aubrey was in love with that same James A. Haley whom John had engaged to audit the estate. It seems probable that she, too, was ambitious —for her future husband. She married Jim Haley in 1943, and he became first vice-president and assistant to the president of Ringling Brothers.

After the noisy argument the voting went as expected—up to a point. My brother and I and George Woods voted to accept John's proposal; Robert and the two ladies voted against it. Then, to our shocked surprise, Bill Dunn voted to continue operating the circus. Until then he had always thrown his deciding vote to us. Why he suddenly shifted puzzled and saddened us at the time, though I can now understand his reasons.

Having no actual experience in running a circus, Dunn could not envision the difficulties and dangers of operating it shorthanded. He probably thought John was overstating them. He was basically a financial man, being a vicepresident of the Manufacturers Trust, and as such, could see no sense in closing up a profitable operation. Especially since he knew that by the time the board met again in April the voting trust would have ended and the ladies would be able to elect anybody they chose.

As soon as the vote was recorded John resigned, his black eyes snapping with anger. Robert Ringling was elected president of Ringling Brothers–Barnum & Bailey Combined Shows.

As everybody had foreseen, at the stockholders' meeting in April the ladies elected five of the seven directors. My brother John and George Woods continued as minority directors with no power to control policy. I was off to the wars. The officers of the company were Robert Ringling, president, and James A. Haley, first vice-president and assistant to the president (my old spot). Bill Dunn continued as treasurer.

Thus the management of The Greatest Show on Earth was entrusted to Robert, who had made his career in opera; a certified public accountant who had never ridden a circus train; a banker; and to two matriarchs who actually owned control of it.

(Now, for three years, everything I write is hearsay—backed by documents—for I was overseas. My war memories have no place in this book. I will only say that, not caring for the desk job the Navy had in store for me, I wangled my way into the OSS and was engaged in some exciting cloak-and-dagger work, which included participation in the African, Italian, and Normandy campaigns and a brief appearance at the Battle of the Bulge. On the whole I found it more agreeable to be shot at by the Nazis than sniped at by my relatives.)

Naturally Robert Ringling's first acts as president of the circus were to get rid of two of our top men. Leonard Bisco was replaced by Karl Loos as legal counsel, and George Smith returned as general manager, replacing Concello, who, however, continued to stage the aerial acts.

George Smith had pulled himself together. In the summer of 1943 he was loaned to the Army. Because of his vast experience with the circus, he successfully directed the train movements of hundreds of thousands of troops across the United States to ports of embarkation. In 1944 he returned to the circus, to his lasting regret.

Robert Ringling's first season as president was a qualified success. The Big One made big money. However, he set up a smaller, European-type circus called "Spangles" to play in the Garden, which was a dismal flop. In spite of this there was a considerable over-all profit.

A great deal was made in the circus publicity of the return of a "real" Ringling to head the show. The circus program featured a photograph of Robert beneath the famous picture of the five mustachioed brothers. The caption was:

RINGLINGS ALL

A Ringling son has taken his rightful place in the circus sun.

The mantle of the Ringling Brothers, the famous founders of the Ringling Circus, has been draped on the broad shoulders of Robert Ringling, son of the late Charles Ringling, one of the most brilliant showmen that ever lived.

Raised with the circus under the tutelage of his illustrious father, Robert knows the Big Show inside out. . . . His father and uncles (see picture), . . . the most powerful and successful group of amusement purveyors in the world, have a worthy scion.

In Robert Ringling the circus dynasty lives on as they would have it.

Even in a book as outspoken as this one, Brother John's comments on this flimflammery are unprintable.

The season of 1944 started well for the circus. As usual, it made a nice profit in the Garden. On the road it was playing to near-capacity audiences. However, the manpower problem had become even more acute. This was the very peak of the war effort—D Day and our armies pouring into Normandy, and the great steppingstone advance through the Pacific islands toward Japan. There was virtually no such thing as unemployment. What men could be recruited as razorbacks and roustabouts were almost unemployable except for a few faithful old-timers.

Nevertheless, Robert Ringling was satisfied with the results, and sure that the decision to carry on the show had been a wise one. However, he was not in good health, and after a bit, he went to his home in Illinois, leaving Jim Haley in command of the train.

On July 6, 1944, the circus was playing Hartford, Connecticut. The forty-one tents stood on a lot close to town. It was admirably situated for accessibility; but there were only two fire hydrants on it. Since our fire-resistant Big Top had proved to be unsatisfactorily waterproofed, the new management had abandoned it in favor of the old paraffin-benzene-treated canvas, which was admittedly more watertight. On that day boss canvasman Leonard Aylesworth was in Evanston conferring with Robert Ringling.

The standing rule was that during the performance tractors with the circus' fire-fighting equipment were to be marshaled outside the tent with engines turning. For some reason tractor boss David Blanchfield had not ordered them into position. Fire extinguishers were normally placed under the seats. Because the show was so shorthanded, they had not been unloaded from the train at Hartford.

It was a typical July day, hot and muggy with thunder over the horizon. Because of the threatening storm George Smith and Fred Bradna wisely decided to shortchange the customers. Three of the opening displays were canceled.

Despite the unpleasant weather the people of Hartford were in a holiday mood. Many of them had taken a long Fourth-of-July weekend. It was a wonderful opportunity to take the children to the circus. There were eight thousand people in the tent when the opening spec began its triumphant procession around the arena.

After the spec the clowns kept the kids roaring with laughter while the cage was rigged for Alfred Court's wild-animal act, which had been moved back from first to sixth place that year. A runway of steel mesh through which the cats entered and left the cage led across the back hippodrome track, which was partially blocked while it was in place.

In the condensed schedule decided upon, the Wallendas followed the clowns with their tremendously dangerous high-wire act. The show had now been running for about twenty minutes.

Photographer Dick Miller was standing near the end of Clown Alley looking up at the Wallendas. He saw a tiny spurt of flame running up a guy rope and yelled. A policeman on duty outside noticed a circle of flame "like the glowing end of a cigarette" burning the roof of the Big Top. It seemed to widen slowly. "Then it suddenly burst through in a big common flame and went roaring all around the place." It was, in fact, like the terrible flash of billowing fire when a gasoline tank bursts.

Inside the tent Fred Bradna saw smoke at the main entrance. His shrill whistle stopped the Wallendas in mid-air.
They came sliding down the guy wires. Fred yelled to Merle
Evans. Somebody made an announcement over the public-
address system asking the audience to leave quickly, and the
band burst into "The Stars and Stripes Forever," the traditional circus signal of disaster. That was the last moment of
order. Complete chaos ensued.

With sun-baked canvas roaring in hundred-foot flames
above them, the crowd went crazy. They stormed toward the
main entrance toward the fire, and piled up against that fatal
animal chute. Thousands more pushed behind, trampling
every small thing in their way, building up tremendous pressures that crushed and ground the life out of those in front.
Others saved themselves by crawling out under the sides of
the tent. Many tried to crawl back again to save beloved
children lost in that first blind panic.

Inside the tent performers and roustabouts were heroically
saving lives. Fred Bradna, with his hair aflame, dragged eleven
children out of "the monstrous pile in front of the animal
chute" and shoved them to safety. Dick Miller, who gave the
first warning, rescued many more. Countless others performed
acts of heroism.

But thousands of people stood trapped and helpless like
cattle packed in a slaughterhouse pen while the holocaust
above their heads made the interior of the tent a furnace. To
the helpless onlookers, watching the soaring, roaring flames
and black billowing clouds of smoke, it seemed impossible
that anyone could still be alive in that inferno. After eight or
ten minutes the great main poles began to waver. Moaning in
anguish, people watched them totter and crash down like tall
pines in a forest fire; down in fountains of sparks bringing the
remnants of burning canvas upon the heads of those within.

Five minutes later it was all over. Where the Big Top had

stood was a devastated oblong of blackened earth, with Court's great cage rising crazily above it, and against that fatal chute, a ghastly heap of humanity piled four and five deep. The living were writhing under the dead. And beneath them again were the small crushed bodies of the kids who had come to see the circus.

I read about the fire in the *Stars and Stripes* at an OSS advance base in Normandy. I have no words to describe my sickened reaction—the "horrors of war" paled by comparison. One hundred and sixty-eight persons were killed—more than half of them children. Four hundred and eighty-seven were badly injured.

John got the news in New York and immediately telephoned Robert offering to help in any possible way. He was curtly refused. Robert was in a state of shock, from which he never completely recovered. Poor Jim Haley bore the brunt of the storm. That night he, George Smith, David Blanchfield, seat boss James Caley, and lighting boss Edward R. Versteeg were arrested and charged with involuntary manslaughter. A warrant was served on Leonard Aylesworth when he reached Hartford.

Before the scorched ground was cool the damage suits began. Attachments were slapped on all that was left of the circus. It was evident that the claims would run into millions. The liability insurance carried by the circus was only $500,-000. In this situation the sensible thing was to let Ringling Brothers go into bankruptcy and then buy it back at auction.

I am proud to say we did no such thing. For once our entire family was in agreement that, cost what it might, our circus would pay its just debts. Our lawyer spoke for all of us when he said, "The Ringling family is not interested in escaping liability. It wants to help and it wants to carry on."

In the crisis Jim Haley acted with prompt decisiveness. The

first step was obviously to get the circus on the road again
as rapidly as possible or nobody would get anything. Bonds
were promptly posted to secure the release of the attachments
—the officers were out on bail. The circus then retired to
Winter Quarters and reorganized. It went out again in August,
playing in stadia and ball parks without a Big Top, and ended
the season with a small operating profit.

Meanwhile circus lawyer Karl Loos called in an eminent
colleague, Daniel Gordon Judge of Engel, Judge and Miller,
to attempt to work out a plan for paying the claims. In con-
sultation with dozens of lawyers representing the claimants
and the Hartford Bar Association, he was able to negotiate
the arrangement known as The Hartford Arbitration Agreement. Under it the circus accepted full responsibility for
damages and left it up to a local arbitration board to decide
what was to be paid. The circus was then to pay a "receiver,"
out of earnings, the amounts necessary to pay off these claims.
The circus further agreed not to enter into any unusual expenses during the term of the agreement and to pay every
cent of net profit to the claimants.

At first John thought this was a bad deal, but he afterward
changed his mind. Eventually the circus paid out nearly
$5,000,000 in damages.

A condition of the circus' assuming these vast liabilities was
a "gentleman's agreement" that Haley, Smith, and the others
would not be sent to jail. However, the Connecticut officials
were not that gentlemanly. I suppose public outcry for
vengeance was too great for politicians to ignore it. Haley,
Smith, Aylesworth, Caley, Versteeg, and Blanchfield were all
brought to trial late in 1944. Robert Ringling was not in Connecticut at the time of the fire and did not go there.

When the trial began, the defendants threw themselves on
the mercy of the court. Counsel for the defense claimed that
Haley and the others were indispensable for keeping the

circus running so that it could earn the money to pay the damage claims. Nevertheless, they were sentenced to jail terms but allowed to go to Sarasota to get the show on the road.

In April 1945 they all returned to Hartford to surrender to Judge Shea. Their counsel had entered motions for suspension of the sentences, again on the grounds of indispensability. They had brought Robert Ringling on an interstate subpoena to testify on their behalf. Robert made a poor witness. He did, indeed, testify that circus operation would be "desperately jeopardized" without these men. All he said about Jim Haley was "He is a great help to me."

My brother had also been subpoenaed. He was far from unwilling. He gladly testified to his extremely unfavorable opinion of the management of the circus—he was beginning suit against Robert and Jim Haley for mismanagement. When asked if he considered "that the accused were indispensable to the running of the circus," he said that none of them was.

Counsel for the defense attacked John's testimony on the grounds that he was anxious to regain control of the circus—which he was—and implied that he thought himself the indispensable man—which he did.

However, Judge Shea agreed with John. Jim Haley got a year and a day. The others were given more or less severe sentences. Only Blanchfield got off. He had testified that he was not indispensable and Judge Shea commended him as "the only one who told the truth."

CHAPTER XXVII

HOW JOHN WON THE CIRCUS

Never for one moment had John stopped trying to regain
control of the circus—that was his Everest, his Promised Land.
His first move was a very canny one. He went to see Jim
Haley in jail in Connecticut.

At first Haley absolutely refused to see him. John persisted and Haley finally agreed to talk to him if the warden were present.

When the two men met in the warden's office of the jail, Haley naturally blew his top about John's testimony. My brother allowed him to let off steam for a while. Finally he said, "Now Jim, I was under oath to tell the whole truth. Everybody knew damn well I didn't think you were indispensable. What could I say?"

Haley glumly admitted that John could not vouch for him. Then with real anger he started to talk about Robert Ringling. Jim thought that the president of Ringling Brothers had let him down; that he was interested only in saving his own skin. He believed that had Robert's testimony been more forcefully in his favor he would have been given a suspended sentence.

Until then John had thought that calling on Jim Haley was a futile gesture, which he made only because he would leave no stone unturned to regain the circus.

I came home from the wars in the summer of 1945, expecting to be reassigned to the Pacific. Then came the Bomb and V-J Day. I became a civilian again. The first thing I did was to try to get some sort of work with the circus—the only thing I was fitted to do. I was turned down cold. But from here on I was in the thick of things.

Meanwhile John was trying to see Aubrey Haley. He failed. It appeared that Aubrey had an understanding with Robert that neither would talk to John without the other present. John thought that this was due less to hostility on Aubrey's part than as a legal precaution because of his suit against them all for mismanagement of the circus, which was progressing favorably.

On Christmas Eve 1945 Jim Haley was released from jail. He had a deep sense of disgrace and dreaded returning to Sarasota. His fears were unjustified. His loyal friends there

were convinced that he had unjustly taken the rap. They
canceled a banquet for General Jonathan Wainwright, and
instead, gave Jim a royal welcome home. A few years later he
was elected United States Congressman from that district, a
position he still holds.

Two extraordinary things happened in the spring of 1946.
First Aubrey sent for me. When I met her in Washington,
D.C., she said, "How would you like to be president of the
circus? I think I could get the others to agree if you want it."

I was dumfounded. Then my brain began to work. "I'm
awfully flattered by your confidence, Aubrey," I said, "but I
wouldn't be a good choice for you. You want me to help you
get rid of John. The first thing I'd do as president would be
to turn the operation over to John, who has a lot more ability
than I have."

That was that.

Then John's friend Karl Bickel came to him and said that
Haley was still very bitter against Robert, who had never gone
to see him in jail or even written to him. Bickel indicated that
Haley would make a deal that would put John back running
the circus. There were, however, two conditions. The first
was that Haley was to be president of Ringling Brothers. The
second was that I was to have nothing to do with the show.
Haley was still brooding about a caustic letter I had written
him from North Africa. This was a weird switch from my talk
with Aubrey.

Just about then Haley and Robert had a real dingdong
blazing row. Red-eyed with anger, Haley sent for John and
told him that he wanted to be president of the circus for only
one year, as a sort of vindication; that he wanted to pay the
Hartford debt and then go fishing. John agreed to these
conditions provided he could run the show.

In 1946 the stockholders' meeting again took place in

April. This time it was Aunt Edith and Robert who got the unpleasant surprise. Aubrey, who was ill—either really or diplomatically—was not present. Jim Haley, holding her proxy, voted her stock with Brother John. What an unholy row ensued! Robert and Edith in outraged voices demanded that the stock be voted in accordance with The Ladies' Agreement. The arbitrator, Karl Loos, ruled that this must be done. Jim Haley told Loos where to go and voted with John. A new board of directors was elected, which named Haley president and John Ringling North executive vice-president of Ringling Brothers–Barnum & Bailey Combined Shows.

John and Jim Haley went over to Madison Square Garden, where the circus was playing, and took over. When Robert and Bill Dunn came in stating that the election was illegal and demanding their rights as president and treasurer, they were politely but firmly ejected.

So John once more came into control of his beloved circus. But for how long? He was in the saddle by courtesy of Jim and Aubrey Haley, who had voted against him before. Their right to vote their stock for him was challenged by Edith and Robert suing in Delaware under The Ladies' Agreement. Three hundred shares of the stock John had voted himself belonged to the estate of John Ringling. His own holding was still only seventy shares, a measly 7 per cent of the total. In plain fact, his position was more precarious than that of the Wallendas balancing a human pyramid on a bicycle traversing a sixty-foot-high wire with no net.

John's authoritarian ways did not sit well with Haley. It soon began to appear that he was not content to be president in name only. Some heated arguments developed over policy. In spite of this the circus had a very good season. There were no profits taxes to pay because there were no profits—all the net earnings went to the victims of the Hartford fire. At the end of the 1946 season we paid over $1,000,000 to the receiver on their behalf.

But John was involved in more lawsuits than a hyena has fleas. Robert was suing in New York for his salary as president; Edith in Delaware to declare the April election void. John, in turn, was suing them and the Haleys for $5,000,000 damages for mismanagement of the circus at the time of the fire. Also, the John Ringling Estate was not yet settled. The federal government, the state of Florida, and a lot of private individuals were suing it and John as executor.

In comparing John with the Wallendas I may have erred. He was more like a juggler trying to keep a sixty-four-piece dinner service in the air while standing on his head. How he ever kept it all straight in his mind I do not know.

Ringling Brothers had been chartered in Delaware. Aunt Edith's suit to declare the April election void came to trial there in the fall of 1946. The lower court held in her favor. So Haley and John were thrown out and Robert came back as president—for three weeks. John appealed the case and got an injunction temporarily reinstating Haley and himself.

At this point poor Robert, who I am convinced had never really wanted any part of this family squabble, had a stroke.

John went off to Europe to sign new acts for the circus.

Nineteen forty-seven was the year of decision. It began very badly with a flare-up between John and Haley. The latter wanted him to fire John Murray Anderson as producer of the show. John liked Anderson and thought that he made a great contribution to the beauty of the circus. In the course of the argument my brother said, "Anderson needn't worry you, Jim. After all, I'm going to be president of the circus this year."

"The hell you are!" said Haley.

There went John's understanding that he was to succeed Haley at the end of a year. John immediately tried to induce

Aubrey and Jim to sell him 140 shares of their Ringling Brothers stock, which, added to the 70 shares he owned and the 300 shares he controlled through the John Ringling Estate, would give him control of the circus with 51 per cent of the total stock. They refused to do so. Instead, Haley told Robert's son, young Jim Ringling, who was serving his apprenticeship with the circus, to write to his father that he, Haley, was ready to bounce John.

Meanwhile, Daniel Judge had replaced Loos as adviser to Aunt Edith and Robert. Robert, recovering from his stroke, had lost all desire to run the circus. Therefore, Judge was faced with the problem of choosing between Haley and John. This was a splendid opening for John's "divide and rule" policy.

John decided to leave the circus train at Dallas and fly to New York. Evidently Jim Haley had an unhappy prevision of a triple cross. At the airport he said to John, "Don't make a deal with your Aunt Edith!"

Of course, that is exactly what John did. In New York he called on Mr. Judge, with whom he had a long discussion. At their next meeting Leonard Bisco was also present. In these meetings John had tremendous leverage because his mismanagement suit for $5,000,000 had won in the lower courts and was being appealed. He had no desire to wreck the circus or impoverish Aunt Edith and Robert. He only wanted to run the show.

In these circumstances an accord was soon arrived at. All suits were dropped. John personally agreed to pay Robert $7500 as partial compensation for his loss of salary as president, and Robert was to be chairman of the board at a nice salary. In return, he and Aunt Edith formally agreed to vote with John.

When they heard of this new alliance, the Haleys knew they had been outmaneuvered. Almost immediately they agreed to sell their stock at a fair price to John and Robert. Robert agreed to buy 175 shares for $243,055.55, giving him and Aunt Edith a total of 490 shares, or 49 per cent. John agreed to pay $194,444.45 for 140 shares, which with the 370 shares he already voted gave him 510 shares, or 51 per cent. The Haleys thus received $437,500, which in view of the tremendous fire claims still outstanding against the circus was more than fair.

The only thing wrong with this deal was that John did not have $194,444.45. He had to raise it somewhere in a hurry. Eventually John and our mother put up $100,000. He raised the rest with the help of his favorite flier, general manager, and true friend, Arthur Concello.

If the affairs of the circus seem complicated, they were like the child's game of musical chairs compared to the intricacies of the settling of Uncle John's estate, which was proceeding simultaneously. Although John and Mother were performing all the duties of executors of Uncle John's will, their right to do so was not finally settled until July 22, 1947. Meanwhile, throughout the years most of the claims against the estate had been settled very advantageously to it. As I have said, the federal government's tax claim for $13,500,000 was settled in 1946 for $850,000.

However, as some suits were settled new ones cropped up. About 1945 the state of Florida suddenly sued the executors and trustees on the ground that the museum and pictures were not being properly cared for. John proposed the idea to his fellow trustees, Randolph Wadsworth and myself, that we give it outright to the state, who would then be responsible for it. We agreed and wrote to Governor Caldwell of Florida making the offer. He referred our letter to former Governor Frank Carleton, who was prosecuting the suit against us. Carleton wrote us, "I am glad you have reached this conclusion. I am sure it is to the best interests of all." He suggested February 9, 1946, would be a good day for the transfer.

The proposal was an obvious solution of the problems. The state officials did not wake up to the disadvantages until the deed was done.

John was taking no chances on their changing their minds. He set the presentation up in a blaze of publicity, and on the appointed day he and Mother and I formally and with lots of pictures gave Florida the museum, Ca' d'Zan, and the stock of the Rembrandt Corporation, which owned the pictures.

Thus Florida now owned the whole works, but as yet there was no trust fund to maintain it. The officials suddenly realized that they had assumed a heavy financial responsibility. It made them awfully anxious to get the estate settled.

This was still a tremendously complex holding, consisting of the circus stock, oil wells (about depleted), Florida real estate, a part interest in Al Ringling's theater in Baraboo, Wisconsin, and a great many odds and ends. If the normal administrative procedures were followed, all assets would have to be liquidated piece by piece, all pending litigation would have to be consummated, and, after a final accounting and payment of all legacies, the residue—if any—would be turned over to the trustees to be administered for the state of Florida.

A few days after the presentation ceremony John was called to a meeting with Governor Caldwell at Tampa. The governor was decidedly unhappy. John describes him as "impatient, gruff, and annoyed." He realized that the estate still owed a great deal of money, including some $960,000 to John and our mother for statutory executors' fees, and claims of Newman and Bisco for legal fees of $640,000.

They discussed ways of winding it up quickly. The more the governor heard about the complicated holdings, the less hopeful he became of a quick settlement. Finally he said, "Why don't you fellows buy out the state of Florida and wind it up yourselves?"

John kept a poker face, but I am sure there were sparks in his eyes. This was his chance to get that circus stock.

It had not been possible for the estate to pay legal fees during the course of the prolonged litigation, so the next step was a meeting between John and Leonard Bisco and the latter's partner, Sydney Newman. As a result of this discussion, it was agreed that if the residuary estate was purchased from the state of Florida, the lawyers would share in the purchase on a 40-60 per cent basis.

Then began the long, delicate negotiations with the Florida officials. The museum and the works of art—assessed at $15,000,000—were the greater part of the estate. What remained after the settlements so far made was valued as follows:

Sarasota real estate	$2,000,000
Oklahoma oil interests	800,000
300 shares of circus stock	500,000
Theaters in Wisconsin and miscellaneous	100,000
TOTAL:	$3,400,000

Against this were estate liabilities of about $2,000,000, leaving a dubious net worth of approximately $1,400,000. I say "dubious" because at that time it was doubtful if the assessed valuation, which was higher than the depressed values of the time, could be realized if the holdings were sold.

John's first offer to Governor Caldwell was to give the state $500,000 clear and assume all obligations of the estate. Robert got into the act and bid $550,000. Both offers were turned down by the Florida officials. The negotiations continued from March 1946 to October 1947. The state jibbed and jibed, and John's syndicate, which consisted of Mother,

John, and Newman and Bisco, kept up a steady pressure. There were offers and counteroffers, as state officials whirled like weathercocks under the shifting winds of public opinion and local political pressures. Various outside interests tried to muscle in.

Finally, on August 19, 1947, John and Bisco went to Florida for a showdown meeting with Governor Caldwell and his cabinet. The weather that day was hot and humid, but in the cabinet room the atmosphere was icy. Hostility was written on all but a few faces. Governor Caldwell looked implacable. He immediately suggested that the session be private.

John, thinking fast, said, "I believe it is customary for the press to be present at cabinet meetings in Florida. We have nothing to hide. We are going to make a fair offer. I think the press should stay."

The press stayed.

John and Leonard Bisco then made a series of alternative proposals. Each one was buffeted around the table getting nowhere. It was evident that the officials did not want to make any agreement. To force their hands, John said in a very stagy whisper to Bisco, "Find out how much they will take." He said it four times, loud enough for the governor to hear, loud enough for the reporters to hear. Thus prodded, Caldwell proposed that he and his cabinet withdraw to confer in private on a price.

After twenty minutes or so they marched back into the room and took their places at the table. Somewhat triumphantly, Governor Caldwell announced, "Gentlemen, we have decided on a figure. We will accept $1,250,000."

Bisco shot to his feet as though stung by a bee. "We can't do it!" he said.

John hauled him down. "We've got to," he whispered fiercely. "It's our last chance."

"There isn't that much cash," Bisco said.

"We'll raise it," John countered. "Tell them we accept."

Reluctantly Bisco stood up. "Governor and gentlemen," he said, "Mr. North and I accept your proposition."

From then on things moved rapidly. The Florida press had given our offer great publicity. The tone of their comment was that the governor had made a fine deal for his state. Warmed by their approval, Caldwell became enthusiastic. Details as to how the fund was to be set up and when the installments were to be paid into it were quickly ironed out. The final contract provided that $500,000 would be paid into the state fund within ninety days of signing; and that the remaining $750,000 was to be a mortgage against the assets of the estate payable over a period of five years. The contract was signed on October 8, 1947.

Now all that remained to be done was to find the money. By this time some of the assets had been sold, so there was $200,000 in cash. That left $300,000 to be raised, of which, according to the 60-40 deal with Newman and Bisco, John and Mother had to raise 60 per cent, or $180,000.

Remember that all this time John had also been involved in the negotiations with Aunt Edith, Robert, and the Haleys over the circus stock. That deal went through almost simultaneously, and he had to get the money to finance that purchase as well. Nobody but a rampant optimist would have dreamed of trying. No one but a supersalesman could possibly have pulled it off.

John's next move was to talk with Newman and Bisco about the circus stock. While they were willing to let John have the voting rights without any payment, he wanted to own the stock. "I've got to have it all," John said.

"If you want it that much you'll have to buy our forty

per cent interest in it or assign other assets," Newman said.

"What do you consider it worth?" he asked.

Newman answered that the 300 shares were worth $500,-000, which was the release value in the Florida agreement. John said it was worth no more than $450,000. This was in accordance with the facts. After arguing for a while, John said, "All right, we'll toss a coin to see if it's $400,000 or $500,000."

They tossed and he lost.

This was the one serious blunder my brother made in all these very intricate negotiations. He was so emotionally involved in securing control of the circus that his customary shrewdness completely deserted him. He was, in fact, a sucker for the circus. Since the valuation of $500,000 forced him to pay $200,000 instead of $160,000 for Newman and Bisco's 40 per cent share, that little coin flying through the air cost him $40,000.

An agreement was then made between the lawyers and John giving him an irrevocable option to buy their share of the circus stock and an irrevocable proxy to vote it meanwhile.

Somehow John and Mother and I and Arthur Concello raised the money to complete these transactions. How it was done is too involved a story to tell here, and is beside the point in a book about our circus. It's enough to say that we mortgaged everything we had, including our immortal souls.

However, it was worth it. Due to an era of great prosperity, John's good judgment, and a lot of luck, the properties acquired from Uncle John's estate have increased enormously in value. Most important of all, John at last owned a controlling interest in the circus. And peace descended upon our embattled family—for a while.

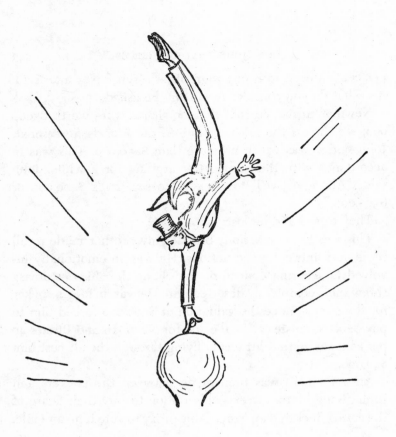

CHAPTER XXVIII

"GEARED FOR GLORY AND FOR GOLD"

As soon as John was definitely assured of control of the circus he and I set about modernizing it further. Though its gross earnings were climbing due to increased prices for seats, expenses were going up at a much higher rate. We would not try to counteract this by cheapening the show. The only answer was greater efficiency. For a while this policy was effective, but in an inflationary era it was like building sand forts against a flood tide.

In the 1948 *Circus Magazine* I wrote, "Ten years ago we thought we had done quite a job of modernization. When I look back now and see what has been accomplished it appears to have been only a beginning. . . ."

Of course, from 1946 on all our canvas was flameproof. Then Arthur Concello brought to the circus a portable steel grandstand, which is generally considered the greatest innovation in circus techniques since Barnum put the show on rails. This invention, which we used for the first time in 1948, consisted of big dual-wheeled trucks which looked like stainless-steel van trailers. When we came onto a lot the Big Top went up first with its sides bare. Jeeps backed the trucks into it at uniform intervals around its perimeter. Their machinery began to grind, and great steel wings carrying upholstered seats and bleachers rose up and spread gently out until they almost touched those of the trucks on either side. The pitch of the grandstand was supported by the main frame of the trucks and sixteen tubular-steel wing jacks. These were adjusted to inequalities of the ground and the decks dovetailed to form a single steel-floored structure broken only by spaces for exits. Steel safety stairways were part of the package.

The twenty-seven units for a grandstand to seat ten thousand people cost us $250,000. Never was money better spent. I have described the laborious business of building a wooden grandstand every day. That took over four hours and dozens of hands. The new grandstand could be erected in fifty-five minutes by comparatively few workers. As a fringe benefit, the enclosed part of the trucks could then be used as dressing rooms.

Concello's innovations did not stop with the new grandstand. He designed aluminum side poles and quarter poles—

the latter weighed 50 per cent less than the 675 pounds of the wooden quarter poles—and he persuaded the Aluminum Company of America to design a machine that would extrude them. The only reason the main poles were not made of the same light metal was that the Aluminum Company was not able to devise a method of making a pole sixty-seven and one half feet long.

Another change in which Concello had a hand was using steel cables and a winch on the main falls for hoisting the bail rings, instead of the inch-and-one-half manila rope we had always used. Before this it took fifteen men to handle their 1500-pound weight dry. When wet, they were almost twice as heavy.

Other improvements of this period were a light, easily assembled steel-mesh cage for the animal acts, and the new method of bringing the cats into the arena in small individual cages which were then hooked together to form a chute which did *not* obstruct any exit.

We increased efficiency in many less noticeable ways. In the cookhouse, which still served over four thousand meals a day, we put all the mechanization of a big hotel, steam kettles, dishwashers, and so forth. We devised improvements in loading and unloading the trains and dozens of other smaller things, which for a time enabled technology to keep pace with inflation.

In fact, 1948 was our best postwar year. Our somewhat overenthusiastic press agent Frank Braden wrote:

"Spectacular has been the Big Show's 1948 season— spectacular in its triumphant coast-to-coast tour, . . . its phenomenal grosses, and in its never-to-be-forgotten performance.

"The Madison Square Garden engagement was out of the cosmic dream books. Enough people were turned away during that epochal run to fill the Yale Bowl thrice over. In Boston,

. . . Washington, Baltimore, turnaways reigned. The Midwest was equally profitable. . . . The take-off for the first big railroad zooms—Kansas City to Denver and more stampede business . . . Spokane, Seattle and Portland. . . .

"Like a river of platinum, the four long railroad trains, silver-enameled and stream-lined in Ringling Red, swept majestically down from the high North to San Francisco. In the Cow Palace we had an all-time record intake in seven performances there, with thousands turned away each night. . . . [And so on and so on around the whole big country.]

"'Twas a long, hard season, a glorious season, but if you don't think it was a tough one, you weren't with it.

"But, Brother, will it stand out long after all of us are gone as the One for the BIG PLUSH BOOK, the Master Ledger.

"Here are the top reasons why:

"John Ringling North produced for 1948, the greatest, the finest circus performance ever seen on land or sea. His policies were Big Show, Big Business, Geared for Glory and for Gold.

"Arthur Concello's expert management . . . Henry Ringling North . . . a tower of strength while his brother was in Europe engaging attractions . . . Frank McClosky ever poised to meet crises and go to town like a bat out of hell . . . Pat Valdo . . . wise and funny. . . .

"There are so many good men who should be mentioned here. Big Executives and big agents, too, and the guys who moved Big Bertha, put her up and down, advertised her, railroaded her; and cherished her welfare above their own."

Thus Frank Braden, a man we paid to write for us and a good friend; so, of course, traditionally exaggerated and overly fulsome. Nevertheless, it does give a reasonably accurate description of that wonderful year in which John introduced for the first time in America such famous stars as Unus, "Upside-down gravity-defying, equilibristic Wonder of the World"; the great juggler Francis Brunn; Cucciola, the midget

equestrian clown; and nine other new imports from Europe
and the Orient in addition to our grand old stand-bys.

The charming opening spec "'Twas the Night Before
Christmas" featured "Santa Claus and His Merry Artisans"
and "The Noel Gnomes' Night Out," while one of the production numbers was the "Monte Carlo Ballet" with sixty girls
whirling on spin riggings, "Roulette Revolves in Rhythmic
Flights"; and the finale, "The Circus Ball," in which the stag
line consisted of high-hatted dancing elephants supported by
"enchanting debutantes and Careening Clowns."

As Braden implied, I had the train for three months that
summer; and I thoroughly enjoyed it. For all its modernization
and Broadway production numbers this was still the old
circus that I loved. Many friends whom I had known since
boyhood were still with it; and all those wonderful new
people had joined us.

Of these, Unus, whom my brother found working in a night
club in Barcelona in 1946, was perhaps the most astounding.
He was originally a Viennese named Franz Furtner, who took
the name Unus from the Latin for the number "one." I think
that his hand-balancing act was one of the greatest of its kind
the world will ever know. He always wore white gloves when
working, but for the finale of his act he would take them off
and exhibit his bare hands to the audience to show there was
no gimmick. Then he would put them back on, and getting
on top of a huge electric-light bulb, made especially for him
by General Electric, he would balance himself on his index
finger with his feet straight up in the air.

We never knew whether he applied some sort of brace by
sleight of hand when he put the gloves back on, but as Aunt
Edith, who adored watching Unus, said, "Even if he has got
a gimmick, it's a whale of an act."

We still had Bill Heyer and his horses with the show, and

John brought over Roberto de Vasconeallos, a former Portuguese bullfighter who was also a superb horseman. Both these men trained their own horses, not only for dressage but also liberty horses. They would work as many as sixteen liberty horses at one time. Another great horse trainer, who is still with us, was Polish Charlie Moroski. His real name was impossible—Czeslan Mroczkowski.

Liberty horses are very difficult animals to train; in some respects more difficult than elephants or cats. It takes great patience, skill, and an intimate knowledge of horses: a horse is not terribly bright, and at the same time he is big, so much bigger than a man that you cannot place him as you would a dog. You cannot use fear, as with the larger wild animals, for if you punish a horse too much you'll break his spirit and thereby ruin a good performer. So you have to do it just right.

First you must make him ring-wise. Then you train him singly to do simple tricks. After that you make your horses perform two at a time, then three, four, and five together, building it up to as many as sixteen, all performing in unison. The patience required for that sort of training is unbelievable. I love horses myself and I have often watched Heyer, and Roberto, and Moroski working up an act. It is a wonder to me that they did not lose their minds long before the horses acquired a similitude of sense.

Then there were the clowns. I have always loved clowns. There is nothing unique about that; I think almost everybody does. I suppose the most famous one we ever had was sad-faced Emmett Kelly, the incarnation of the tramp in all of us, who succeeded in combining the techniques of the great European clowns with the American walk-around style. This was very difficult to do. The classic clowns of Europe, wearing their traditional costumes, are often fine musicians and jugglers as well. The great ones, as typified by the Fratalini

Brothers and the late Grock, also use a great deal of dialogue and work to the whole audience for as much as fifteen minutes or even half an hour.

But such as these have seldom succeeded in America. On several occasions John has imported fine European clowns. They were wonderful performers, but they got lost in the vast spaces of our three-ring arenas and their talents were wasted on our audiences, who were not used to having their attention commanded for so long a time. They prefer the walk-around type of clowning with laughs based on quick sight gags and comic properties such as three-foot cigars, water-spouting hats, and wired-on pursuing skunks.

That Kelly was able to establish something of the European clown's rapport with his audience was a tribute to his greatness. Otto Greibling, who works for us now, is one of the great European clowns who succeeded in adapting himself to American techniques.

Every year we used to have some amateur clowns with the show. Since the run-of-the-mill, walk-around type of clowning requires no great experience, you can dress a person up in an absurd costume and other clowns can show him how to put on a white face. We have had many friends throughout the years who lead perfectly normal lives most of the time, but have an overpowering urge to join the circus. These people take their vacations by working for us as clowns. To live the ordinary life of a clown is part of their enjoyment.

I remember a man called Harper Joy, a vice-president of one of the big banks in Spokane, who joined the circus every fall for the ten days or two weeks of his vacation. Joe Ward, a rich building contractor from Texas spent his vacations clowning for many years.

The best and most serious of our temporary clowns was Bill Ballantine. I met him in Clown Alley and learned that he was an artist who had decided that he loved the circus. He joined it for his own amusement and in the expectation of getting background material for his art. He was with us for several seasons, at the same time doing his art work successfully on the side. In later years he also worked at his regular profession for the circus. He did some very good display work for the menagerie and redesigned the side shows for us one year.

Bill Ballantine went even further in his affair with the circus. He fell in love with one of our circus girls. He married her and so far they have produced five little circus fans. I have hardly spoken of one great traditional adjunct of the circus—the side shows. They appeal to the barbaric side of human nature, which enjoys looking at the distortions of the human form. A few of those we had with the show at one time or another included:

Fredia Bushnick, The Armless Wonder

Mr. and Mrs. Fischer, Giants

Miss Musette, The Legless Marvel

Lorina, Sword Swallower

Major Mite and Family of Midgets

Ima Sight, Fat Girl

Cliko, Wild Man from Borneo

Iko and Eko, Ambassadors from Mars

When you knew them as well as I did, these freaks, or "strange people," as Barnum billed them in England in deference to British susceptibilities, were neither freakish nor strange, but nice ordinary people with extraordinary physiques. Many of them became close friends of mine. I have spoken of my long friendship with Cliko. Iko and Eko were weird-looking albino Negroes from Richmond, Virginia. Their skins were a glistening white, much whiter than white folks, and their hair looked like lamb's wool.

I always felt sorry for the giants, who were apt to be unhappy and unhealthy—they seldom lived very long. Robert

Wadlow was the tallest man on record—nearly nine feet—but the poor fellow could hardly walk. My favorite giant was Jack Earl, who stood eight feet three in his cowboy boots. Jack, whose real name was Jacob Erlich, was a nice Jewish boy from El Paso, Texas. He happened to walk onto the lot there one day and Clyde Ingalls said, "Come over here, boy. I want to talk to you."

"Yes, suh," said Jack.

"Now stand up against that side wall."

Clyde got a tape measure and checked what he thought he saw. Then he said, "Boy, how'd you like to be a giant?"

"I reckon I am one already."

"Yes, but how would you like to work at being one for us? There's good money in it."

That is how we got our second-tallest giant. Jack worked for us for many years. He was quite a clever sculptor and used to take lessons at the art school Uncle John had founded in Sarasota. Like so many of his kind, he died in his early forties.

Midgets, or the "little people," as they prefer to be called, are usually healthy and gay. They must not be confused with dwarfs, who are misshapen in some way. The little people are perfectly formed, often highly intelligent human beings who just stopped growing. The smallest one we ever had was Major Mite, who we claimed measured only thirty-one inches in height—though that may have been shrinking things a bit. Unlike most of his colleagues, Major Mite had a wretched disposition. Great big men were frightened by his towering temper.

Quite different was my close friend Harry Earle. Most midgets have perfectly normal brothers and sisters, but the Earles, who were known professionally as the Doll Family, were an exception. They were four delightful little people— though they had several regular-sized brothers and sisters.

In addition to Harry, there was Gracie and Tiny (the smallest) and Daisy, who was very pretty. Daisy grew quite a bit in her twenties, after most people stop, so she became quite a big midget.

Harry was the most talented member of the family. He was an excellent actor and in wintertime made a number of pictures in Hollywood, including a part with Lon Chaney in *The Hunchback of Notre Dame*.

I think the greatest side-show attraction we ever had was back in the days when Uncle John was running the show and I was serving my apprenticeship. It was the Ubangis, or Big Lips. Uncle John rented these ladies, who wore wooden disks as big as dinner plates in their lips, from their tribal chief and brought them to America in 1931. They came out of the Congo to civilization with absolutely no preparation. They were miserably lonely and unhappy and did not even get paid —the chief took all. The poor things were always cold. One time they built a fire to keep themselves warm in their railway car and set it afire. In fact, they behaved like naughty children.

When they ate they took the disks out of their lips, so they hung down like great fleshy awnings over their mouths. They lifted the awning with one hand and poked food in with the other.

But we had some gay experiences with these ladies. When anything annoyed them they shed the few clothes they wore. One time in Boston they were up on their platform in the menagerie when something made them mad. They took off all their clothes and ran through the crowds stark naked with some of us dashing after them with blankets in an endeavor to salvage Boston's well-known propriety.

The youngest and prettiest was Princess Camala. Perhaps she was not the prettiest by Ubangi standards, for her lips were not as large as those of the others. She took a liking to me because I talked a little primitive French with her. I used to bring her insignificant little presents from the ten-cent store —glass beads and lengths of copper wire, which she liked to wind around her arm. My most successful present was a child's straw hat with a rubber band to hold it on, a toy umbrella, and dark glasses with white rims. She insisted on wearing the whole works in the spec that evening so that everyone could see her finery.

Naturally this did not please Uncle John and I caught hell. But the Princess was so enchanted that she tried to seduce me. Much as I hated to hurt her feelings, I had not the stomach for it. But we were friends.

If I have neglected many of my good friends among the workers, it is not for lack of affection on my part or lack of picturesque qualities on theirs. I could write another whole book about them—Waxy Panzer, our wonderful old harness maker, who went blind and still made the best harness ever; Mike Kerry, who painted the wagons and was a specialist on sunburst wheels; Captain Curtis, our great boss canvasman; dozens and dozens more whom I hold close in my memory.

The reason I knew all our people so well and had such a warm feeling for them was that I was their foster father. The circus was a paternalistic institution—it had to be. For most of the performers and workers were, by the necessities of their way of life, homeless, rootless people. In joy or trouble they had no one to confide in or turn to for help except the circus management. Keeping them happy was one of my jobs. I helped them with quantities of good advice, small loans from the red wagon, and big hospital bills. Sometimes I lectured a performer's rambunctious child; or congratulated one who had gotten into college; or arranged a quick marriage for a girl who had gotten into trouble. The fact that they trusted me and confided in me made me love them. It was, as I said, just one of my many jobs with the circus. But it was the most important and the most rewarding.

Of all the strange and wonderful people whom I knew in the circus at one time or another, one of the most extraordinary did not belong there at all. He was Cecil B. De Mille, who produced the film called *The Greatest Show on Earth*.

For a long time John had been talking with David Selznick about a circus picture, and contracts were actually signed for it. However, Selznick had difficulty financing it, and in 1948 he told John that it was only fair to release him from the contract though he still hoped to do it some day.

Word of this got around Hollywood, and while we were in the Garden that spring De Mille approached us. Contract negotiations took a long time, but they were finally signed. De Mille joined the show on the road in the summer of 1949. He had quite an entourage with him, including his woman Friday, Miss Gladys Rosson, who was secretary-treasurer of Cecil B. De Mille Productions; Fred Frank, a top screen writer; and C.B.'s freckle-faced, wide-eyed granddaughter, Cecilia De Mille Calvin, aged thirteen. What fun we had showing her our wonderful world and reliving our own youthful rides on the circus train!

C.B., short and stocky, big nose, white hair, red face, always dressed in a white open-collar shirt, gray riding breeches, and field boots, which were the uniform of his profession back in the silent days. But that was the only thing uniform about him. He was indefatigable and unpredictable. At every show, every afternoon and every night, he mingled with the circus crowds as they poured in, listening and making notes. While the show was on he was running around the Big Top, followed breathlessly by Miss Rosson and Fred Frank, squinting through his finder to study camera angles, giving suggestions to Frank, dictating to Miss Rosson, and scribbling notes for his own use.

At Madison, Wisconsin, on August 12, his sixty-eighth birthday, he had himself hoisted in a bosun's chair to the very peak of the Big Top, where he remained for more than an hour, swaying gently as he peered down on the aerial and high-wire acts. He was like a kid seeing the circus for the first time in his delight.

And what a companion he was at our little dinners in the Jomar! Every place we stopped reminded him of stories of the time at the turn of the century when he had trouped over this same ground in a Shakespearean road company. When we played Bemidji, Minnesota, he addressed the chamber of commerce and they made us all honorary members of the Paul Bunyan Association.

He could stay with us for only two weeks, but we welcomed him back when we got to California and he was just as energetic. His genius, in part at least, really was "the capacity for taking infinite pains."

Meanwhile his writers had been busy on the screenplay. C.B. wanted a thrilling, Hollywood-type plot set against the bizarre, exciting background of the circus world. And that, of course, is what he got. We can hardly quarrel with his judgment as far as the popularity of the picture is concerned.

After the writing came the shooting, much of it in Sarasota. We had a fine time with it that winter of 1949–50. Mother, who was nearing eighty, enjoyed it as much as any of us. They came to Sarasota with a tremendous crew, including, of course, the stars Betty Hutton and Cornel Wilde, who were fliers in the picture. We devoted all of our facilities to De Mille, putting up the Big Top and staging the show day after day, while the city of Sarasota co-operated enthusiastically, permitting us to put on the great circus parade in the grand old manner.

De Mille could be very different on the set from the gregarious, socially lovable man we knew. He stalked about followed by his special chair boy, who carried a high-cushioned stool, which could also be turned on its side to make a low, comfortable seat. C.B. used it for leaning or sitting and since, like Queen Victoria, he never looked back when he sat, the poor boy had to be nimble and quick to decide whether he wanted the high stool, low stool, or leaning stool. He never missed. But I shudder to think of his fate had he guessed wrong and allowed that Very Important Bottom to crash to earth.

I remember watching De Mille's technique in getting the best out of his actors. As a director he was as deliberately schizophrenic as Jekyll and Hyde, changing in a flash from a soft-spoken gentleman to an absolute demon. I first saw his Hyde with an actor who was playing one of the daring fliers. In the first scene, where the actor had to get up on the trapeze, he did so with all the agility of one of Pallenberg's bears and sat looking utterly miserable although the net was rigged only a few feet below him. De Mille yelled at him, "Act! Act! Don't just sit up there looking scared to death."

In a resigned way, the actor said, "But Mr. De Mille, I am an actor, not a circus performer."

To which De Mille shouted back, "That's a matter of opinion."

I am convinced that the great director was deliberately needling him as a good horseman uses spurs to bring out his stud's mettle. He wanted to enrage the man to the frenzy of determination to show De Mille that he was an actor, a circus performer, and as daring as any young man who ever rode a flying trapeze. As a result, the actor eventually turned in a truly fine performance.

Betty Hutton was another matter. It was not a question of spurring her on, but of holding her back, keeping her from taking unnecessary risks. Tony Concello taught her the ropes, literally speaking. Betty insisted on learning really to fly. Tony put a "mechanic"—a safety belt like a child's harness—on her and taught her some of the simpler tricks. Betty got so she could perform the crossover, flying from the swinging bar to the hands of the catcher, and back to the pedestal, and did it in the picture with no mechanic. De Mille was consistently gentle with her and she, too, turned in a great performance.

Of course, the stars of the show had doubles for the more difficult feats. Fay Alexander flew for Cornel Wilde and performed one really hair-raising stunt. This was in the scene where the Great Sebastian falls to the ground performing without a net. Concello set the stage by having a bulldozer dig a tremendously deep pit in the center ring. The net was slung in it and a light surface covering was spread with sawdust to seem part of the floor. Fay performed his tremendous flying feats. Then came the final fatal miss and he plunged headlong to apparently solid earth. Even though the net was there, it had to be beautifully timed and executed.

Other mechanical tricks were used to give the public thrills without risking the stars' precious necks. In one scene an elephant was supposed to almost step on Gloria Grahame's head, a thing no elephant would knowingly do. To avoid risking a valuable property, De Mille had his people build a mechanical replica of an elephant's foot, and in the close-up you saw Gloria's pretty nose a scant millimeter from destruction.

C.B. also demanded an exciting scene of a circus train wreck. This was accomplished by trick photography with model trains. But to add verisimilitude to the scene of carnage, he bought some old coaches from the Southern Pacific Railroad and painted them like circus cars. Then a huge crane lifted them high in the air and dropped them on the tracks with a most gratifying crash.

The last location shooting was done under the real Big Top while the circus was making its scheduled dates in Philadelphia and Washington in 1950. The big crew of technicians and the uncertainties of filming an actual performance made it a very expensive process. But there is no substitute for reality. The live audiences, the sense of excitement, and the solidity of the background gave the picture the final touch of authenticity.

The Greatest Show on Earth was a tremendously successful picture. It grossed over $20,000,000, and the end is not yet in sight. For a while this figure made it the second-greatest money-making picture of all time, surpassed only by *Gone with the Wind*. Then *The Robe* and *Around the World* passed it, but it is still in fourth place. The circus received over $1,300,000 in royalties. The money came just when we needed it most. You might almost say that *The Greatest Show on Earth* saved The Greatest Show on Earth.

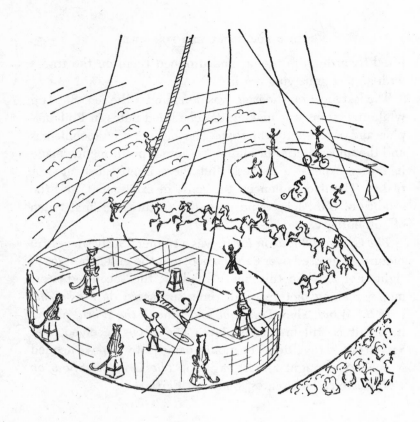

CHAPTER XXIX

THE DECLINE AND FALL
OF THE BIG TOP

The end was written plain in our ledgers for years before it
came. But we were deliberately blind. Nineteen forty-eight
was the last of the really good times. Then the tide began to
ebb; slowly at first, then flowing out fast. The highest-attend-
ance year had been 1942, though our gross in 1948 was higher

due to increased prices for admission. But inflation was flood-
ing in and we were gradually drowning in a sea of increased
costs.

In the Garden we could take in $80,000 in two sellout per-
formances; and on the road we could take in $50,000 in the
later days, when our prices had gone up. But we could have
$4000 days, too, when it rained or you had a bad lot someplace
which people could not get to conveniently. And big day or
small, our expenses were the same. They rose to over $25,000
a day.

The cost of every phase of our operation was going up.
Naturally labor costs increased with social security and with-
holding taxes to pay. But this was not all. The cost of food for
our 4000 meals a day—2000 pounds of meat, 1500 loaves of
bread, 2800 eggs, 5000 pancakes, 1000 quarts of milk—had
doubled. The price we paid the railroads for hauling our four
long trains had tripled, from about $180,000 in 1941 to
$580,000 in 1955.

But it was not only a question of money. We could no
longer get the right kind of men to head our departments. The
secret of the smooth functioning of the intricate circus operation was that it was completely departmentalized—trains and
loading, canvas, cookhouse, tractors, seats, menagerie, side
shows, red wagon, and so forth. The boss of each department
was absolute in his sphere; all he had to think about was getting his section on the lot and running on time.

Our old-time bosses could be trusted to do it, because they
were as dedicated to their jobs as we were. Even when they
were drunk they managed to do it. As Braden said, they put
the welfare of the circus above their own.

One of my boyhood heroes was Happy Jack Snellen, who
had been boss canvasman with Barnum & Bailey 'way back in
the nineties, and then for us. He was promoted to lot superintendent with the job of getting the circus on difficult lots.

Sometimes he had to do fantastic pieces of engineering, such as building a bridge over busy streets because the menagerie was on one side and the Big Top on the other. Happy had no formal education—he had been with the circus since he was a boy—but he was certainly a genius. The only thing he needed to figure out complicated problems of engineering were some numbers, secret formulae, that he kept written in the sweatband of his hat—he had the same hat for years. It was his equivalent of the modern slide rule.

Happy had some delightful whimsicalities. I can see him now, sitting at the staff table in the cookhouse putting away a platter of boiled cabbage. He always said the same thing, "I love cabbage—but it repeats."

He died of cancer of the throat, and we certainly missed him.

Jimmy Whalen—the Whale—succeeded Snellen as boss canvasman. He was short and stocky with a white walrus mustache, and he had a voice you could hear from one end of the Big Top to the other. How he drove those gangs with it! Jimmy was completely responsible and will go down in circus history as one of the great boss canvasmen of all time. Captain Curtis, who succeeded him, was also a fine boss.

These, and men like them, were the irreplaceable characters around the circus. It is often said that no one is indispensable for anything in this world, but I am afraid those old-time bosses were indispensable to the operation of the railroad show. For as they died off in the later years of the road operation, there were no young men coming along to take their places.

We had personal losses in our family, too, in that time I think of as the twilight years. Robert was the first to go, and though we had had our differences, Bob had many lovable qualities. So we sincerely missed him and sorrowed at his passing.

In November of 1950 our mother suffered a massive stroke from which she never recovered. Until that moment she had been as keen and gay as ever, ready to play bridge all day and poker all night. The circus was her first love, and there was nothing she enjoyed more than the exciting conferences at Bird Key as Anderson and White and Max Weldy and John and I planned the new show, with the whole floor of the big hall covered with designs for production numbers and costumes.

Aunt Edith was the last of the older generation to go. Though I have spoken harshly of my aunt Edith at times, it was only for the factual aspects of this record. In my heart I loved her dearly. She had a tremendous strength of character. What she did not choose to believe she would not, in the face of whatever proof. An example: When Mother had her stroke, my sister Salomé called on Aunt Edith in her pink marble palace. In the course of their talk Sally asked her about certain of our mother's symptoms. Aunt Edith, whose husband had had two strokes and died of them and whose son had had two strokes and died of them, replied, "I would not know about that. You see, we never had anything like that in our branch of the family."

An indomitable lady indeed!

In those years of diminishing returns, the only thing that did not diminish was the show itself. We kept it going in its full glory, cost what it might; for we knew that any let-down of quality, or even quantity, would be the end.

In every other way we tried to combat our failing finances. In 1949 John gambled on taking a one-ring European-style version of the circus to Havana. It was a considerable success, which we repeated for several years. This helped to defray the cost of maintaining Winter Quarters when little money was coming in.

To save expense Max Weldy set up his own costume factory in Sarasota. Much of the work was done in people's own homes. Sewing on sequins for the circus became a very fashionable occupation, which many of the *grandes dames* of Sarasota practiced to earn pin money or gifts for their favorite charities. We also began to build our own floats for the spec. In this way we saved several hundred thousand dollars a year.

We also engaged engineers to survey the show for complete mechanization. They came up with a plan which would have required a capital investment of $2,000,000. Where could we get that kind of money? Though the last of the Hartford-fire claims had been paid off, that $4,000,000 plus had drained our treasury. We had no reserves. In any event, the engineers' plan would have saved $500,000 a year, and by 1955 we were losing $1,000,000. We grossed $5,000,000 and it cost $6,000,000 to run the show. In the great days our uncles had made a net profit of $1,000,000 on a gross of about $2,700,000.

The losses were made up in part by the royalties from De Mille's picture. We plowed $1,300,000 of them back into the show.

At the close of the 1953 season Arthur Concello and John came to what fortunately proved to be only a temporary parting of their ways. On John's return from his annual European talent hunt Artie faced him with at least a quasi ultimatum— he insisted on drastically cutting the 1954 presentation of the circus to a fifty-car operation. John agreed with him that some reduction in overhead was timely and in order, but he felt that to reduce the size and splendor of The Greatest Show on Earth to such an extent would not be commensurate with its title; nor would it be keeping faith with our public. He talked with Arthur as he had previously about the day when there would be enough adequate buildings in the country for continuous operations of the Big Show, but until such a time he was determined to carry on with our time-honored annual boast of "bigger and better than ever." They didn't agree and Artie left.

We put Concello's assistant, Frank McClosky, in as general manager. He was an able man for the physical movement of the show, getting it up and taking it down. But he lacked Concello's spark and his firm discipline. Things ran raggedly in 1954. We lost money, of course.

In the winter of 1955–56 I went before the eastern railroads and told them our sad tale of diminishing returns and increasing expenses. They listened very patiently to me; they were certainly sympathetic, because they were more or less in the same fix themselves. After several weeks of discussions they agreed to a reduction of almost 25 per cent in our rates, but they made it clear to me that they were doing it not on a basis of good business, but from their emotional involvement with the circus, with whom they had done business for so many years. The southern railroads followed suit.

In return they demanded and got some things they wanted, too. One of them was a promise from the circus that within two years we would move the show in two sections instead of three. In deference to the railroads' problems we had already cut the trains from four to three, making each one heavier. That did not give us the time needed for the staggered operation of setting up the show. I did not see how it was possible to handle the peculiar logistics of our movements in two sections—not and keep the circus as big as it had always been. And if you started reducing it from what the people expected, you would be cheating them, because it would no longer be The Greatest Show on Earth.

The western railroads refused even to give us a personal audience. Because of their own problems of increased competition and costs, the railroads were unable to move us right. All our efficiency and streamlining enabled us to get the circus off the lot, down to the yards, and loaded onto the trains much earlier than in the old days. But sometimes it would sit in the yards for hours and hours, sometimes all night long, ready and waiting to be moved; and we would get to the next town late. The circus could not meet its overhead on one performance a day, so we would give the matinee anyhow. But more and more often in the last two years, instead of starting at two-fifteen, the matinee would begin at four-thirty. This meant inconvenience and exhaustion for the performers with no time to rest or eat between shows; and annoyance to our public.

They had been faithful to us for a long time. The circus had survived wars and depressions because people needed entertainment even in those trying times, especially in trying times. It had survived the movies and the talkies and the radio. But television—which hit all the amusement industries, and all professional sports except horse racing—had an effect on us, too.

In spite of everything, we started the season of 1955 with a bang. On the opening night in the Garden, Marilyn Monroe led off in the spec riding a pink elephant. The publicity was tremendous and we played in New York to a turnaway business. That pulled us through the season.

My friend Michael Burke joined us as general manager in 1955. He was a thin, dark, vibrant blade of an Irishman who had been my buddy in the cloak-and-dagger days with the OSS. He was a wonderful man to have beside you in a tight spot, and a good public relations man; but I am afraid he was not circus-wise enough for the job.

So we came to 1956, and our moment of truth.

We had as fine a show as ever that year. Unus was with us, and that magnificent horseman Captain Alexander Kŏnyŏt had returned; the Nocks Trio from Switzerland did terrific acrobatics and chilling crossovers on sixty-foot-long masts that swayed like palm trees in a hurricane. John brought in fourteen new acts from Europe, and we had many old favorites, the Loyal-Repenski equestrians, the Flying Palacios, and Pinito del Oro reading a newspaper while standing on her head on a free-flying trapeze with no net under her. We also had two hundred tons of "Ponderous, Performing Pachyderms."

In Madison Square Garden we made a substantial profit after all expenses. By July 15, midway in the season, we had lost it all and close to a million dollars besides.

On that day, while I was in Europe, I received a cable from John telling me he had decided to close the show. Though long expected, it was a grievous piece of news. I thought and thought, as I often had before, about what had gone wrong and if it was we who had failed. There were the obvious things, such as the cost of labor and its inefficiency, the cost of transportation and everything else. Even so, we could have kept going a while longer if we could have filled the Big Top every day.

The circus, as a railroad show, was a vestige of the past which we had been fighting to keep alive. Gone were the days when the Shuberts owned a hundred theaters all around America and filled them every night; when the Keith-Orpheum Circuit operated in half a thousand cities. You could see all those things on television now.

Certain as I was that the American people still loved the circus, they never endowed it like that other grand relic of the past, the Metropolitan Opera. Nor would they any longer fill our tents. Yet when we played in coliseums, the Garden, Boston, St. Louis, and San Francisco's Cow Palace, we turned them away. Yes, they still loved the circus.

Then I realized the final basic reason why the road show had to go; why the people no longer came to see it. They simply could not get there. It took a fifteen-acre lot to hold the forty-one tents in which the circus lived and showed. And you needed another big lot to park three thousand cars. With suburbs ringing every city in America from three to thirty miles in depth, where on earth could you still find a fifteen-acre lot that could be reached by public transportation or even conveniently by automobile? The answer was: virtually nowhere. Thus we had been gradually pushed farther and farther from the urban centers until we were practically pitching our tents in the sticks. It was not the American people who were forsaking us. We had forsaken them. The thought gave me passing comfort.

The truth of this proposition had been dramatically demonstrated to me one time when our manager went to Pittsburgh the day the show closed. He told a taxi driver to take him to the circus. *He did not know where it was.* It took him nearly an hour to find it. If our own manager could not find the circus, how could the public?

In Pittsburgh, Pennsylvania, on the night of July 16, 1956, the show went on as scheduled at 8:15 P.M. In their radiantly beautiful costumes the whole company, about seven hundred strong with fifty elephants and all our beautiful horses, paraded around the arena in the opening spec while the band gave out furiously with John's gay, brassy tunes. Then came the clowns and children's high-pitched screams of laughter and their fathers' deep guffaws. Everybody gave a little extra that night—fliers flying more daringly than ever the daring young man; equestrians performing with the exquisite grace of smiling desperation; the laughing girls in the aerial ballet; elephants doing their stuff, old Modoc in her ponderous waltz; jugglers insanely versatile; Pinito del Ora serenely standing on her head flying in great arcs over the audience; and the crashing, thumping magnificent brassy band mingling with the yells of delight and awe and fear of ten thousand children of all ages. It was almost just as it had always been since ever so long ago. Al and Alf T., Otto and Charles and John would have recognized it and felt at home.

All just as it had always been, except at the end, the grand finale with almost the entire company in the arena. The band played "Auld Lang Syne." Daring young aerialists and the funny old clowns began to cry. Pretty girls streaked their mascara. The Loyolas buried their faces in their horses' necks and roustabouts and razorbacks crowded around the exits and barricades were embarrassedly wiping at their faces.

But John, standing alone in his box, was thinking not of the past but of the future. He had done all he could, and more. He had made his decision and bravely put it behind him. While emotions ran rampant in the arena his mind was already busy planning the circus of tomorrow.

At 11:15 P.M., July 16, 1956, we struck the Big Top for the last time.

CHAPTER XXX

THE NEW AND FUTURE CIRCUS

John brought the show back to Winter Quarters to be disbanded. Despite his courage in making the decision to abandon the Big Top and his confident announcement that "the circus will be in Madison Square Garden next year," he was badly shattered.

The last night of the Big Top his feeling had been almost one of relief that the long, hopeless fight was done. But now that the excitement was over, he was left with a great emptiness. The mainspring of his life seemed broken. For the next few weeks, while he listlessly attended to the melancholy details of the great dispersion of performers and workers, he was almost in a state of shock. He retracted himself into his shell, the Jomar, and saw hardly anyone.

Gradually his enormous vitality surged up. He began to make tentative plans, and as he did so his natural optimism and imagination took fire.

The first clear sign of his recovery appeared one night when he entered the Plaza Restaurant—the 21 Club of Sarasota. Arthur Concello, who was sitting at a table, said to him, "I'm sorry the circus had to be closed, John."

"Sit with me, Artie," John replied. "Let's talk about it."

When they were seated at a corner table John said, "You were right, Artie. We couldn't swing it. We'll have to do a modern setup. Play the coliseums. We can keep the old girl alive if we do it. I want you with me, Artie."

Concello thought it over. He was amusing himself by dabbling in real estate in Sarasota with no financial worries. Why take up the exhausting grind again? "I don't know, John . . ." he said.

Enthusiasm was crackling out of John as though he'd never known defeat. "It's a challenge," he said. "If it's a challenge, it will be fun. Let's do it!"

Concello was still dubious. They talked until 2 P.M. the following afternoon, with John doing most of the talking, outlining ideas, making glittering, optimistic plans. He saw Arthur beginning to catch fire and slipped him the clincher. "I want to do it with you, Art," he said. "If you won't come along I'll sell out."

Perhaps he really would have, though I doubt it. But he convinced Concello. "All right," Arthur said, "I'll go along. But what about the capital we'll need?"

"I'll arrange the financing," John said confidently.

They were both crazy by any standards but their own up-side-down, sentimental logic. As I have said, Concello was very comfortably fixed—whether he was happy doing nothing in particular is another matter. John was a comparatively rich man. All the assets he had bought from Uncle John's estate were beginning really to pay off. The oil wells were spouting again; and the fantastic rise in Florida real estate had made the islands in the bay worth millions. He had nothing to gain financially, and a great deal to lose, by keeping the circus going.

For the past two years the credit of the circus had been zero. Nobody would lend the corporation a dime. But they would still lend money to John Ringling North on his personal notes. He had signed them in the amount of several hundred thousand dollars to keep the show from going under. In addition, the Forty-niners, as the minority stockholders were called, because they owned 49 per cent of the stock, were getting restless and threatening a mismanagement suit. In the face of all that, he went out and borrowed $286,000 more to put the new show together. Later he put up $400,000 more of his own money. Like Uncle John, he was a splendid gambler.

Meanwhile Concello was planning the physical side of the show and reorganizing it to fit the new conditions, working like a small demon. He designed an entirely new type of aerial rigging, which did not depend on tent masts or girders to hold it up. It was to be used in ball parks and outdoor stadia and could be assembled and interlocked on the ground and hoisted aloft by a single-cable action. Portions of it were also used in coliseums, where it could be raised to the ceiling in one operation, saving many man-hours.

When it was first set up at Winter Quarters, Fay Alexander, a fine young flier, started up the ladder to test the safety net. "No, you don't," said Artie.

He ran up the ropes like a monkey in a business suit, swung high and far on the flying bar, and sailed off it into the net. He bounced beautifully with nickels, dimes, quarters, cigarette lighter, and oddities showering out of his pockets. The net was safe.

We were all busy planning the logistics of the new operation. Here is the way it worked. We figured we were in five different businesses: the railroad business, moving 67,000 tons of equipment, animals, and people 20,000 miles a year; the restaurant business, serving at least 900,000 meals a year; the hotel business, providing sleeping accommodations for 1300 people for eight months; the construction business, building an amphitheater and a tented town every day or so; and show business. The only one that brought in any money was show business. The rest had to go.

Our first premise was that the show must still be the greatest on earth. The only things we cut out were the side shows and the menagerie, but not the performing animals. The menagerie had been anachronistic for a long time. Gone were the days when people gaped in wonder at a polar bear—there were so many animals in zoos and moving pictures and TV shows that people were sated by the sight of them. We loaned the menagerie to the Providence (Rhode Island) Zoo and borrowed it back once a year for Madison Square Garden.

As we planned our moves, and as they are done today: instead of the great eighty-car train, we use three-system baggage cars, in which the elephants and some other trained animals ride. The circus does not even own the cars any more, but leases them from the railroads. The physical equipment of the show—rigging, properties, and costumes—moves in ten big trailer trucks. The performers get travel allowances and they go places under their own steam. They live and eat in restaurants and hotels of their choice. Some use planes, trains, or buses, but a great many have their own cars and trailers. The smaller trained animals, including the cats, travel much more comfortably in motor vans than they ever did by rail.

Thus we chiseled our overhead down from $25,000 a day to less than $10,000, and our labor force from 800 to 100 men, while still holding to John's edict: "No expense will be spared to give a performance as lavish and spectacular as imagination and money can make it."

Now we were in a position to earn profits if we could hold our public, but this was fogged by doubt. For one thing, there had been a tremendous outpouring of lamentations in the press when we closed the tent show. It almost amounted to a period of public mourning for the passing of a beloved national institution, a little like that for a President who dies in office. We were up against the task of convincing people that the circus was still very much alive and undiminished in splendor and excitement.

This was very difficult to do, and we were not entirely successful. Even three years later people were still talking as though the circus were dead and my brother and I had murdered it, though by then it was the liveliest corpse in history. Even those who realized that the show was going on felt uneasily that it could never be the same indoors. In a nostalgic sense they were right. On the other hand, we had not started a new or unprecedented operation, but had, in fact, gone back to an earlier time. The Aztecs had watched a sort of circus *inside* the Halls of Montezuma. The first real American circus was put on by John Bill Ricketts in a specially constructed amphitheater in Philadelphia in 1793. He made so much money that he built another amphitheater for his show in New York. Many of the famous European circuses have always played indoors.

The wagon shows and, later, the great railroad shows were an interim thing to meet the special circumstances of a pioneering era. Changing conditions made the Big Top as incapable of survival as the dinosaur, which, indeed, it resembled in its ponderous giantism. We had simply gone back to the good *older* days of circus tradition. But it was hard to convince people of that.

For another thing, we had great difficulty routing the circus the first two years indoors (1957–58). The cities had been building their own Big Tops, so to speak. Nearly one hundred and fifty urban centers in the United States and Canada had amphitheaters large enough to house the show, but some of them were booked a year or two in advance for the dates we needed. This resulted in our making uneconomic jumps back and forth across the country, and playing fill-in dates in ball parks, which were always in danger of being rained out. This was a situation which would clear up as soon as we could start making bookings two or three years ahead, but it made those first years indoors very difficult.

The final trouble was caused by the Forty-niners. In 1957, led by Charles Ringling's daughter, Hester Sanford, and her son by a previous marriage, Stuart Lancaster, some of them sued John, Concello, and me for $20,000,000 for mismanagement of the circus. A curious example of Cousin Hester's mental processes occurred just after they started suit. At a party in Sarasota she rushed up to my sister Salomé and, after greeting her affectionately, asked, "And how is dear Johnny?"

"What do you mean 'dear Johnny'?" Sally asked. "You're suing him for twenty million dollars."

"That's only business," Hester said gaily. "I still love him dearly."

As I pointed out in the statement I wrote for our lawyers: "John Ringling North's determined courage in the face of adversity has enabled him to pilot his beloved circus through many harried years. . . . When he took over the active presidency in 1937, . . . the circus was run down physically and depleted financially. Five years later . . . the Ringling stockholders, other than himself, had received approximately $250,000 in salaries, expenses and dividends. The corporation had paid all its debts and established a cash reserve of $1,400,000. It was then [1943] that he was voted out of management control.

"When he regained control in 1947 he was faced by the enormous debt incurred during the Hartford Fire, . . . a debt that was finally liquidated under his management. . . ."

I then described the manner in which John had streamlined the show and combated the innumerable difficulties of which I have told, adding, "When the financial situation became serious in August, 1955, John made the personal sacrifice of cancelling his annual salary. . . .

"Practically all my brother's waking hours, all of his strenuous business life and great creative effort have been devoted to the service of the circus. It is under his management now, not because he sued for it, but because he won the circus; and not in the courts or at Las Vegas, but by gambling his courage, his energies, his experience of forty years, his love of our great enterprise and his personal fortune to achieve the success which has made his name a proud one, synonymous with the Circus on two continents."

In my own defense I stated that I had served the circus off and on for over thirty years, at salaries ranging from $17.50 a week to $20,000 a year—for one year, 1942. Speaking of that strenuous year, I said: "Though as vice-president and assistant to the president I was responsible for many executive duties, including the Press Department and almost all of the executive correspondence, I worked daily at roustabouts' tasks. I was on the lot helping set up in the mornings and I followed the pole wagon [last wagon] off the lot at night. I helped guy out and tear down; folded chairs and loaded them; carried bibles, planks, stringers, and jacks; helped to set up poles and quarter poles; rolled canvas, shook, pushed and folded canvas in rain storms, snow storms, sand storms and tornados. . . .

"I knew the name of every performer and hundreds of working men, and I lent them thousands of dollars over the years and was seldom repaid except in the most precious way, by their loyalty and respect—a loyalty that enabled me to stave off numerous strikes. . . ."

I added that, since my return to the circus after the war in 1947, I had never been paid more than $6200 a year, which did not seem a great amount.

Though the mismanagement suit seemed hopeless—and became more so when the new indoor circus planned by John eventually began to make profits—the threat of it and then the actual suit, in which they asked for a receiver, caused us great inconvenience. The Forty-niners not only made refinancing the circus difficult but they stopped us from selling all our railway cars, tractors, and other machinery at Winter Quarters which were no longer needed for the show. We wanted to sell them to raise additional capital. For three years they stood on the sidings, rusting and melancholy, doing no one any good.

When we came into Madison Square Garden in the spring of 1957, the circus was $1,300,000 in debt. But no one in our audiences could have sensed any diminution of its greatness. There were such stanch old favorites as the Loyal equestrians, our famous clowns, the Flying Alexanders, and Harold Alzana, whom I regard as the most daring high-wire artist of them all; and many of our famous animal acrobatic and juggling acts.

Our new producers, Richard and Edith Barstow, had provided, and Max Weldy had costumed, a lavish and beautiful spec and production numbers that included "Carnival in Venice," "The Coronation of Mother Goose," and the "Enchanting Ethereal Extravaganza Cherry Blossom Time," an aerial ballet featuring Galla Dawn standing on her head on a high trapeze while spinning hoops on *both arms and both legs*. Somehow John had found time to write the charming music which accompanied them, including the hit tune "Those Maracas from Caracas."

In addition, he introduced from Europe Hugo's unique combination of a trained elephant, zebra, and llama; "Miss Elabeth" in "A Desperate Dive from the Top of the Arena"; Sciplini's chimps, who were very funny natural comedians; and a number of other performers never seen in America before. In short, a show that justified our cherished superlative.

In New York the public gave us a thundering vote of confidence, expressed not in written ballots, but in those beautiful green engravings exquisitely etched in the United States Mint. The gross in the Garden was the second-largest up to that time.

Armed with these figures, John went confidently to the directors' meeting in June 1957. It turned out to be another of those unhappy family fracases where, after hearing the good news that the "Old Girl" had survived her drastic operation and was, so to speak, doing a financial mambo, our cousins grimly announced that they were going ahead with the mismanagement suit. In other words, the patient had recovered but, according to them, the operation was a failure.

The 1957 season was encouraging, but it was not all smooth sailing. Those dates we had been forced to make in open stadia were quite frequently rained out. What happened when they were is shown by the figures for our engagement in Syracuse, New York:

Income	$ 1,618.00
Expenses	$20,868.00

The bruit about the mismanagement suit was no help, either. It caused our creditors to press us heavily and made the establishment of new credit extremely difficult. As Arthur Concello puts it, "We twist, we turn, we keep the creditors happy, paying a little to this one, a little to that. I manage to keep peace with the unions. We get through the season."

We did, indeed, get through the season with a small operating profit, which was extraordinary, considering the short time we had to make bookings, due to which the show was idle some 40 days out of a 134-day season, and rained out on many others.

In 1958 the tour included an invasion of Mexico City, where our charming Latin-American neighbors received it with acclamation. Let Arthur also state, in his concise, cocky way, the good news of that year:

"We operate in '58 and it works out considerably better. All trade bills paid. So we open on March 4, 1959, at Charlotte, North Carolina, and we don't owe anybody except our lawyers and the family so much as one little piece of copper with Lincoln's head on it."

The $20,000,000 suit of the Forty-niners was dropped. The year looked bright ahead and bright it was.

John opened the new show in Charlotte, as Arthur said. Until 1958 we had always opened in the Garden to our biggest and most critical audience. It was like opening a play cold on Broadway, which, as everyone knows, is a very dangerous thing to do. But with four months in Winter Quarters to prepare and two or three weeks of rehearsals in New York, it was not too difficult. At that the show often ran four hours on opening night, which, however much one may love it, is too damned much circus. We would cut and prune and condense as we went along until the running time came down to reasonable limits.

However, the new indoor season—weather no object—of eleven months left little time for rehearsing the new show and it seemed wise to shake it down, like most plays, on the road.

So John brought it into the Garden with a polished performance. Among the production numbers was a new aerial ballet. Max Weldy dreamed it up and suggested it to John. Speaking in his heavy European accent, he said, "This year we should have parrots performing on the web."

"Parrots!" said John blankly.

"Parrots," Max enthusiastically repeated. "With very sexy short little pants."

Finally it penetrated John's bewilderment. Max meant pirates, of course.

The "parrot" ballet was a great success, as was the entire new show directed by Concello and staged by Margaret Smith. With the elbow room granted by increasing profits, John was able to introduce splendid new features, including the Stevenson Troupe from Ireland, who were not only fine equestrians but had a whole pack of enchantingly gay little dogs who so clearly enjoyed performing their clever tricks that the audience seemed to be laughing not at them but with them.

Alzana's dangerous acrobatics on the high wire were particularly dramatic that opening night. Only a few days before, he had been struck by a car on the New Jersey Turnpike and had been seriously injured. In spite of this he insisted on performing his act. With the lights dimmed and a single spot focused upon him, he limped painfully to the slanting wire leading upward at an angle of forty-five degrees to the upper heights of the arena, the same wire from which he had fallen two years ago. Slowly, breathlessly, he walked up it with no pole or aid to balance. Once on the heights, he performed with his customary brilliance and apparent ease, and then made the perilous descent on the other side. When he touched ground there was a great whoosh as ten thousand people let out their breath at once. Then they burst into tremendous applause. It was a display of courage and loyalty seldom if ever equaled in the whole history of Ringling Brothers.

In addition to the new acts I have mentioned and our old favorites, John introduced *seventeen* acts never seen in America before. The show ended with a bang—the crash of Zacchini's cannon as it hurled his *two* beautiful daughters in a great parabola across the entire arena into the safety net.

The box office was a bang, too. At Madison Square Garden the show made the record gross of approximately $2,000,000. Now we ended the season with a near-record gross at a handsome profit.

It seemed that the American people still loved the "Old Girl," after all.

I enjoyed this triumphant season only vicariously. In May 1958 I had resigned as vice-president of Ringling Brothers–Barnum & Bailey Combined Shows. You may wonder how, loving it so much, I could bring myself to leave our circus. In a very real sense it had left me.

Though I believe I had performed the executive functions of my job adequately, they were something that any good man could do. My unique value to the circus had been my standing *in loco parentis* to our performers and workers. To have a member of the Ringling family there to whom they could turn in trouble, anger, or joy meant a great deal to them, and their confidence and friendship meant as much to me.

I have told how I interceded for the workingmen with the

bosses and how I arranged loans for all our people in financial difficulties from the red wagon, and lent them my own money as well. Of course, you did not charge any interest, and all this made our people feel that the circus was not just a big, cold, impersonal organization, but a family affair which had their interests at heart. That feeling is what kept the circus going through all the years and vicissitudes.

But in the last days of the Big Top and in the new setup, these paternalistic activities were not possible any more. The Hartford-fire claims, excess-profits taxes, workmen's compensation and social security, and God knows what besides, left us too thin a margin. Our people still thought the circus could do everything, but there just was not enough money.

In the final years of the Big Top I tried to help them as I always had, partly because I wanted to so much and partly because I believed that it was what kept the circus going. My brother's managers would say, "Christ, that Buddy's trying to do things like it was in the good old days!"

That was the only way I knew how to do things. I listened to all the sad stories and tried to dispense justice and charity. I did the best I could, but the combination of changing circumstances was too much for me. When I finally realized that it had become impossible I lost a lot of my enthusiasm for devoting my life to the circus.

That was more or less the reason I resigned, that and the fact that in the new setup, with people scattered in hotels all over town, my particular function had become obsolete.

As I have shown, the circus is a terribly demanding mistress, whose service precludes her people's living a normal life. Nowadays it continues for eleven months a year, and the twelfth month of putting the new show together is the most frantic of all. So after thirty years in her service I felt that I should have an opportunity to live as other people do, for a while at least.

But my resignation does not mean that I have forsaken my love or lost my faith in her. I still scout new acts for my brother and help him in every way I can. Nor does it mean that I will not go back to her if she needs me.

As to her future, it appears brighter than ever before in my time. With the operation on a sensible budget, and bigger and better amphitheaters being built all over the Americas—and in Europe, too—the circus seems assured of solvency for the foreseeable future. Perhaps the economics of inflation will catch up with her again, but not for a long while.

And working in her favor is what the statisticians call the population explosion. All those babies of the future, whose millions only Univac can reckon, hurrying on to the scene to become little circus fans who in the years ahead will thrill to laugh at and love The Greatest Show on Earth.

Our circus has traveled a long road from gaslit Baraboo to the atomic glare of today. It was a difficult and dangerous road, as you have seen, filled with joy and great achievements, too. Indeed, it was as varied and full of interest and wonder as life itself. I am proud and grateful to have been aboard the train for part of the way.

AFTERWORD

Henry Ringling North's great family chronicle, *Circus Kings: Our Ringling Family Story*, is the most significant memoir ever published about the lives and achievements of leading American circus proprietors. It is a unique document, a family member's articulation that reveals the Ringling brothers' lives as private individuals and public amusement magnates. It affirms their honesty, hard work, and unified ability to progressively advance—the means by which the brothers achieved the pinnacle of the circus business against all adversity and competition. North's chronicle also details to a degree the second generation of Ringlings, particularly himself and his brother John. It's a well-written chronicle that spans the Ringling family and circus existence from the mid-nineteenth century to 1960.

In a broader context, the most enlightening aspect of the book, beyond the insights that it provides to outstanding Ringling brothers success, is the accounting of the turmoil that ensued from a failure to plan for their own succession. Charles Ringling kept a daily diary throughout the show season, a so-called Book of Wonders, notations about what to improve, to retain or to avoid in the future, especially in regard to conducting business with railroads, local suppliers, elected officials, newspapers, and others. He shared the contents with his brothers at their annual Christmas-time planning meetings. Henry North's volume is perhaps a cautionary Book of Wonders for multiple-generation families engaged in their own closely held business, given the high profile failures of such entities in recent times.

The Ringling brothers commenced their entertainment careers with nothing more than a dream and their determination, having no real estate, property, capital, or experience. They acquired performing skills in their spare time, while practicing other trades, and joined other troupes to see how it was done. In their winter stage shows of 1882 and 1883 they sang and danced, made music and cracked jokes, earning and saving enough money so they could inaugurate a modest overland circus in 1884. Five brothers started and owned the circus; two joined it later as employees, while their sister remained outside the entire operation.

By 1907, the brothers owned the three largest circuses on earth, the physical plant of the biggest Wild West troupe, four winter quarters operations on two continents, and a lease on Madison Square Garden. In late 1929, the remaining brother, John Ringling, owned six of the nine largest circuses in North America, along with five winter quarters and an interest in a newer Madison Square Garden. These are achievements that cannot be equaled because the traditional circus is no longer the governing amusement enterprise in a changed America. The world has moved on and of necessity so has the circus.

Were it not for North's memoir and the road map that it provides to their study, we'd have difficulties learning about the Ringlings as people. They left no substantial personal papers and only limited corporate records from the 1910s can be consulted. Other publications that usually form the basis of biographical work, newspapers and magazines, are silent about them to a large degree because they granted few lengthy interviews until the 1920s.

Henry Whitestone Ringling North, author of the family memoir, was born in Baraboo, Wisconsin, in 1909, six years after his older brother, John Ringling North. It was the small town the Ringling brothers' parents had moved away from, to Rice Lake, Wisconsin, on the eve of the brothers commencing their circus careers. The North brothers' mother, Ida Ringling North, was

386   AFTERWORD

solicitously protected by her seven brothers but also developed
an iron will. She exchanged the small-town provincialism and
brothers' domination for Chicago to secure her music education
and also a husband, Harry North, a railroad engineer. Naming
their first son for her brother John, the dominant but not the
leading brother, was a gambit to regain family acceptance, their
second son being named in honor of the boys' father. A daughter
named Salomé arrived in 1907, named for her recently deceased
grandmother. Young Henry North's maternal grandparents and
his Uncle Gus were already dead by the time he arrived, and Uncles Otto and Al Ringling, the leader, would be gone before he
reached seven. Uncles Henry, Alf T., and Charles were deceased
by his seventeenth birthday, but Uncle John remained alive until
1936, when North reached twenty-seven. Henry North's mother
survived until 1950.

The Norths periodically traveled with the family circuses
(two between 1908 and 1919, save for 1910–11 when there were
three, and then just one starting in 1919) and were also invited
to spend time at Uncle John's ranch in Montana. Their quarters
were aboard their uncles' multiple and comfortably appointed
private railroad cars. They also lived amidst the winter-time circus activity of Baraboo until it left town for good in the spring of
1918.

John and Henry North each had opportunities to work for the
circus as young men, with results that varied with their tempera-
ments. The Ringling staffers watching over the Norths became
something of an extension of the brothers in assuring that Ida's
boys were schooled in the ways of the circus and protected from
its hazards. The Ringling brothers had been expert at identify-
ing the best men for management positions, and Henry North's
well-chosen words reflect the admiration and appreciation that
the family had for these trusted lieutenants who often served
decades in their jobs and were sometimes remembered in the
brothers' wills.

The older Ringling brothers had moved away from their parents' various cities of residence as young men, leaving the family household as they established themselves in their initial working trades in Minnesota and Wisconsin. The young men returned to Baraboo when their show was organized. As the needs of the circus, prosperity, and their own family desires dictated, they moved on again. The death of mother Salomé Ringling in early 1907 also removed some of the structure that brought them together as a family. John went to Chicago about 1890 and between 1908 and 1910 established residencies in New York City and Alpine, New Jersey. Otto went to New York City in late 1907; Charlie relocated to Chicago about 1908; Alf T. moved to New Jersey in the mid-1910s. Gus and Al were Baraboo boys.

The relocation to Florida of the majority of the surviving family members took place between 1911 and 1922. Even Henry changed his principal residence to Florida in the 1910s, but he bought near Orlando, while the others were all around Sarasota. The five surviving brothers started to come back together in Florida, enjoying a near full family assembly at Charles's home in 1915. Courtesy of the brothers, led by John, the Norths resided in Baraboo in increasingly larger homes until after Henry North died in 1921, when they were relocated to Sarasota.

It was largely in the sunny Gulf Coast city where young Henry North garnered most of the knowledge and insights that were employed in *Circus Kings*. In the 1930s he spent many enjoyable hours with his Uncle John, as well as later with his mother and aunts. During the preparation of the book, he was supported by his sister and her husband in the search through family documents, the stories related by his elder brother John, and contact with his cousins Hester (Charles's daughter) and Alice (Gus's daughter). The contributors were noted by name in his acknowledgments, which are headed by a tribute to the entire North family. Thereby Henry North became the spokesman for the family in telling their story, hearing family lore firsthand as a boy, teenager, and young man, and then garnering more during research for the actual writing.

Overall, Henry did an excellent job in his chosen task, providing a text that remains a valued resource nearly a half-century after it was originally distributed. There are, as is typical in family memoirs stretching over several generations, some errors in *Circus Kings*. The fact that there are so few errors in a fact-filled study speaks well of the volume. We do not believe that they are intentional in any way, but the good-faith result of working without primary and written documentation. Further, there's no assurance that family members told Henry the entire story, but at least they confided in him the most important points. If there is an Achilles heel in North's work, beyond a reliance on some orally perpetuated family lore, it is North's borrowing from other memoirs, specifically Fred Bradna's, for critical coverage on the merger of their two great circuses for 1919 and the relocation of the winter quarters from Bridgeport to Sarasota in 1927.

The most significant error is the date Henry North provided for the passing of his grandmother. Her death took place on January 27, 1907, and not January 16, 1908, as stated in the book. It was the absence of grandson Richard T. Ringling, and not son John Ringling, which caused the postponement in late 1906 of the annual family Christmas gathering and dinner at Salomé's Baraboo residence. The dual mistake suggests a general memory lapse by whoever recalled the episode for North. A closure of the Carnival of Fun was dated 1889, when it should have been 1884, and the opening date of the 1890 tour was May 3, not May 2. On the other hand, North was correct in providing the year 1903 for the marriage of his Uncle John and Aunt Mable, which subsequent writers have placed in 1905 due to a misreading of the marriage license. A search of the text revealed seventeen simple spelling mistakes, most of which should have been corrected in proofreading. The extended and poignant account of John Ringling's last viewing of a circus parade was certainly composed with writer's license. A rational analysis of the entry, utilizing a 1952 letter wherein North commented upon the actual event, points to him and his Uncle John witnessing the Hagenbeck-Wallace Circus street procession at Pensacola, Florida, on Monday, October 31, 1933.

The tradition-bound, romantic tent operation of RBBB, on the ropes for several years financially, was brought to a close by John North near Pittsburgh, Pennsylvania, on July 16, 1956. It was a victim of labor union activism, difficulties with railroad transport and unrelenting expense escalation. The loss of the iconic big top, in use since 1825, was traumatic, but the circus had always maintained an indoor presence, if only to open the annual season and play engagements in a few selected cities where it was advantageous to do so. In a few years, the circus men learned how to exploit the dozens of arenas and amphitheaters that housed major sports and other events. It was a time to rein in tradition for progress into the future.

During the next decade, experienced manager Art Concello and others transformed Ringling-Barnum from a labor-intensive tent and blue sky operation to an efficient, indoor venue attraction. The menagerie and side show, established with the big top show as part of the triple-feature concept of the traveling circus business between the 1830s and standardization in 1871, were relegated to history after occasional indoor use. A number of event promoters, including two brothers named Feld, were part of the transition, their collective bookings supporting a conversion from tents to buildings that *Billboard* circus columnist Tom Parkinson had advocated in the early 1950s as a means of survival and expansion in a changed entertainment landscape.

The circus prospered modestly under various management regimes, but North was increasingly an absentee owner, the details entrusted to others. For some observers the show had become formulaic, each new sensation harder to advance before an audience increasingly jaded by other entertainments that had moved ahead of the three-ring extravaganza. In addition to moving from tents to buildings, the circus altered transportation methodology, changing from trains to trucks for 1957 to 1959 and then back to railroads for 1960. As part of cutting its roots, the circus also departed the longtime winter quarters community of Sarasota, where it had resided since the fall of 1927, and moved down the coast to Venice. North and his experienced staff continued to operate the circus for seven years after *Circus Kings* appeared. For several good reasons, John Ringling North sold the family circus to outsiders in 1967. The Norths continued to be affiliated with the circus for some time thereafter, in both productive and honorary roles. James Conway Ringling, Robert's son, also served as a show employee.

John Ringling North passed away in 1985, having achieved a wealth far beyond his more famous uncle. His passing enabled Henry North to provide for the long-delayed interment of John and Mable Ringling on the grounds of their home in Sarasota. Henry died in Geneva, Switzerland, on October 2, 1993. Most of the Ringling brothers' grandchildren are now deceased, except for Paul Ringling, who still operates the Montana ranch that John Ringling sold to his father, Richard Ringling, in 1916. Much of the remaining family, except for Gus's line and the Norths, gathered together for a great reunion at Charles Ringling's home in Baraboo during the summer of 2005. It was a flashback to the last such event in the same community in 1907. The family feasts must have been legendary, because they were described to North as being "an enormous meal [with] joyous expressions of their deep affection for one another." The observation is part of the enduring feeling that the Ringlings, via Henry North, wanted to give about their family.

Henry North's son, John Ringling North II, made a remarkable move in 2007 by buying the highly respected Kelly-Miller Circus and operating it, successfully, for the first time that year. No other member of the family has been a show owner since

1967. His name is circumspectly seen in only a few places around the lot of this fine motorized tent circus. Many threats challenge the circus business today, and for how long and in what ways Mr. North will make his mark remain to be seen.

Roughly, there have been three eras to the Ringling–Barnum circus existence. The Ringling brothers, their widows and offspring, and their children's widows owned and controlled the Ringling circus enterprise from 1884 through 1932, a total of 49 seasons. Incorporation and governance change resulted in outsider Sam Gumpertz being elected to be in management control for five tours, from 1933 to 1937. His service was essentially an extension of the Ringling-managed years, there being little deviation from the established patterns of prior management.

The ascent of second generation Ringling brothers' nephew John Ringling North commenced a new era, spanning 1938 to 1942 and 1948 to 1967, a total of 25 tours, with his cousin Robert Ringling and his cousin-by-marriage James Haley at the head for the five intervening years. Ringling widows, or their progeny, remained involved throughout this three-decade period.

The third era commenced in 1967. For the immediate past 41 seasons, Ringling Bros. and Barnum & Bailey, the Greatest Show on Earth, has been under the ownership or contractual control of the Feld family. The men who replaced the Ringling family were Irvin and Israel Feld, proprietors of Super Attractions, Inc., via which they parlayed their promotion of records and personal appearances by early rock stars into a modest fortune. They recruited Judge Roy Hofheinz, owner of the Houston Astrodome, for the cash to make the circus purchase, but it truly was a Feld takeover. P. T. Barnum had mostly "brass" when he acquired Scudder's Museum in 1841, and John North had no major cash to gain control of Ringling–Barnum for 1938. The bold Feld takeover of the circus in 1967 seems to share something in common in that regard. North and the minority owners, all veterans of battles for control, split the $8,000,000 paid for the family legacy. The deal was signed on November 11, 1967, in Rome's Colosseum, a photogenic locale that was inspirational. It was also totally unconnected to the modern circus that started in Great Britain in 1770 and which was transplanted to the United States in 1793. The widely publicized event should have served as notice that things would change. Henceforth, there would be magic in the rings and also in the marketing.

The Feld brothers set about taking the circus to a new level, rapidly buying Circus Williams of Germany and forging ahead with two completely independent, railroad-based circus troupes, the Red and Blue Units, in 1969. The concept of two circuses operating nationally to cover the nation had been articulated in 1888 by P. T. Barnum to James A. Bailey, who then put it into practical use in 1891. The Ringlings embraced the methodology to an even greater degree between 1908 and 1918. The Felds also undertook an immense expansion of souvenir and food sales, which garnered enormous profits beyond the ticket sales revenue. Sharp-minded concession and privilege men did the same thing with circuses in the past and used it to springboard to circus ownership. As under the Ringling, Gumpertz, and North regimes, every year an entirely new three-ring production was created, but the Felds were much more personally involved in everything. Continuing the performance formula established under North, the show was highlighted by high quality acts and ever more sumptuous ensemble production numbers. The Felds knew modern marketing better than North and showcased a leading aspect of the presentation in their publicity. RBBB publicity quickly made a household name of superstar Gunther Gebel-Williams and brought about a renaissance in traditional circus audiences across the country. The press picked up on a story line that the Felds had "saved" the circus, an engaging simplification of their overall expansive efforts that didn't seem to bother John Ringling North. He readily invested his proceeds in gold and easily jumped into the nine-figure worth levels of the super-wealthy.

In 1971, after developing RBBB into a financially remunerative enterprise more than double the North-era size, the Felds sold the circus operation for $47,000,000 to toy maker Mattel. The lucrative concessions and command over performance production remained with the Felds. After Mattel failed to exploit the circus via synergy with their toy line, the Felds bought the circus back in March 1982, at a price far less than it had sold for in 1971. Irvin Feld offered, "The good Lord never meant for the circus to be owned by a big corporation." In the future, ownership by the family's huge privately held company has also brought its share of challenges.

In subsequent years, additional touring shows have been created, generally in response to opportunity, competition, and niche fulfillment. These included the Monte Carlo (1979) and Barnum's Kaleidoscape (1999) operations, which were responses to new wave, one-ring circuses like the not-for-profit Big Apple Circus and the Canadian government–backed Cirque du Soleil. The Gold Unit (1988) was assembled to play for several seasons in Japan, and the Hometown Unit (2002) was framed to play smaller arenas. Some lasted a single tour, while others have exhibited staying power. There have also been multiple Disney-titled ice shows, and Siegfried and Roy in Las Vegas was under the Feld banner.

Israel Feld passed away in 1972, followed by Irvin in 1984. His son, Kenneth, joined the firm in 1970 and inherited leadership upon his father's passing. The dates work out to 18 seasons for Irvin and 24, and counting, for Kenneth. Feld Entertainment, Inc., was organized in 1996 and Ringling Bros. and Barnum & Bailey became a subsidiary of that organization. The Feld enterprise of today conducts business on six continents and in at least fifty countries, a global coverage beyond what James A. Bailey had accomplished in his career by touring Australia, South America, and Europe. The multiple circus units are just a fraction of the Feld operation, which derives a far greater percentage of its revenues from a larger number of traveling ice shows. With avowed commitment, the Feld organization characterizes itself as the "caretaker" of the 137-year-long circus heritage.

The American Bicentennial (1976) and the centennials of the Barnum and Ringling Bros. circuses (1970 and 1984, respectively) all served as lead themes for Feld-era productions. The headliners for Ringling–Barnum have varied in the past four decades, including notable individual stars (animal trainer Gunther Gebel-Williams [1969], crocodile hypnotist Tahar [1988], animal trainer Flavio Togni [1990], Italian clown David Larible [1991], Airiana, The Human Arrow [1996], clown Bello Nock [2001]); group performers (Shanghai Acrobatic Troupe [1986], Mongolians [1992]); and noteworthy animals (performing giraffe Dickie [1981], Living Unicorn [1985], King Tusk [1987], rhinoceros Thor [1990] and hippopotamus Zusha [1997]). Despite anti-animal propaganda, the American public still turns out in large numbers to see trained elephants, horses, dogs, and exotics demonstrate their intelligence and abilities derived from co-operative human interaction. Performing artists with skills that amaze the best Olympians and reckless daredevils who truly defy death serve up spine-tingling thrills beside others whose grace and beauty in motion are unsurpassed in other entertainments. Advances in sound systems, lighting, and projection and computer controls for everything have changed the arena activity into something that in many ways no longer looks like the circus of the Ringling and North periods. The 2006 abandonment of the defining nominal 42-foot diameter circular performance ring takes Ringling–Barnum into new territory where the word "circus" is no longer applicable to its productions. Indeed, the descriptive word circus has been dropped from the RBBB title as the company's leadership struggles to satisfy an ever-changing public and American lifestyle with an arena show. Purists should note that P. T. Barnum's epochal 1871 enterprise had a long, feature-filled title that hardly included the word "circus."

The P. T. Barnum circus was founded in 1871 and implemented the anonymously conceived "Greatest Show on Earth" trademark in 1872. There had been many "Great Shows" in circusdom before it, but the Barnum enterprise inaugurated the heyday of the circus in America, a period of gigantic expansion into a national institution of daily importance. In constant use thereafter, the famous phrase passed to the ownership of the Ringling brothers in 1907; was selected for continued use over the brothers' own "World's Greatest Shows" at the time of the combine in 1919; and then rolled into Ringling Bros. and Barnum & Bailey Combined Shows, Inc., when it was incorporated in 1932. Worldwide legal right to the acclaimed phrase, owned by Feld Entertainment, Inc., is constantly challenged by governmental bodies, private enterprise, and individuals. To maintain the unique identity, "top of mind" consciousness and internationally recognized status of the branding requires constant and keen monitoring of the printed word and the full-time attention of lawyers specializing in intellectual property. The world is now an international market, united by the Internet. Branding often loses meaning with a disconnection between product or service origin and perpetuation by others. Yet, after 136 years, being "The Greatest Show on Earth" still resounds every time its familiar ear-pleasing cadence is proclaimed during the circus opening.

The passage of time and loss of icons of the circus was countered by the Felds with the 1968 founding of RBBB's Clown College and the construction of a Center for Elephant Conservation in 1995. Keeping the shows rolling caused Feld to organize a state-of-the-art rail car recycling plant in Palmetto, Florida, acknowledged to be one of the best in the nation, and part of an extensive consolidated operations support facility. In 2006, Kenneth Feld's daughter, Nicole, became the first of the third generation of Felds to participate in RBBB production management.

The circus performance that debuted in December 2007 was the 137th edition. The counting starts with the formation of the Barnum circus in 1871. Being the longest-running live show production entity in the United States is both a formidable heritage and a challenge, as there is a bifurcated expectation within the audience for both traditional and modernistic presentation. Mixing elephants, clowns, and acrobats with computer controls, laser lights, and contemporary music is not child's play, nor is it an animal-free, high tech, avant-garde version of Commedia dell'Arte. The proliferation of computer technology that facilitates cultural awareness and advancement has educated the audience far beyond its predecessors, imposing ever-increasing expectations on Feld's creative staff and hired consultants.

Circus purists decry some of the changes that have been implemented, but to embrace only tradition and not to evolve would be contrary to circus tradition itself. It was for good reason that Earl Chapin May termed it the "Ever Changing Never Changing Circus" in a 1927 magazine article title. The challenges that the Felds face (Gen X and aging audience segments, digital era, restrictive animal laws and governmental regulations, rising expenses, terrorism, railroad limitations, nuclear family division, lessened circus activity and interest) are as diverse and as threatening as those that confronted the Ringling brothers (peer competition, vaudeville, film, World War I), Sam Gumpertz (film, Great Depression) and the Norths (union activity, dramatic expense escalation, cultural and technological advances, World War II, suburban development, television).

Henry North's memoir occupies a unique niche among many other works that document selected aspects of the Ringling brothers' lives and circus. His publication falls about two-thirds of the way through the 125-year existence of the circus that made the name Ringling internationally famous.

The basic family genealogy and peregrinations under patriarch August Ringling, consulted by Henry North, was capably presented by J. J. Schlichter in "On the Trail of the Ringlings," *Wisconsin Magazine of History*, September 1942. The seminal event in the brothers' careers, seeing a steamboat-based circus in McGregor, Iowa, in the 1860s, was not explored in detail until circus history doyen Stuart Thayer published his analytical "The Circus That Inspired the Ringlings," in *Bandwagon*, journal of the Circus Historical Society, May–June 1996. It would appear that the boys were influenced by exposure to more than one circus.

The first published summary about the Ringlings appeared in a local volume, William H. Canfield's *Outline Sketches of Sauk County, Wisconsin* (1891). Alf T. Ringling, the ink-spreading scribe of many Ringling press releases and route books, penned the Horatio Alger–style account of their existence in *Life Story of the Ringling Brothers* (1900). It did little to provide broader understanding of their rise but makes great juvenile instruction. Another period recounting of the brothers' story, prepared under their supervision, also appeared in programs that were sold at the circus. A local history volume, *A Standard History of Sauk County, Wisconsin* (1918), contains entries on both the brothers collectively and Al alone, likely meaning that he or his widow had subscribed to the publication.

Articles about Ringling personal activity appeared infrequently in weekly amusement trade periodicals, especially *Billboard*, *New York Clipper* and *Show World*, which also provided detailed news on performances and all sorts of circus minutiae. These were seen largely by amusement industry employees and not the general public. The daily newspapers provided some public coverage of their lives, but the Ringlings evaded most

ERWY

reporter efforts and had a dislike for any type of paperwork or governmental control. Notable for the insights that it provides on Ringling management philosophy is an extended piece presumably ghost written after interviews with John Ringling, "We Divided the Job--But Stuck Together," *The American Magazine*, September 1919. This essay, more than any other, confirmed the success of their "one [circus] for all and all for one [circus]" management as well as the unity and admiration that they mutually enjoyed.

The keenest insights on John Ringling's private life aboard his private railroad car are in *Born to Be* (1929), penned by his former valet and porter Gordon Taylor shortly after he achieved fame as a Harlem singer. In the 1920s, publications by trade press and article authors Earl Chapin May, Courtney Ryley Cooper, and Edwin P. Norwood captured the essence of the 1920s railroad tent circus experience when the word ubiquitously meant Ringling Bros. and Barnum & Bailey Combined Shows. They wrote especially about behind the scenes activity, logistics, animals, and star performers for children and adults alike. Some of these works were dedicated to John and Charles Ringling, who were much revered as "Mr. John" and "Mr. Charlie" in their own time by staff, performers, and workingmen.

The business press first took a long look at the circus and its sole remaining member when *Fortune* printed "To Make a Circus Pay" and "Portrait of Mr. John" back-to-back in the April 1930 issue. The initial extended study of the Ringlings for popular consumption appeared as four chapters in Earl Chapin May's faulted general history of the American circus, *The Circus from Rome to Ringling* (1932). With writer or publisher timing aforethought, it was issued on the eve of the family's golden anniversary in the business. It was followed by a small flurry of articles, like that published in the July–August 1933 issue of *White Tops*, the journal of the Circus Fans Association. Alvin F. Harlow's reasonably researched *The Ringlings, The Wizards of the Circus*

(1951) was the first postwar Ringling book. Despite his readily apparent library work and interviews, Harlow was led astray in significant ways. He termed Alf T. Ringling's marriage with Della Andrews a "happy match." Della loathed the circus and they divorced.

The year before North's book became available, horse enthusiast turned circus history promoter Charles P. Fox issued *A Ticket to the Circus* (1959). It's a well-illustrated volume that still holds value today for an extended memoir by one of Gus Ringling's daughters and a topical analysis of the circus enterprise. The least reliable of the Ringling accounts is Gene Plowden's *Those Amazing Ringlings and Their Circus* (1967), with its created dialog. Two broad studies of Wisconsin's substantial circus heritage, newspaper man Dean Jensen's *The Biggest, the Smallest, the Longest, the Shortest* (1975) and *Badger State Showmen*, by Fred Dahlinger Jr. and Stuart Thayer (1998), each include extended chapters on the brothers and their circus operations from different perspectives. The intricacies of building and managing the Ringling circus when it was a Baraboo, Wisconsin, institution is solidly covered in *Ringlingville USA* (2004), by regional Wisconsin author Jerry Apps. Supporting references and a bounty of illustrations make it stand out. The first thirteen years of the Combined Shows have yet to be analyzed, but the seasons of 1932 to 1956 were the subject of an extended series of articles by Joseph T. Bradbury published in *White Tops* between 1974 and 1991.

The first of two studies devoted solely to John Ringling is Richard Thomas's suspect *John Ringling* (1965), a vanity press issue of which some content cannot be verified. The subsequent *Ringling, The Florida Years, 1911–1936* (1993), by David C. Weeks, was the first attempt to unravel John's complex and often convoluted Florida dealings. John's namesake nephew, who reflected his uncle's character and demeanor in many ways, is presented in Ernest C. Albrecht's *A Ringling by Any Other Name, The Story of John Ringling North* (1989). David Lewis Hammarstrom's subsequent interview-based *Big Top Boss, John Ringling North and the Circus* (1992) complements it in a variety of ways.

Rooted in the Ringling family circus story is the origin of the John and Mable Ringling Museum of Art in Sarasota, Florida. John Ringling's bequest of his home, grounds, and art museum to the State of Florida was accomplished in 1936, with complete transfer of control achieved in 1946. Following several decades of difficulty, the Venetian-inspired mansion, Cà d'Zan, has been restored to the elegance of John and Mable's occupancy. The long-term stability of the Ringling site was achieved when a governance change made the John and Mable Ringling Museum of Art a campus of Florida State University. As a center of learning, the cultural facility has recently been substantially enhanced with many millions of dollars given by private donors, matched with equal amounts provided by the State of Florida. The art museum, the state's designated facility, was expanded. New facilities were erected for collections care and exhibition, visitor comfort and convenience, and staff utilization. The modest circus museum addition of 1948 was immeasurably augmented with the erection and opening of the Tibbals Learning Center in 2006. Amongst treasured circus archival items and artifacts, it showcases the Howard Bros. Circus, an incredible, exacting, and mind-boggling scale model of the Greatest Show on Earth in its greatest manifestation during the railroad and tent era. A further expansion providing for additional exhibition space and a circus research center has just been announced (2008).

John Ringling was of the opinion that the circus enabled all people to regain the innocent joy of their youth. That magical transformation still happens at the circus and the benefits that it provided to him are evident in his personal compound on Sarasota Bay.

Fred Dahlinger Jr.
Circus Historian, John and Mable Ringling Museum of Art